# Many Faces of Mexico

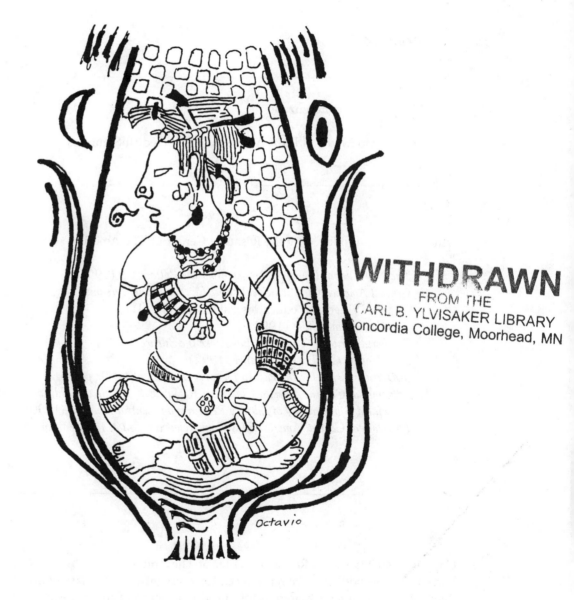

Octavio

By Octavio Madigan Ruiz, Amy Sanders, Meredith Sommers

Resource Center of The Americas
317 - 17th Avenue Southeast, Minneapolis, MN 55414-2077
612 / 627-9445

*Many Faces of Mexico*

Published August 1995 by

Resource Center of The Americas
317- 17th Avenue Southeast
Minneapolis, MN 55414-2077
Telephone 612 / 627-9445
Fax 612 / 627-9450
E-mail: rctamn@maroon.tc.umn.edu

ISBN 0-9617743-6-3

Cover design by Ivett Lorenzano

Authors: Octavio Madigan Ruiz, Amy Sanders, Meredith Sommers

Other Materials Produced by the Resource Center of The Americas

*The New Global Economy: A View from the Bottom Up* (1995)
*Central America Children Speak: Our Lives and Our Dreams,*
        Video and educators guidebook (1994)
*The Cost of Your Shirt* (1993)
*Rigoberta Menchú: The Prize that Broke the Silence* (1992)
*El Salvador: Conflict and Change* (1992)
*500 Years: Exploring the Past to Discover the Present* (1991)
*Directory of Central America Classroom Resources K-12, Second Edition* (1990)
*Annotated Bibliography of Library Resources on Central America* (1990)
*Directory of Central America Classroom Resources, K-12, First Edition* (1987)

# Many Faces of Mexico
## Table of Contents

# Introduction

*M*any Faces of Mexico braids together the cultural, political and economic realities which together shape Mexican history. As Jorge Castañeda wrote in an article comparing Mexico and the United States, "Mexican history appears to be one long continuum, with great and long constants and underlying continuities and only sporadic bursts of compressed, highly intense events." He goes on to say, "For the United States, history is folklore, plus the recent past; for Mexico, it is the essence of the present".

Indeed, as we wrote *Many Faces of Mexico*, a guiding question was, "What do we need to know about Mexico's past in order to understand its present and future?" This question led us to an interdisciplinary approach which includes geography, history, economics, sociology, politics, literature and the arts.

In the process of creating *Many Faces of Mexico*, we have identified key themes that help us understand the continuities in Mexican history from before the Spanish invasion to the present day. These themes include the following:

- **Land and Resources** - examining who controls or has access to land and resources and how they are used
- **Borders and Boundaries** - understanding the nature of borders and how continuously changing boundaries affect people's lives
- **Migration** - considering why people move, where they go and the consequences of migration
- **Basic Needs and Economic Issues** - examining how people meet their need for housing, food, education and work
- **Social Organization and Political Participation** - analyzing how people and governmental systems are organized and reflecting on whose voices are heard or not heard
- **Popular Culture and Belief Systems** - considering how people express themselves through language, arts, literature, sports and games
- **Perspective** - understanding how people view, interpret and react to issues and events in their lives, communities and nation

We wrote *Many Faces of Mexico* in response to numerous requests of the Resource Center of The Americas for curricula and other materials about Mexico. Despite the close geographical proximity of the US and Mexico, we were able to locate few resources about Mexico. Those that did exist seemed to put their emphasis on "food, fiestas and famous people". The high quality lessons seemed to focus on ancient Mayan or Aztec civilizations, or be limited to one or two concepts. We could find no up-to-date, comprehensive curriculum describing the reality of Mexico from past to present. Thus began our journey to create *Many Faces of Mexico*.

## Goals and Objectives

Our goal is to help learners in the US and Canada develop awareness and understanding of Mexican reality and an appreciation for the rich diversity of the Mexican people. Our guidelines state that the resource/study guide should:

1.  Develop an attitude of respect for the dignity of all people.
2.  Build a recognition of both differences and similarities among people.
3.  Use the arts to help develop compassion and a sense of connection.
4.  Arouse curiosity and teach analytical thinking.
5.  Present multiple perspectives.
6.  Acknowledge and discuss major inequalities of wealth and power within Mexico and the US and question why those inequalities exist.
7.  Explore the wide diversity of the Mexican people, ethnically and culturally, and give special emphasis to the indigenous heritage of the nation.
8.  Encourage a vision of a future which is more equitable and just, and to act upon that vision.

## Teaching Strategies and Techniques

*Many Faces of Mexico* helps participants identify perspectives and examine how differing perspectives influence a person's understanding of events. To bring Mexico's history to life, we incorporate several short narratives or stories about people from different social, economic and ethnic groups, who also live in different regions of the country. These original stories help readers identify with the lives of people in the colonial, revolutionary and contemporary eras.

The resource/study guide is designed so educators do not need to be experts on Mexico, rather facilitators and co-learners in the study of Mexico. Numerous handouts are included that may be reproduced. These include a number of original writings, as well as primary and secondary source materials from books and periodicals. Many of the primary sources are not commonly available. We found them in the Penny Lernoux Memorial Library at the Resource Center of The Americas, in libraries at the University of Minnesota and in various global computer networks.

We have tried to incorporate numerous innovative teaching techniques to stimulate student interest in the material. Many lessons encourage small group work and require active participation. We have included a number of simulations and role play exercises, which provide excellent opportunities for students to work with information and analyze situations and issues. Role plays enable learners to empathize, analyze and rehearse ways they might respond to situations. These participatory teaching strategies require more preparation than more traditional methods, as well as a willingness to "let go" of the outcome. However, the rewards can be great as participants begin to understand that history is a living narrative, not the rote memorization of facts. Allowing students to process their impressions and understandings is as important as the actual activity, and requires plenty of time.

We frequently use a teaching strategy known as "jig-sawing" throughout the curriculum. In jig-sawing, small groups of learners focus on separate parts of an issue or story. They then teach others about what they have learned, and together construct a picture that forms a whole. This technique relies upon a collective effort in which everyone teaches and everyone learns.

We wrote **Many Faces of Mexico** in the **active voice** as much as possible, to indicate that people are active and instrumental in their own history. To write in the active voice, we were challenged to identify the subject. Instead of writing "war broke out" we included, whenever possible, information about who made decisions to fight and why. We also have tried to specifically name who initiates an action. Instead of saying "Mexico decided to nationalize the oil industry", we identify the decision makers. By focusing on people's critical decisions and their responses to decisions of others, we hope students become active learners and respond to what they have learned.

### Description of Contents
A number of lessons in **Many Faces of Mexico** are designed as *"Exploring the Connections"* lessons. These include information on topics that link Mexico, Canada and the US. These lessons encourage students to realize that learning about Mexico includes learning about other countries—that political, economic and cultural systems are interrelated. It also encourages students to understand that learning about other people means learning about oneself.

The curriculum consists of five units and 24 lessons. Many of the lessons require more than one class session to complete.

#### Unit I — Introduction
This unit locates Mexico so students develop a mental map of its location, understand its relationship to the region, and explore language and terminology appropriate to the study of Mexico. It includes questions such as "Who is an American?" Students also may construct a large scale map of Mexico to use during their study.

#### Unit II — Pre-contact to 1521
This unit begins with a survey of six major indigenous groups whose societies flourished before contact with the Spanish. We ask students to engage in "historical imagining" to consider where they might have settled within a given region. We then focus on daily life in the Aztec city of Tenochtitlán, before chronicling the Spanish invasion of the region.

#### Unit III — 1521-1810
This unit covers the colonial era, during which new systems of social stratification, exploitation and inequality were established in New Spain. Participants portray the effects of these systems through a socio-drama. Through story, we visit the families of six people who lived during the colonial era. The unit ends with the struggle for independence from Spain in 1810.

#### Unit IV — 1810-1940
The first lesson of this unit covers the years during which Mexico lost more than a third of its land to the United States. This is followed by a study of the Mexican Revolution, which draws on primary source documents for debate on the issues and to dramatize the human aspects of the war. The concept of national identity also is addressed here, raising the question of "who are the Mexican people?" We examine how Mexican people are viewed and stereotyped in the US, as well as the historical

roots of stereotypes. We include a lesson on Frida Kahlo and Diego Rivera, artists who influenced greatly the concept of a Mexican identity. Finally, descendants of the six families tell their stories about their lives during the revolutionary era.

### Unit V — 1940-present
This unit begins with an examination of Mexico's governing system. The first lesson chronicles the 1968 Student Movement, in which Mexican university students demanded a more open and democratic political system. There is a lesson on analyzing media coverage of Mexico — using the 1994 uprising in Chiapas as the topic. This unit contains a simulation exercise about the economic culture in Mexico, a voting simulation to learn about Mexico's electoral system, and a "story about a tomato" which demonstrates the economic integration of the Americas. There is a lesson on migration, which includes case studies of Mexican living in Mexico and the US, and a structured controversy on US policy initiatives on immigration, such as Proposition 187. We take a contemporary look at the families we met in other historical epochs, and read examples of how Mexicans today are working to improve their own lives and that of their communities. The concluding lesson is a powerful analysis of Mexican society today, providing participants with tools for understanding Mexico's future.

## Alternative Ways to Use *Many Faces of Mexico*
Because *Many Faces of Mexico* is a comprehensive resource, it is lengthy. If all lessons are used, it can take eight to ten weeks, including time for research and presentations. **If you have less time and still want to cover the major historical events and issues, we suggest you use the following lessons: 5, 6, 8, 10, 11, and 12, plus the stories that bring history to life, Lessons 9 and 15.**

If you wish to incorporate lessons about Mexico into other courses or as part of a study of The Americas, we suggest:

### For Geography
| | |
|---|---|
| Lesson 1 | Mapping Mexico |
| Lesson 2 | Locating Mexico |
| Lesson 3 | Defining Mexico |
| Lesson 4 | Historical Imagining |

### For Pre-Columbian History
| | |
|---|---|
| Lesson 4 | Historical Imagining |
| Lesson 5 | Exploring Tenochtitlán |

### For an Economics Course
| | |
|---|---|
| Lesson 18 | At What Price? |
| Lesson 19 | Who is Being Fed? |
| Lesson 24 | Understanding Mexico's Future |

**For a Political Science or Government Course**
    Lesson 16    Political Reform
    Lesson 20    Casting a Vote

**For an Art History Course**
    Lesson 6    The Spanish Invasion
    Lesson 14    Frida Kahlo and Diego Rivera

**For a Study of Immigration**
    Lesson 21    Mexicans on the Move

**For Contemporary Mexico**
    Unit V    All lessons

Participants are encouraged to keep a journal throughout the course, and many lessons use journal writing as a teaching strategy. For evaluation after a journal writing assignment, we suggest that educators randomly select and read five or six journals, and to continue the random selection, so students keep their journals current even after they have been read once. Two self-evaluation forms are included in the appendices, one for participants to assess their own learning and one for small groups to evaluate the process of working together.

A map of Mexico, a chronology, and a glossary are also included in the appendices. A pronunciation guide is at the bottom of the glossary. Although Spanish is a phonetic language, some vowels and consonants are pronounced differently than English. Indian names appear frequently in the curriculum, and they also are also generally phonetic.

We recognize that it would be impossible to adequately represent the history and contemporary reality of Mexico in one curriculum. Therefore, we approached the subject with a sense of humility and a belief that learning is a process which never stops. At the same time, we have attempted to convey as much information and insight as possible, hoping that *Many Faces of Mexico* will be a beginning point to engage people in a study of both Mexico and the wider world around them. At the Resource Center of The Americas, we consider the process of educating young people and adults to participate in and challenge the world in which we live to be a most exciting and important endeavor. We hope that you will find in this curriculum some of the tools to encourage young people and adults together to work for justice, equality and democracy in our world.

August, 1995
Resource Center of The Americas
317 17th Avenue Southeast
Minneapolis, MN 55414
612/627-9445

Three people were the authors of *Many Faces of Mexico*.  They share their thoughts below:

**Octavio Ruiz**, a Mexican citizen and native of Chiapas, brought to the project his knowledge of Mexico's history and experience, a profound sense of the issues of Indian people, and a capacity to tell stories as a way of keeping memories alive. He writes:

> *As a Mexican living in the United States I realize that our lives are so tied to yours that we can no longer see each other as separate entities. The study of Mexican history is very connected to the history of the US and vice versa. In the past, large sections of what is now the US were part of Mexico, and in the present day many people who live in the US and Canada are of Mexican heritage. Our future depends on the interrelationship of the three countries. Many Faces of Mexico offers a perspective that connects the people of North America. My work on the project is my best effort both to contribute to an understanding of Mexican history and to help all people better understand our shared history.*

---

**Amy Sanders**, a secondary social studies teacher and researcher, brought a strong commitment to historical accuracy, great organizational skills, and a sense of the needs of classroom teachers. She writes

> *A friend and mentor sent me a poem years ago entitled, "We Have Been Told Many Things But We Know This To Be True." It tells of the relationship between the land and the people — how the land has given life and how we must give life back to it. The words encourage one to engage in creative work to generate new life and new relationships. These thoughts reflect my commitment to, and purpose for, work on Many Faces of Mexico. As an author and educator, I view my work as an opportunity to explore my connections to the land and the people of Mexico, and to foster these same opportunities for others. After all, our histories and our futures are inextricably linked. In this body of work, we have tried to provide a context for understanding Mexico. My hope is that we will provide provocative ideas and encourage you to question, ponder, reflect and act on what you have learned. We must be encouraged to conceive of ourselves and our actions in the world community — to think about how to live in our world with a measure of decency and responsibility.*

---

**Meredith Sommers**, staff person from the Resource Center of The Americas, provided critical leadership to the project. She brought creative energy, patience, passion, perseverance and years of experience in participatory education to the effort.

> *As the team has worked together to produce Many Faces of Mexico, we often have been challenged and frustrated , but always encouraged by what we have learned about the people of Mexico and each other. We started with a few questions that lead to observations, research, new discoveries, and lively discussion. We learned to listen intently to one another and to take the time to read and learn from difficult materials. We used our imaginations, as well as our emotions, in order to understand the topic and each other. It took persistence, discipline and trust. We want to pass on our conviction that working and learning together can break down barriers that separate people.  Knowledge of the other can be deeply enriching. It is our hope that this resource can guide you through a process to build bridges among the people of Americas.*

# Acknowledgments and Credits

Many individuals and organizations have participated in the production of *Many Faces of Mexico*. We are extremely grateful for their generous contributions. It was truly a labor of love, involving the thoughts, suggestions and expertise of dozens of people:

- **For vision, clarity, fund raising, editing and production work**, Pam Costain, Resource Center Executive Director.
- **For help with editing and final production**, Pam Keesey, Larry Weiss, JoAnna Villone.
- **For creative layout and final design**, Jane Austin.
- **For an extraordinary cover design**, Ivett Lorenzano
- **For general support when most needed**, staff of the Resource Center of The Americas including Mary Swenson, Darla Baker, and Kay Dunne, along with Jay Dregni, Paul Dobbins, Jean and Warren Sanders, and Sandra Lindstrom.

Research and written contributions:
Oakley Biesanz, Macalester College
Karen Carlson, Southwest High School
Katy Egan, University of Minnesota
Laurie Nelsen, De Colores Project
Barbara Rogers Bridges, University of Minnesota
Elena Thomas, Midwest Farmworkers Employment and Training, Inc.
Wendy Vasquez, Macalester College

Reading, comments and consultation
Patricia Avery, University of Minnesota
Sara Damon, Columbia Heights High School
Juanita Garcia-Godoy, Macalester College
David Flannery, Elk River Schools, Elk River, MN
Paul Kramer and Apple Valley High School Students
David Lanegran, Macalester College
Bob McCaa, University of Minnesota
Peter Martín Morales, College of St. Benedict
Pamela Nice, University of St. Thomas
Joanna O'Connell, University of Minnesota
James O'Neill, St. Cloud State University
Mario Quintero, Mankato State University
Guillermo Rojas, University of Minnesota
Ramón Eduardo Ruiz, Rancho Santa Fe, California
Shelley Sherman, St. Paul, MN
Kathryn Sikkink, University of Minnesota
Kaia Svien, Minneapolis, MN
Gilberto Vasquez, University of Minnesota
Jenny Zanner, Hopkins High School

**Artwork and graphic design**
SuzanneDel Oro
Octavio Ruiz
Amy Sanders
Nancy Svien
Jay Dregni
Jan Landin

**For generous financial assistance**
Center for Urban and Regional Affairs (University of Minnesota)
Children's Haven Foundation
Minneapolis Foundation
Minnesota Humanities Commission
Samsara Foundation
Unity Avenue Foundation

**Permissionfor the use of ideas and material was provided by:**
Beacon Press, 26 Beacon Street, Boston, MA 02108
Bill Callahan, Quest for Peace,
    3502 Varnum, Brentwood, MD 20722; 301-699-0042
Caren Caraway and Stemmer House Publishers, Inc., (graphics)
    2627 Caves Road, Owings Mills, MD 21117
Center of US-Mexican Relations, University of California at San Diego
    0510, La Jolla, CA 92093-0510
Columbus (Ohio) Dispatch,
    34 South Third Street, Columbus, OH 43216
Patti DeRosa, Cross-Cultural Consultations,
    28 S. Main #177, Randolph, MA 02368; 617-986-6150
Ecumenical Coalition for Economic Justice,
    11 Madison Ave., Toronto, Ontario, Canada M5R 2S2
Jorge Enciso and Dover Publications, Inc. (graphics)
    180 Varick Street, New York, NY 10014
The Houston Chronicle, PO Box 4260, Houston, TX 77210
The Milwaukee Sentinel, 918 N. 4th St. Milwaukee, WI 53201
Minneapolis Public Library, Children's Services,
    300 Nicollet Mall, Minneapolis, MN 55401
Minneapolis Star Tribune,
    925 Portland Ave. So., Minneapolis, MN 55402
SouthWest Organizing Project,
    211 Tenth Street, SW., Albuquerque, NM 87102; 505-247-8832
St. Paul Pioneer Press, 345 Cedar Street, St. Paul, MN 55101
Rini Templeton and the Real Comet Press (graphics)
    3131 Estern Svenue #410, Seattle, WA 98121
VIDEA, 407-620 View Street, Victoria, BC, Canada V8W 1J6
Viking Penguin, a division of Penguin Books, USA Inc.
World of Difference, 1111 Third Ave. So., Minneapolis, MN 55404

# Mapping Mexico
## *Perceptions and Reality*

This curriculum begins with the question, "Where is Mexico?" At first glance this might appear a simple question, but in reality it is very complex. It involves notions of time, space and location; the relationship of one territory and people to another; and the understandings and perceptions one carries about this relationship. The first lesson asks students to begin to engage in a process by "mapping" Mexico, first as an exercise using their own perceptions and knowledge and later using concrete information.

An effective way to begin to become geographically informed is to work with "mental maps." Mental maps usually are a mixture of knowledge and perception. They may contain knowledge about the location of geographic features such as countries, oceans, mountains, and cities, but they may also contain less precise information, such as impressions about the relative size, shape, location and connections between places.

To create a mental map, students draw a freehand map from memory. They draw the outline of the place in question, include as many details as they can, and show the relationships to other land and bodies of water. Such mental maps provide students with a means of storing and recalling information about the shapes and patterns of the earth's physical and human features. They are also an excellent diagnostic tool to gauge students' prior knowledge. Mental maps represent ever changing knowledge. Students should be encouraged to update and refine their mental maps as they continue to learn about Mexico. As their maps increase in complexity and accuracy, students often feel a sense of satisfaction as more places and events are placed into meaningful spatial context.

In the second part of this lesson, students construct a large map of Mexico that can remain on the wall of your classroom during your study of Mexico. The wall map divides Mexico into six regions, determined according to geographic and cultural characteristics. In future lessons, students will work in small groups, becoming very familiar with one of these regions.

Don't be intimidated by this project. The directions walk you through each stage of the map production and it is an easy and fun projects which engages students! This project will be chaotic if all students work on these various stages at once (a maximum of six students working on each stage is preferable). Therefore, we suggest that groups of students alternate work on the map with other classroom activities. The map project can be an ongoing project for a rotating group of 4-6 students over several days.

| | |
|---|---|
| **Learner Objectives** | • To draw a sketch map of Mexico and compare it with atlas maps to determine the accuracy of place location. <br> • To construct a map of Mexico using the grid method. <br> • To participate in a group activity to construct a map of Mexico. |
| **Concepts** | • Region <br> • Location |
| **Major Question to be Addressed** | What does the current political map of Mexico look like? |
| **Teaching Strategies** | Mapping |
| **Materials Provided** | • A Regional Map of Mexico (Handout 1) <br> • Instructions for Drawing the Map (Handout 2) |
| **Materials Needed** | • blank sheets of paper (½" x 11") <br> • scissors <br> • 2 thin black markers for labeling <br> • 6-8 pencils <br> • 6 erasers <br> • pencil sharpeners <br> • masking tape or packing tape (at least 2" wide) <br> • large roll of butcher paper (newsprint tears easily) <br> • 6–12 rulers (12, 18, or 36 inch—the longer the better) |
| **Time Required** | 2 class periods |
| **Preparation for Lesson** | Determine the size of the map you would like to construct and cut the paper. See Handout 2 for complete instructions on determining map size and paper needed. NOTE: If you have |

little time to complete this project, you may wish to do much of the preparatory work, such as cutting the paper and drawing the grid so that students begin drawing right away.

# Sequence of Lesson

*Anticipatory Set*
*10 minutes*

Distribute blank paper to students and ask them to draw a "mental map" of Mexico. Without referring to any materials in the classroom, ask students to sketch a map of Mexico, adding as much detail as they can from memory, making their best effort. Students may compare their maps with one another without adding to them. Collect the maps, which are an excellent diagnostic tool to gauge students' knowledge of Mexico's geography. (Later in your study of Mexico, you may wish to ask students to complete this exercise again. Then distribute the student's first map, and ask her or him to compare the first and second maps. This often results in a tremendous feeling of accomplishment as students realize how much they have learned!)

*Body of Lesson*

1. Explain to students that in this class period, they will be constructing their own map of Mexico to place in the classroom. Discuss briefly the procedure for drawing the map, and then ask for 4-6 students to begin the project. Only a few students may work on the map project at a time; otherwise, the process becomes too chaotic. All students will eventually work on the map.

2. The rest of the students should continue with other classroom activities. They may, for instance, work on the first activity in Lesson 2, locating places in Mexico and Central America. This is an activity that the 4-6 students working on the map can complete at another time. Continue to rotate students working on the map as you complete the activities in Lessons 2 and 3.

*Extension Idea*

The grid method can be used for numerous other projects, such as enlarging and reproducing other maps and educational posters for school or community center walls.

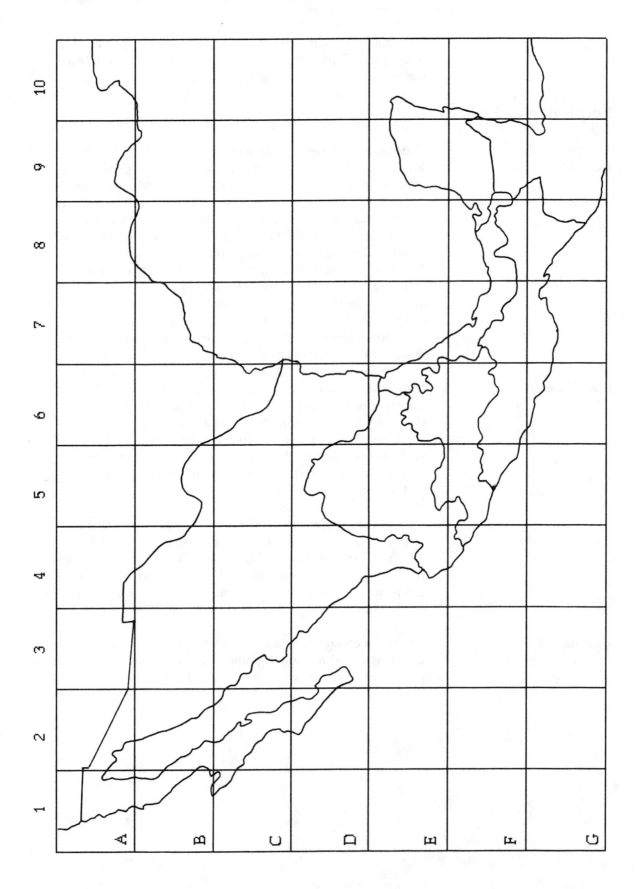

# Instructions for Drawing the Map

The grid method is simply a method of enlarging drawings or images while maintaining proportional size. Whereas freehand drawing of maps may lead to distortions, the grid method increases the proportional scale of an image. In the first stage of the map drawing process, draw a grid that looks like a giant sheet of graph paper. The size of your grid blocks will determine the size of your map. Larger grid blocks will increase the dimensions of the map, and smaller grid blocks will decrease the size of the map. The calculations for determining map size follow.

## DRAWING THE GRID

### Block Size

The map in Handout 1 is 7 blocks tall and 10 blocks wide. To determine the final dimensions of your map, multiply the number of blocks by the size of the blocks. Your calculations are given for a map 5.25 feet tall (63 inches) and 7.5 feet wide (90 inches), using 9-inch square blocks.

If you choose to make a map of a different size than the one described here (either larger or smaller), you can determine its final dimensions by multiplying the number of blocks by the size of blocks you desire.

### Preparing the Paper

You will need large rolls of white butcher paper to complete this project. Brown paper will be too difficult to see, and newspaper will tear too easily. Roll out an 8 ft. piece of paper and cut the paper from the roll. Continue rolling out pieces of paper and placing them so that they touch but do not overlap the adjoining paper. Tape the papers together lengthwise with masking or packing tape until the total piece is at least 6 feet tall.

### Drawing the Grid

The basic goal here is to end up with what looks like a giant sheet of graph paper.

### Setting Reference Lines

LEFT-HAND LINE: Using a yardstick and pencil, make a vertical straight line that is perpendicular to the bottom edge of the paper. This line should be at right angles to the top and bottom edges of the paper. Make this line one or two inches indented from the left-hand edge of the paper, since this edge is likely to be jagged from cutting.

BOTTOM LINE: The bottom line of your map will simply be the approximately 7.5 ft. bottom edge of the paper.

TOP LINE: Measure 63" (or 5.25 ft.) up from the bottom line in several locations on the paper and make a mark. Connect these points to make a straight line along the top of the paper. This will be the top of your map.

### Vertical Grid Lines

Starting at the lower left-hand corner, make a light mark every 9". Repeat this process, marking every 9" at 2 or 3 locations in the middle of the map. Using rulers or yardsticks, make parallel vertical lines between these marks (making light but legible pencil lines).

*See diagram below.*

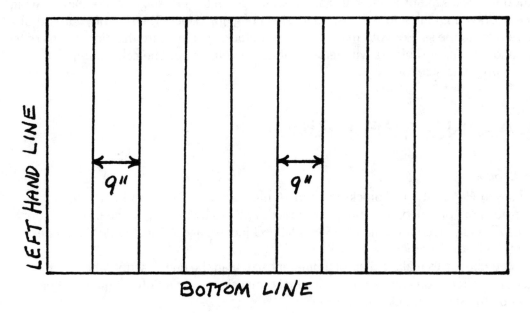

### Horizontal Grid Lines

Starting at the bottom line, make a light mark every 9" above the line. Repeat this process several times across the paper. Using rulers or yardsticks, make parallel horizontal lines between these marks (making light but legible pencil lines).

*See diagram below.*

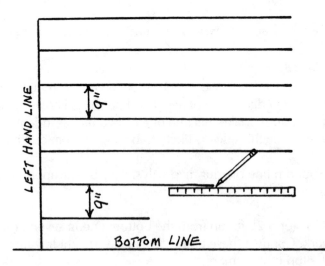

### Numbering the Grid

Numbering the grid keeps you from losing your place when drawing the map in the next step. Number and letter the grid blocks (A to G down and 1 to 10 across) LIGHTLY in two or three places on the grid.

# DRAWING THE MAP

The basic goal here is to end up (eventually) with what looks like a giant (5.25 by 7.5 foot) map. Using the grid lines as guides, you can draw the whole map freehand. Almost everyone can draw and enlarge well using the grid method, but to find out just how adept you are, take this simple test!

First, look in the "Original Map Block"; now look in the "Enlarged once" block and see how the form was enlarged while still retaining its original shape and proportions. Now try it in the "Practice Block."

 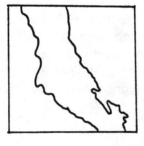 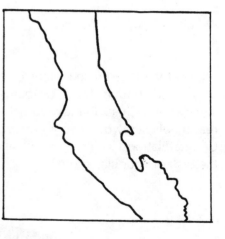

## Drawing Tips

Notice where lines cross on the original map block and make marks in proportionately similar places on your paper block. Then, work your way in, making similar lines as in the original map block. Remember to keep the junctions where lines meet in proper perspective as well.

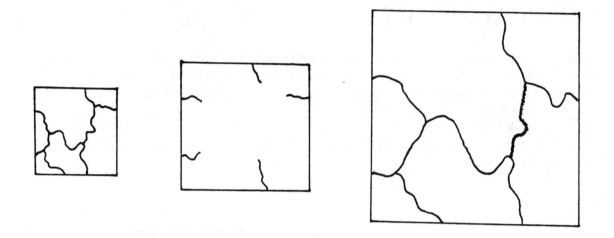

One of the biggest map-making disappointments is being "off one." Don't be overly concerned about it. This is a creative project, and the map of Mexico is bound to change somewhere. Check to make sure the block you are drawing is the right one. When you are reasonably sure your map is correct, trace over border lines with a fine-point black marker. Congratulations! You're finished, and have a wonderful LARGE map of Mexico to place on the wall of your classroom.

# Locating Mexico
## *Maps, Places and Relations*

I f you ask Mexican people to locate places in the United States or Canada, you probably will be pleasantly surprised. In Mexican high schools, most students memorize the states and provinces and major cities of their neighbors to the north. They learn that Mexico's northern geography—its rivers, mountains, and deserts—extend across the border and impact ways of life north of the border in a similar fashion to their own country.

This lesson introduces students to the location of Mexico in relation to other countries in the region and world and asks students to label Mexico, the United States, the countries of Central America and their capitals. Students will then participate in an activity, *Geography Bingo*, designed to reinforce some of the information learned during the map exercise.

For classroom maps, we suggest you use a variety of projections, including the maps of the Peter's Projection. Also turn maps upside down or sideways to demonstrate different perspectives.

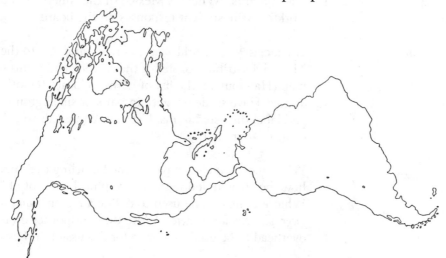

| | |
|---|---|
| **Learner Objectives** | • To identify and label the locations of certain physical and human features on a map and answer related geographic questions.<br>• To identify and define conventional map symbols |
| **Concepts** | • Region<br>• Location<br>• Spatial relationships |
| **Major Questions to be Addressed** | • What are some of Mexico's physical features?<br>• Where is Mexico located in comparison to other countries in the region?<br>• What are some of the criteria used to define a region? |
| **Teaching Strategies** | • Mapping<br>• Discussion |
| **Materials Provided** | • Mexico & Central America map (Handout 1)<br>• Where is Mexico? (Handout 2)<br>• Geography Bingo (Handout 3) |
| **Additional Materials Needed** | • Colored pencils (optional)<br>• Atlases<br>• Maps: World Map (Peter's Projection); Map of the Americas (an upside down map of the Americas, optional)<br>• Students journals |
| **Time Required** | 1 class session |
| **Preparation for Lesson** | Make one copy of each handout for each student. |

# Sequence of Lesson

| | |
|---|---|
| *Anticipatory Set*<br>*10 minutes* | 1. Ask students, "Where is Mexico in the Americas and in the world?" Write student responses on the board. |
| *Body of Lesson* | 2. Use a classroom world map to orient students to the location of Mexico. Distribute copies of the Mexico and Central America map (Handout 1), the list of items to locate (Handout 2) and atlases. Have students work in pairs or small groups to locate and label the listed items. Use colored pencils to color each country (optional). |
| | 3. When most students have finished labeling their maps, ask how they would define the geographical concept of "region". What are the criteria used to define a region? (*language, geographic similarities, etc.*) Write these responses on the board or overhead to be used as a basis for discussion in Lesson 3. |

4. Distribute a copy of *Geography Bingo* (Handout 3) to each student. Students should ask each other the questions posed on the grid and write responses on the sheet. For larger classes, we suggest students only solicit one response from another student before moving on, to encourage greater student interaction. Encourage students to fill as many squares as possible.

**Closure**

5. Check student understanding by discussing which countries border Mexico. Collect Mexico and Central America map if desired for grading.

**Assessment**
**(Optional)**

Give students a blank map (Handout 1) and ask them to label all of the countries.

**Assignment**

Ask students to draw an outline of "America" in their journals and to write a brief explanation of why they included what they did in this outline. Students should bring journals to class for Lesson 3.

# Map of Mexico and Central America

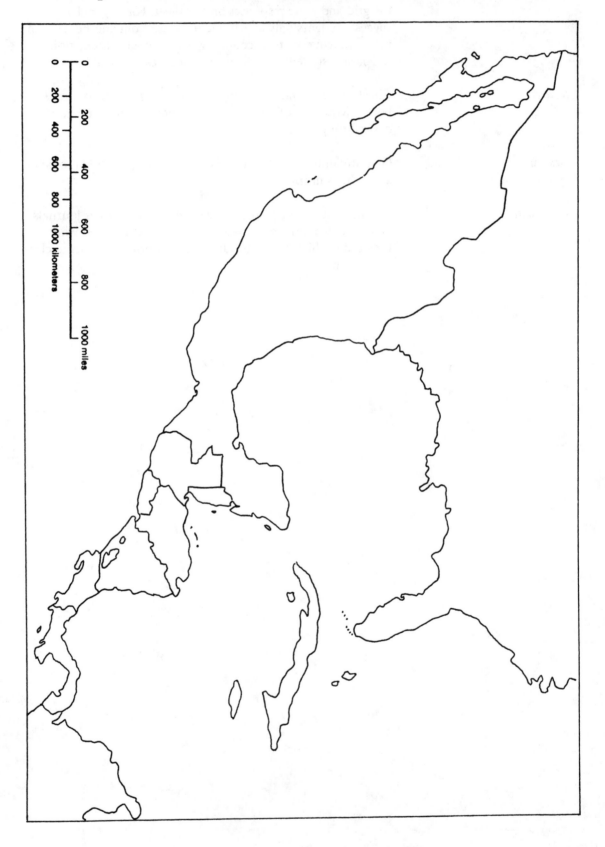

# Where is Mexico?

Locate and label the following items on the map of Mexico and Central America.

## COUNTRIES
Belize
Costa Rica
El Salvador
Guatemala
Honduras
Mexico
Nicaragua
Panama
United States

## PHYSICAL FEATURES
Baja California
Caribbean Sea
Gulf of Mexico
Pacific Ocean
Sierra Madre Occidental
Sierra Madre Oriental
Valley of Mexico
Yucatan Peninsula

## CAPITOL CITIES
Belmopan
Managua
San José
San Salvador
Panama City
Tegucigalpa
Guatemala City
Mexico City

## OTHER CITIES
Acapulco
Tijuana
Monterrey
Guadalajara
Mexico City
San Cristobal del las Casas
Cancun
Oaxaca
Cuernavaca

# GEOGRAPHY BINGO

**Find answers to all of the questions below by asking others for help.** Each person who answers a question on your sheet should sign their initials next to their answer.  (Each person may answer only one question on your sheet.)

| | | | | |
|---|---|---|---|---|
| Name one of the three countries bordering Mexico. | Name a US state that borders Mexico. | Which major body of water borders Mexico's east coast? | Name a city in Mexico that has a population greater than 1 million. | Name another US state that borders Mexico. |
| Which major body of water borders Mexico's west coast? | Which body of water lies between the Yucatán peninsula and Cuba? | What is the capital of Mexico? | What is the name of the peninsula in northwestern Mexico? | Which body of water lies between Baja California and Mexicali, Mexico? |
| What is the name of the mountain range in western Mexico? | What is another name for Lower California? | What is the river that creates the border between Texas and Mexico? | What is the capital of Guatemala? | Name another US state that borders Mexico. |
| What is the name of the peninsula in southeast Mexico? | What is the capital of Belize? | What country borders Guatemala to the east? | What major US city is closest to Tijuana? | What is the name of the mountain range in eastern Mexico? |
| What major US city is across the border from the city of Ciudad Juárez? | Name another of the three countries bordering Mexico. | Name another Mexican city that has more than 1 million population. | Name another US state that borders Mexico. | Name another of the three countries bordering Mexico. |

# Defining Mexico
## *What's in a Name?*

W hen teaching about Mexico, it is important to reach a common understanding of some key terms and concepts. This lesson introduces students to terminology associated with Mexico and the Americas. We will look at names of places and people to show that terms may mean different things to different people. Sometimes language is problematic, either because people understand words to mean different things or because adequate words do not exist to convey the intended meaning. In both instances, people may not understand each other without a common understanding of the meaning of words and concepts.

The terms that describe Mexico's location in the Americas are an example of this problem. Where Mexico is placed — in North America, Central America, or Latin America — depends upon one's perspective. Dictionaries and atlases differ on their definitions and their perspectives. Some define in geographical terms while others use political, ideological, or even historical definitions for the same word. What is important is the realization that our language or terminology conveys perspective and meaning. For instance, how many of us consider Mexico to be a part of Central America and not part of North America? What does that say about the relationship of the US and Canada to Mexico?

Another problematic term is the name "American." Many people mistakenly use this word to refer only to the people of the United States of America. However, people from Mexico to Chile consider themselves to be *Americans* because they are residents of the *Americas*, and they object to the exclusive use of the term by the people living in the US. Some people use the word United States, but this name also can refer to the United States of Mexico. Language can be problematic!

It is necessary to reach a common understanding of the key terms which will be used during the study of Mexico. How we understand and use language has important implications for the perspective we present.

| **Learner Objectives** | • Analyze the implications of geographic names related to Mexico and North America. |
| | • Assess terminology and agree upon definitions of places and people for the study of Mexico |

| **Concepts** | • Language |
| | • Perspective |

| **Major Question to be Addressed** | • What are definitions of key terms used to define the American hemisphere? |
| | • How is perspective embodied in geographic language? |
| | • How is terminology used to include or exclude people? |

| **Teaching Strategies** | • Small group inquiry |
| | • Discussion |

| **Materials Provided** | • Defining the Americas (Handout 1) |
| | • Definitions (Educator's Background Information) |
| | • *The Origins of "America" and "Latin America"* and *Who is an American?* (Handouts 2a and 2b) |

| **Materials Needed** | • Maps and Atlases (see Lesson 2) |
| | • Student Journals |

| **Time Required** | 1 class session |

| **Preparation for this Lesson** | Make copies of Handouts 1 and 2 for each student. |

# Sequence of Lesson

*Anticipatory Set*
*10 minutes*

1. Ask students to consider the names of places in their community, such as their school, parks, student hangouts, or their town. Why do these places have the names which they do? Who named the places? Did they always have the same name? Do any of the places have "nick names" given by students? Explain that the names we call things influence how we perceive them and the study of terminology is also a study about perspective.

*Body of Lesson*
*40 minutes*

2. Distribute Handout 1 and have students work in pairs to answer the questions about countries they would include in North, Central, South and Latin America. Have maps and atlases available for their work. After about 10 minutes, reconvene the class and discuss their findings. Ask students into which categories would they place Mexico and write this on the board. Read the descriptions of the regions from the Educator's Background Information sheet.

3.   Ask students to describe and show the outlines of America they drew in their journals (see assignment for Lesson 2). What did they include — regions, countries, people? Was the entire hemisphere of America represented? Discuss with the entire class the following questions: What is America? What is American? Where did the term come from?

4.   Have students form small groups and distribute Handout 2 to each student to read. When reading is finished, ask them to discuss in their group the questions raised on the handout. If there is not enough time to complete this portion of the lesson, ask students to write responses as a homework assignment.

**Closure**

5.   Point out that people do not always agree about what to include in definitions. What is important is that we take some time to think about how we define terms and concepts and to be as clear as we can about what we mean. How we understand terms and concepts has important implications in our everyday lives because it represents our perspectives. Now, decide as a group how you are going to use the word "American" in the classroom.

**Evaluation**

Collect and assess the students' work on Handouts 1 and 2.

**Assignment**

Using the insight they have gained about the power of names and the process of naming, ask students to conduct an investigation in their own community about a name which has been changed. This could be a street, a school, a town — any place or thing which a community chose to rename. What was the original name? Who wanted to change the name? Who opposed the change? What was the result? Why are names important?

# Defining the Americas

Is Central America really in the center of the Americas? If so, the Amazon Basin would be in Central America. In talking about the hemisphere of the Americas, we encounter terms such as North America, Central America, South America, and Latin America. It is important to have a common understanding of what is included in these definitions. Take a few minutes to answer the following questions, using maps, atlases and other resources available to you.

1. Where is Central America and which countries would you include in this region?

2. Which countries would you include in North America?

3. Which countries would you include in South America?

4. Which countries do you include in Latin America?
   How is this category different from the others listed above?

5. Which countries are <u>not</u> part of Latin America

6. With which category / categories would you place Mexico?  Why??

# *Definitions*

*Listed below are dictionary and encyclopedia definitions of the regions of the Americas. They define the regions in terms of geographical, political, historical, or ideological perspectives.*

## Central America

This term is used to describe the land which lies between the Isthmus of Panama and the Isthmus of Tehuantepec, and includes Guatemala, Honduras, Belize, El Salvador, Nicaragua, Costa Rica and Panama. (*Longman Dictionary of Geography*)

## North America

This term is used geographically to mean the whole continent north of the isthmus of Panama, including the Caribbean islands. (*Longman Dictionary of Geography*)

Continent (3rd in size) in Western Hemisphere. Political divisions: Canada, United States, Mexico, Central America adjoining South America in the extreme south, and West Indies off southeast coast enclosing Caribbean Sea. (*Webster's New Geographical Dictionary*)

## Middle America

Region including Mexico and Central America; name sometimes used to include the islands of the Caribbean. (*Webster's New Geographical Dictionary*)

## South America

This term is used geographically to mean the continent south of the isthmus of Panama. (*Longman Dictionary of Geography*)

Continent 4th in size, comprising greater part of Latin America. Political divisions: Argentina, Bolivia, Brazil, Chile, Colombia, Ecuador, Falkland Islands, French Guiana, Guyana, Netherlands Antilles (Aruba, Bonaire, Curacao), Paraguay, Peru, Suriname, Trinidad and Tobago, Uruguay, and Venezuela. (*Webster's New Geographical Dictionary*)

## Latin America

This term is widely used to cover those countries in the Western Hemisphere which were explored and conquered by the Spaniards or Portuguese and which became part of the Spanish or Portuguese Empires. This includes South America, Central America and Mexico. (*Longman Dictionary of Geography*)

The expression first came into use in France just before 1860 - refers to the 18 Spanish-speaking republics of the western hemisphere, together with Portuguese-speaking Brazil and French-speaking Haiti. (*The Cambridge Encyclopedia of Latin America and the Caribbean*)

# The Origins of "America" and "Latin America"

In 1492, Guanahaní was an island in the Atlantic Ocean inhabited by a group of people known as the Arawak people. On the vast lands further to the west, there were hundreds of other nations, tribes, and communities of people who had been living on their homelands for thousands of years. When Christopher Columbus landed on Guanahaní and later on the lands to the west, he mistakenly believed he had arrived on the continent of India, his original destination. As a result, he called the people of the new land "Indians", a name which was quickly adopted by the Spanish Crown. From that time forward, the original inhabitants of all the lands invaded by the Europeans have been known as Indians. In many cases, their own names for themselves or their land have been lost.

In 1503, eleven years after the arrival of Columbus, Americo Vespucio used the term "New World" to describe this land of the western hemisphere. For the first time, Europeans acknowledged that there was a new land, or new world, which was different from the one they knew. This new world was a contrast to the "old world" represented by Europe.

In 1507, a German book publisher and map maker, Martin Waldseemüller, named the new continent "America" in honor of Americo Vespucio. Vespucio was considered the first European to explore and map an area of the mainland which is now in northern South America. Waldseemüller printed these maps in a book. From that time on, America became the accepted name of the entire continent — a geographical territory divided into three sectors — North America, Central America and South America. The territories within America existed as colonies of England, Spain, Portugal or France. In 1650, the British began using the term America to refer only to their colonies in North America and in 1781, the term was used to connote only the United States. Nevertheless, many of the peoples throughout the Americas continued to use the word to describe their territory. This created much confusion which continues today.

As ideas of independence spread throughout South and Central America, the notion of *Latin America* came into being. In 1835, the Frenchman Michel Chevalier published a book in which he noted the distinction between South America as "Catholic and Latin"and North America as "Protestant and Anglo-Saxon". Then, in 1856, the Colombian poet and diplomat, José María Torres Caicedo, published a poem entitled "The Two Americas". In his poem, he described the differences between the people of Latin America and those whose heritage was Anglo-Saxon and he first used the term "Latin America". From that moment on, the term Latin America was incorporated into the official language of governments. It did not represent a political or geographical division, but rather the acknowledgment of a different historical development. The term, originally applied to the Americas controlled by the Spanish, was later applied to the southern lands which were colonized by the Portuguese and French.

# Who is an American?

*It is important to remember that the United States is not the only land considered to be "America". It is only one country and is part of the American continent. In the Americas, no country is more "American" than the others. Latin Americans, people of the United States and Canadians — all are Americans. Read the following words of a recent Latin American immigrant to the United States and consider his concerns.*

Since I came to the United States, I have wondered about the term "America" — what the word means here and why it has a meaning so different for people living in the rest of the continent. I don't understand why the term America isn't like the words Asia, Africa and Europe, a concept about which everyone can agree. Many books define AMERICA as the Western Hemisphere, the "New World" found by the European colonizers in the 15th Century. It is the portion of land which divides the Pacific and Atlantic Oceans. I wonder why people living in the US consider themselves to be living in the only "America" or why they feel only they have a right to call themselves "Americans". This is very confusing and sometimes upsetting to me!

Among all the definitions, perhaps we can agree on a few things. The whole continent of America is divided into two parts — North America and South America. Each part is divided into many countries. North America, is made up of Canada, the United States, Mexico, the countries of Central America and the Caribbean nations. South America is made up of thirteen countries from Colombia to Chile.

If we can agree that the people of Canada, the US and Mexico all have a right to call themselves North Americans or simply Americans, what should we call a Mexican person, working in a factory in the US or in a kitchen in Canada? He may be called a North American, a Latino, a Mexican or an American, or he may be called a derogatory name instead. It is important to understand that the terms we use for people have a great deal of power and meaning.

Is it necessary to exclude some people from the term American in order to include others? When politicians give a speech and they begin talking about the interests of the United States, they use such expressions like  AS THE AMERICAN PEOPLE, WE ..... WE MUST CONSIDER THE INTERESTS OF AMERICA ..... AMERICA IS FOR AMERICANS..... etc. All of this language serves to set people apart and gives the impression that the needs of some people are more important than others. Who we include and exclude in our definitions has many effects in the real world.

I hope that people can begin to think of themselves less by what separates them or by what name they are given, and more by their common hopes, dreams and desires. Then when the politicians speak of  "the American people" I will not by afraid. I will know they are talking about me, as well.

View of Aztec island city of Tenochtitlán
Island farms, or chinampas, and temple which connected to the mainland by a causeway

*Many Faces of Mexico*

# Historical Imagining
## *Regions & People Before 1519*

In this two-part lesson, students are first asked to imagine what types of cultures developed in regions of Mexico before the arrival of the Spanish, in what is known as the pre-contact period. Second, students learn about six of the ancient indigenous groups who lived in the various regions of what was to become Mexico.

The purpose of the first lesson, "historical imagining," is to help students visualize another culture and to stimulate their curiosity about how people may have lived many centuries ago. Students will form six small groups and each group will focus on one geographical region. (Students will continue to work in these regional groups in a number of future lessons.) Using information provided about landscape, vegetation, water and climate, students determine where they might choose to settle within the region, how they might meet their physical needs, and what kinds of connections they might have with other peoples.

Next, students conduct research about the people who actually lived in these regions, including their cultural practices and ways of meeting basic needs. Some information is provided here, but they will also need to do library research. They will then teach other students about the people in their region.

An understanding of indigenous peoples' way of life is important for understanding the impact of the Spanish invasion and settlement of Mexico. It also lays the foundation for learning about the ways of life of many of these same people in Mexico today.

| | |
|---|---|
| **Learner Objectives** | • To formulate historical questions that guide student research on ancient indigenous cultures. |
| | • To analyze ways in which human systems develop in response to conditions in the physical environment. |
| | • To describe the ways of life of indigenous people before contact with the Spanish. |
| | • To analyze patterns of trade and interaction between people in the pre-European contact period. |
| **Concepts** | • Culture |
| | • Pre-contact |
| **Major Questions to be Addressed** | • What were the ways of life of indigenous people before their contact with Europeans? |
| | • What was the relationship of indigenous people to the land on which they lived? |
| | • How did various groups interact with one another? |
| **Teaching Strategies** | • Inquiry/Historical Imagining |
| | • Research and Discussion |
| **Materials Provided** | • Six maps providing information for each regional group (Handouts 1a-1f) |
| | • Settlement Survey (Handout 2) |
| | • Ancient Mexican Civilizations (Handout 3) |
| | • Comparative Chronology (Handout 4) |
| | • Map of Indigenous Groups (Handout 5) |
| | • Note-taking Worksheet (Handout 6) |
| | • Regional Descriptions (Handouts 7a - 7f) |
| **Additional Materials Needed** | • Six pieces of heavy paper (8 ½ x 11 minimum size) |
| | • Colored markers |
| | • Large map of Mexico |
| **Time Required** | At least 2 class sessions, plus research time between classes |
| **Preparation for this Lesson** | • Make at least two copies of Handout 1a for Group A, two copies of 1b for Group B, etc. |
| | • Make six copies of Handout 2 (one per group). |
| | • Make one copy of Handouts 3 - 6 for each student. |
| | • Make one copy of Handout 7a for each student in group A, one copy of Handout 7b for each student in group B, etc. |

# Sequence of Lesson

*Anticipatory Set*
*5 minutes*

1. Ask students to enter a time machine and to travel back to a world without today's modern conveniences. Have them close their eyes while you read the following:

   *Envision a world without televisions, VCRs or computers; a world without refrigerators, air conditioners or telephones; a place where there are neither cars nor airplanes, horses nor cattle. A place without tennis shoes, or fast food restaurants.*

   *Now try to imagine yourself standing in a desert, a rainforest, or high up in the mountains. The horizons are uninterrupted by skyscrapers and smoke stacks. What would you smell? Hear? Many people live nearby in this place that is now called Mexico...before the Spanish arrived...*

*Body of Lesson*
*45 minutes*

2. Divide students into six small groups and label groups Region A, Region B, etc. Distribute large paper and markers. Instruct groups to make a poster that gives the name and location of their region. Distribute Handout 1a to Region A, continuing to Handout 1f to Region F. These handouts provides information about the landscape, climate, and other aspects of the respective regions. Also give each group Handout 2 that guides their study of physical and human geography. Ask students to answer the questions on Handout 2 in their small groups. Encourage students to complete this handout during the class period, although they should keep it for their research.

3. To wrap up the first class period, emphasize the importance of learning about the context in which the early peoples of Mexico lived. Hypothesizing about how people lived hopefully will generate student questions about the peoples who actually resided in these areas—the focus of their research for the next part of this lesson!

*Assignment*

5. Instruct students to read Handout 3 to gain an overview of ancient indigenous civilizations. Handouts 4 and 5 will help students gain a more visual understanding of ancient indigenous civilizations. Then, they should begin their research about the peoples who lived in their assigned region before the invasion of the Spanish. Distribute Handout 6 to each student for note-taking and Handout 7a to each student in Region A, etc. This has basic information on one group of people in their region:

*Regions and Indigenous Peoples*
Region A (North)—Tarahumara (tar-ah-ou-MAR-ah)
Region B (North Central)—Otomí (oh-toe-ME)
Region C (South Central)—Toltec (TOLL-tek)
Region D (Gulf Coast)—Olmec (OHL-mek)
Region E (Pacific Southwest)—Zapotec (SAH-po-tek)
Region F (Southeast)—Maya Lacandón
(MY-ah la-cahn-DOAN)

Students should be encouraged to look for information in school or community libraries to learn more about the people who lived in their respective regions. The peoples of some regions will be fairly easy to research, while there may be little information available about others. The note-taking grid is intended only as a guide to the kind of information students should try to gather and it should not restrict their research.

**Extension Idea**

Students may wish to draw the physical features of their region on the large map from Lesson I.

**Class Period 2**

6. Ask students to re-join their regional groups to tell others in the regional group what they learned in the homework activity. Use Handout 6 for taking notes. Add the name of the people of their region to the poster they made during the prior class session. Allow 10 -15 minutes.

7. Return to one large group and ask a representative(s) from each group to "teach" the other groups about their region. You may wish to reproduce the note-taking grid so that students can write the information they present on the board or overhead. To facilitate student learning about other regions, ask students to make brief notes about the other regions on Handout 6.

Students should use the large map of Mexico from Lesson 1 to show the location of the region. Ask students to include information about the physical geography and the site(s) they have chosen to form a settlement and explain why they have chosen it. Ask students to talk about connections to other areas, such as transportation and possible trade. Finally, students should discuss what their group learned about the peoples who lived in the region, as well as other features salient to that site, such as housing, food, and clothing. You may wish to add symbols or drawing from the six cultures to the large map.

**Evaluation**

Evaluate the oral reports. Collect and assess the responses on Handouts 2 and 6.

# Region 1—North

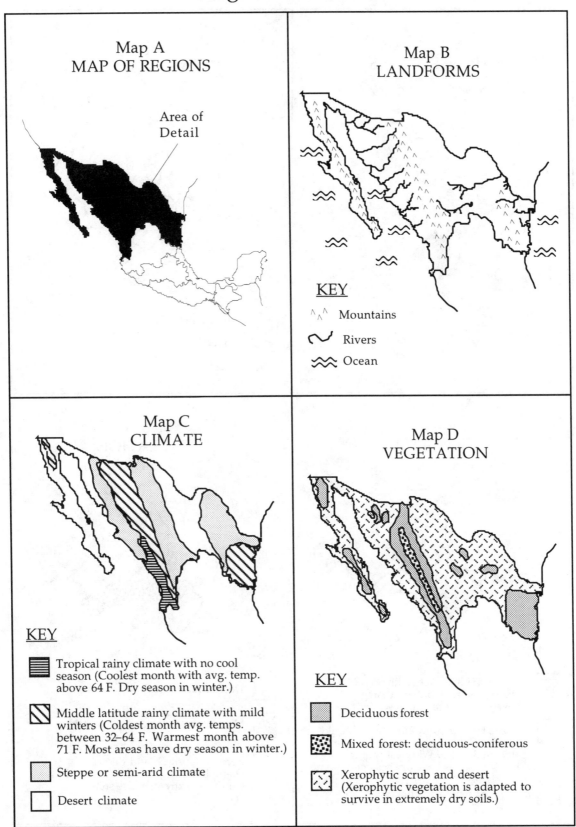

Map A
MAP OF REGIONS

Area of
Detail

Map B
LANDFORMS

KEY

Λ₍Λ Mountains

Rivers

Ocean

Map C
CLIMATE

KEY

Tropical rainy climate with no cool
season (Coolest month with avg. temp.
above 64 F. Dry season in winter.)

Middle latitude rainy climate with mild
winters (Coldest month avg. temps.
between 32–64 F. Warmest month above
71 F. Most areas have dry season in winter.)

Steppe or semi-arid climate

Desert climate

Map D
VEGETATION

KEY

Deciduous forest

Mixed forest: deciduous-coniferous

Xerophytic scrub and desert
(Xerophytic vegetation is adapted to
survive in extremely dry soils.)

# Region 2—North Central

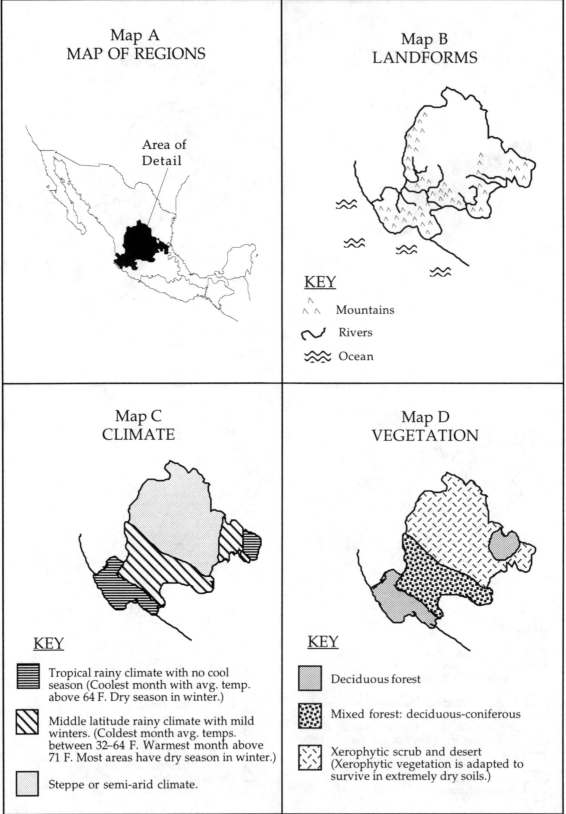

Map A
MAP OF REGIONS

Area of
Detail

Map B
LANDFORMS

KEY

∧
∧ ∧    Mountains

∿    Rivers

≈    Ocean

Map C
CLIMATE

KEY

▤    Tropical rainy climate with no cool
season (Coolest month with avg. temp.
above 64 F. Dry season in winter.)

▨    Middle latitude rainy climate with mild
winters. (Coldest month avg. temps.
between 32–64 F. Warmest month above
71 F. Most areas have dry season in winter.)

▢    Steppe or semi-arid climate.

Map D
VEGETATION

KEY

▦    Deciduous forest

▨    Mixed forest: deciduous-coniferous

▨    Xerophytic scrub and desert
(Xerophytic vegetation is adapted to
survive in extremely dry soils.)

# Region 3—South Central

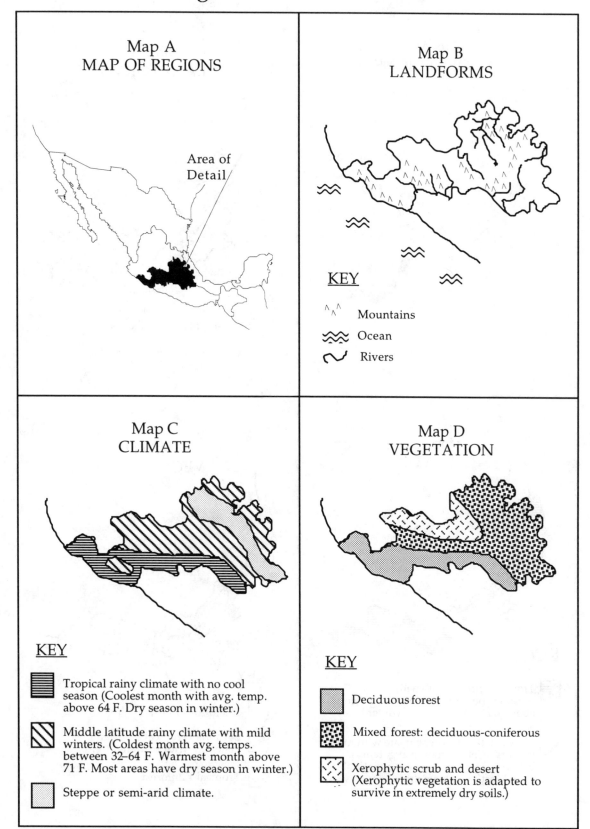

Map A
MAP OF REGIONS

Area of Detail

Map B
LANDFORMS

KEY

^^^  Mountains

〜〜  Ocean

〜  Rivers

Map C
CLIMATE

KEY

Tropical rainy climate with no cool season (Coolest month with avg. temp. above 64 F. Dry season in winter.)

Middle latitude rainy climate with mild winters. (Coldest month avg. temps. between 32–64 F. Warmest month above 71 F. Most areas have dry season in winter.)

Steppe or semi-arid climate.

Map D
VEGETATION

KEY

Deciduous forest

Mixed forest: deciduous-coniferous

Xerophytic scrub and desert (Xerophytic vegetation is adapted to survive in extremely dry soils.)

# Region 4—Gulf Coast

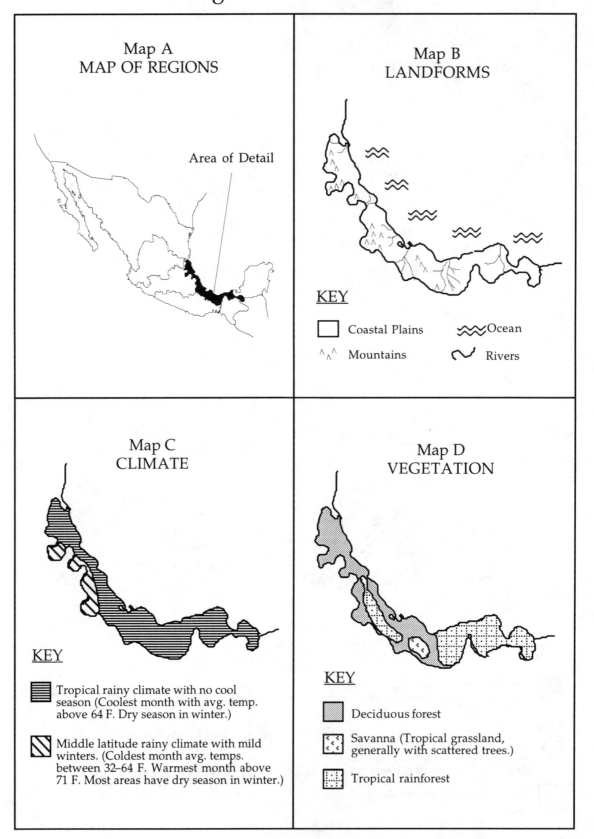

Map A
MAP OF REGIONS

Area of Detail

Map B
LANDFORMS

KEY

☐ Coastal Plains

ᴧᴧᴧ Mountains

〰〰 Ocean

∿ Rivers

Map C
CLIMATE

KEY

▤ Tropical rainy climate with no cool season (Coolest month with avg. temp. above 64 F. Dry season in winter.)

◩ Middle latitude rainy climate with mild winters. (Coldest month avg. temps. between 32–64 F. Warmest month above 71 F. Most areas have dry season in winter.)

Map D
VEGETATION

KEY

▦ Deciduous forest

⊠ Savanna (Tropical grassland, generally with scattered trees.)

⠿ Tropical rainforest

# Region 5—Pacific South

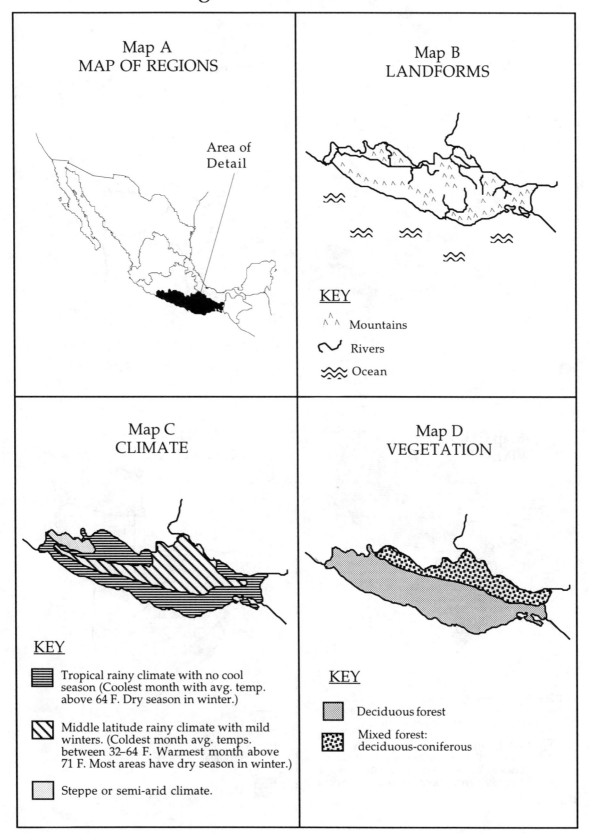

**Map A**
**MAP OF REGIONS**

Area of Detail

**Map B**
**LANDFORMS**

KEY

∧∧∧ Mountains

∿ Rivers

≈≈ Ocean

**Map C**
**CLIMATE**

KEY

▤ Tropical rainy climate with no cool season (Coolest month with avg. temp. above 64 F. Dry season in winter.)

◩ Middle latitude rainy climate with mild winters. (Coldest month avg. temps. between 32–64 F. Warmest month above 71 F. Most areas have dry season in winter.)

▦ Steppe or semi-arid climate.

**Map D**
**VEGETATION**

KEY

▨ Deciduous forest

▩ Mixed forest: deciduous-coniferous

# Region 6—Southeast

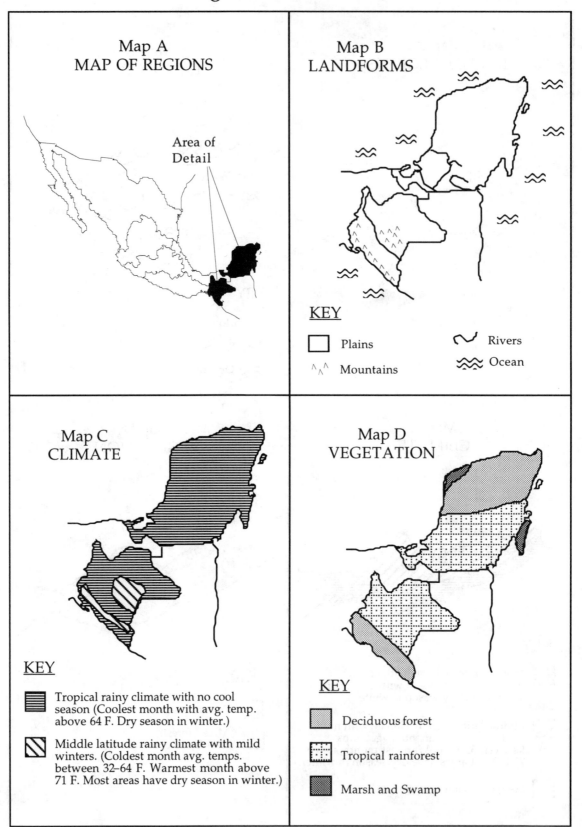

Map A
MAP OF REGIONS

Area of
Detail

Map B
LANDFORMS

KEY

☐ Plains

∧∧∧ Mountains

ᔓ Rivers

≈≈ Ocean

Map C
CLIMATE

KEY

▤ Tropical rainy climate with no cool
season (Coolest month with avg. temp.
above 64 F. Dry season in winter.)

◨ Middle latitude rainy climate with mild
winters. (Coldest month avg. temps.
between 32–64 F. Warmest month above
71 F. Most areas have dry season in winter.)

Map D
VEGETATION

KEY

▨ Deciduous forest

⊡ Tropical rainforest

■ Marsh and Swamp

# Settlement Survey

*You are the scout for a group of people trying to decide where to establish a settlement in your region. You were asked to analyze several locations and make a recommendation as to where to settle. Map A shows your area in relation to other regions. Maps B, C and D simply are enlargements of your region. Each of these maps (B, C and D) contain clues about the landscape, vegetation and climate of your region. Use these clues to find a suitable place for a settlement for your people.*

1. **Look at map B on your handout.** What does this map tell you about the land forms in your region? If you had to choose a place to live based only on the information given in map B, where would it be? *(Discuss this question in your group and mark a dot or region on the map with the group's answer.)*

   **Now look at map C.** What does this tell you about the climate of your region? Is the climate the same throughout the entire region, or does it vary? If you had to choose a place to live based only on the information given in map C, where would it be? *(Discuss this question in your group and mark a dot or region on the map with the group's answer.)*

   **Finally, look at map D.** What does this map tell you about the kind of vegetation in your region? If you had to choose a place to live based only on the information given in map D, where would it be? *(Discuss this question in your group and mark a dot or region on the map with the group's answer.)*

   Now, try to put all of this information together. Discuss the following questions with your group members and write your responses in the space below.

   a) What local conditions would be desirable for people trying to establish a settlement in your region before the year 1500?
   b) What conditions might create problems?
   c) Discuss the best location for a settlement with your group members and after reaching consensus, mark and identify these locations on map D.

| ADVANTAGES of the location | DISADVANTAGES of the location |
| --- | --- |
| | |

2. How do you think people traveled in your region? Where did they go? Why do you think they traveled?

3. How do you think people met their physical needs in this location? For instance, what kinds of clothing would they need? What kinds of food might they grow?

4. Houses directly reflect such things as local climate and geography, family structure and status, cultural preferences, and the availability of building materials. Given the information from the maps of your region, brainstorm with your group what you think houses in your settlement would be like? List below what kinds of materials you think people used to build houses in your settlement. Design or draw a picture of what you imagine houses looked like in your settlement.

# Ancient Indigenous Civilizations

The story of the people of Mexico began long before the invasion by the Spanish and the arrival of the Europeans. Mexican history includes the stories of many people scattered across a vast area of land. Different groups of people at various stages of cultural, technological and social development shared the land. The movement and mingling of these groups of people are part of the Mexican story.

The original inhabitants of the area created communities and established networks of trails and trade routes. They adapted to the land to meet their needs of survival, including food, shelter, clothing, health and security. Notable imperial city states were founded by the Aztecs and Mayans. The Aztec people extended their empire in ways similar to the expansion of the Roman Empire in Europe. They dominated people and land area using force and trade, and eventually established control of these areas.

This region at various times had some of the most highly developed and wealthy cultures in the world. These cultures had very sophisticated political, military, economic and religious systems, in addition to many achievements in the arts. From the northern territories of the country to the south, the major groups of people and their civilizations included the Olmecs, the Zapotecs, the Mayans, the Toltecs and the Aztecs. Other less well known groups, such as the Tarascans, also achieved a high level of development. It appears that these cultures exerted considerable influence upon one another, often blending and merging over long periods of time.

These civilizations did not have wholly separate characteristics, but shared much in common with each other. The periods in which some cultures flourished and waned often overlapped with other cultures.

**The Olmecs** developed their civilization along the gulf coast between 1200 BC–250 AD. They lived mainly in the territory that is now called Veracruz. Mexicans today call the Olmec culture the "mother culture" because of the Olmecs' aptitude and accomplishments in science, art and philosophy. The Olmec are recognized by their gigantic artifacts in the image of the jaguar, a creature with human and feline aspects.

**The Zapotecs** had commercial contacts with the Olmecs. The Zapotec people developed a strong economy and located their center at a place named Monte Albán on the southwestern Pacific coast. This Zapotec center at Monte Albán reached a peak of influence and power at about 500 AD.

**The Teotihuacán culture** developed during the same time period and survived into the seventh century. Their center of power was located approximately 30 miles northeast of what is now Mexico City, the modern capital of Mexico. Although little is known about their civilization, the Teotihuacáns were exceptional in a number of areas including building. The sudden abandonment of their main city has baffled historians and archaeologists. We know about the Teotihuacáns through their influence in art, politics and commerce throughout Mesoamerica.

**The Mayan civilization** also is part of Mexico's history. Mayan people lived in the south as early as 900 BC, and established centers of power that were inhabited by 500 to 10,000 people. One of the most famous centers in the years from 300 BC to 800 AD was at Tikal in the southern low lands, now a part of Guatemala. It was occupied by as many as 50,000 inhabitants and may have been one of most populous cities in the world at that time.

**The Toltec people** established themselves between 900 and 1100 AD in the region around the city of Tula in central Mexico. In that time, the Toltecs became a dominant force throughout Mesoamerica and were known primarily for their military might and their heroic deeds which made them appear mystical. During its brief 200 years of dominance, the Toltec culture influenced people as far south as what is now Costa Rica and up into what is now the southwestern United States. Although Toltec power diminished after 1200 AD, many aspects of their culture were incorporated within the expanding Aztec civilization.

**The Aztecs** are the most well known of the indigenous civilizations. The Aztec people and their empire extended from the middle highlands of Mexico to as far south as what is now Nicaragua and El Salvador. In 1325, the city of Tenochtitlán was founded as the center of the Aztec empire. The Mexico City which we know today is built on the ruins of Tenochtitlán. The city flourished for about 194 years until the arrival of Spaniards in 1519. It has been calculated that the city of Tenochtitlán housed between 200,000-300,000 inhabitants.

Estimates on the number of people in this entire region on the eve of the 1519 invasion vary greatly, but most scholars estimate that approximately 20 million people lived in the region. By 1600 — less than 100 years after the arrival of the Europeans — the Indian population had declined by 95 percent.

There were few land areas where people had no contact with Europeans and where populations did not decrease significantly. Major causes of the decrease in population were death from new diseases, over-work, ill treatment, and systematic killing. Like the Black Plague that was taking lives in Europe, this was called the "Black Legend."

By 1650 the Indian population began to increase again. This was primarily due to the introduction of new laws that abolished some of the worst excesses of exploitation. Those who survived had also developed resistance to diseases, improved their diet, and made some adaptation to the demands of a new way of life under Spanish rule.

However, the conquest begun in 1519 by the Spanish broke up the dynamic development of indigenous cultures in Mesoamerica. As a result, the destiny of the inhabitants of this region and the entire western hemisphere changed forever.

Chart below: Gerhard, Peter. *A Guide to the Historical Geography of New Spain*. Norman, Oklahoma. University of Oklahoma Press. 1993.

——— Indians
------- Others

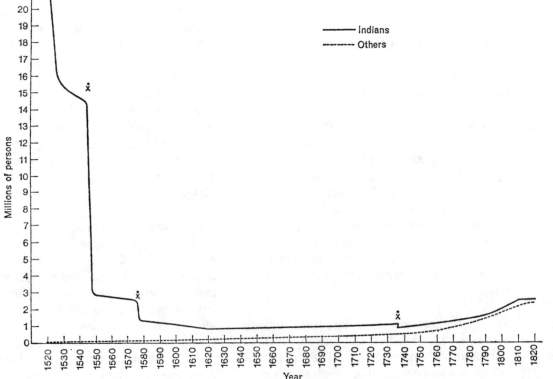

FIGURE I. The decline and recovery of the native population

*Many Faces of Mexico*

# COMPARATIVE CHRONOLOGY

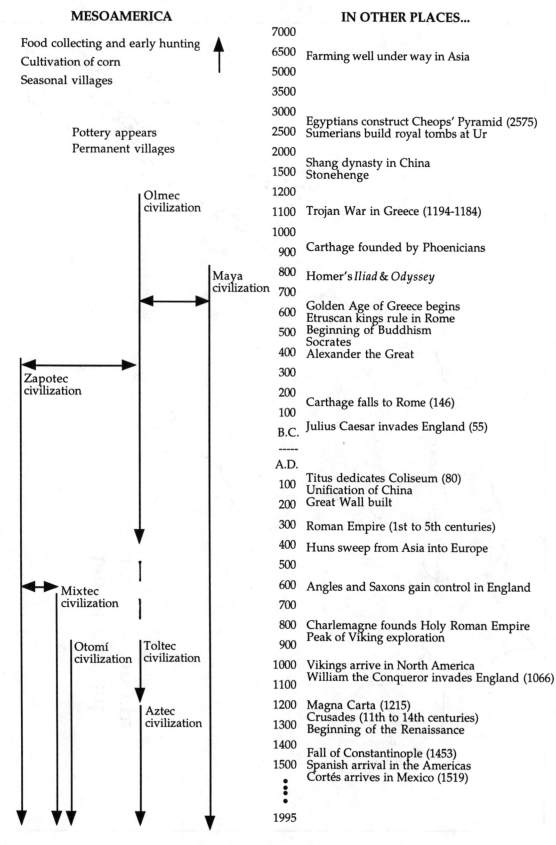

**MESOAMERICA**

**IN OTHER PLACES...**

| | | |
|---|---|---|
| | 7000 | |
| Food collecting and early hunting | 6500 | Farming well under way in Asia |
| Cultivation of corn | 5000 | |
| Seasonal villages | 3500 | |
| | 3000 | |
| | | Egyptians construct Cheops' Pyramid (2575) |
| Pottery appears | 2500 | Sumerians build royal tombs at Ur |
| Permanent villages | 2000 | |
| | | Shang dynasty in China |
| | 1500 | Stonehenge |
| Olmec civilization | 1200 | |
| | 1100 | Trojan War in Greece (1194-1184) |
| | 1000 | |
| | 900 | Carthage founded by Phoenicians |
| Maya civilization | 800 | Homer's *Iliad* & *Odyssey* |
| | 700 | |
| | 600 | Golden Age of Greece begins |
| | | Etruscan kings rule in Rome |
| | 500 | Beginning of Buddhism |
| | | Socrates |
| | 400 | Alexander the Great |
| | 300 | |
| Zapotec civilization | 200 | |
| | | Carthage falls to Rome (146) |
| | 100 | |
| | B.C. | Julius Caesar invades England (55) |
| | ----- | |
| | A.D. | |
| | 100 | Titus dedicates Coliseum (80) |
| | | Unification of China |
| | 200 | Great Wall built |
| | 300 | Roman Empire (1st to 5th centuries) |
| | 400 | Huns sweep from Asia into Europe |
| | 500 | |
| | 600 | Angles and Saxons gain control in England |
| Mixtec civilization | 700 | |
| | 800 | Charlemagne founds Holy Roman Empire |
| Otomí civilization / Toltec civilization | 900 | Peak of Viking exploration |
| | 1000 | Vikings arrive in North America |
| | | William the Conqueror invades England (1066) |
| | 1100 | |
| Aztec civilization | 1200 | Magna Carta (1215) |
| | | Crusades (11th to 14th centuries) |
| | 1300 | Beginning of the Renaissance |
| | 1400 | |
| | | Fall of Constantinople (1453) |
| | 1500 | Spanish arrival in the Americas |
| | | Cortés arrives in Mexico (1519) |
| | 1995 | |

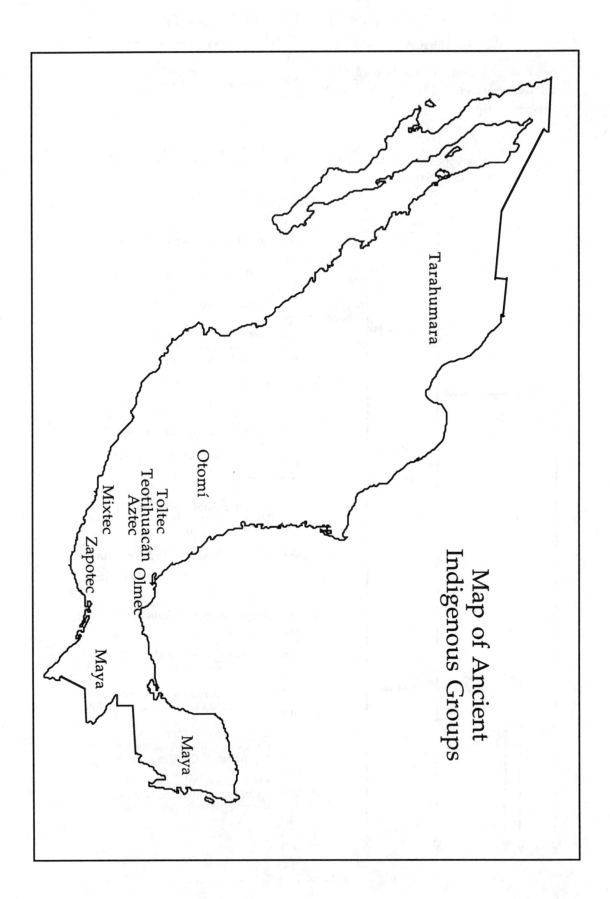

Map of Ancient
Indigenous Groups

Tarahumara

Otomí
Toltec
Teotihuacán
Aztec
Olmec
Mixtec
Zapotec
Maya

Maya

| | **REGION 1**<br>North | **REGION 2**<br>North Central | **REGION 3**<br>South Central |
|---|---|---|---|
| Who lived in the region? | | | |
| Where did they live? | | | |
| How did they live? What kinds of houses, food and clothing did they have? | | | |
| What were some of their cultural practices? | | | |
| What kinds of transportation did they use? | | | |
| Did they migrate or have permanent settlements or cities? | | | |
| What kinds of trade did they engage in with other people? | | | |

|  | **REGION 4**<br>Gulf Coast | **REGION 5**<br>Pacific Southwest | **REGION 6**<br>Southeast |
|---|---|---|---|
| Who lived in the region? |  |  |  |
| Where did they live? |  |  |  |
| How did they live? What kinds of houses, food and clothing did they have? |  |  |  |
| What were some of their cultural practices? |  |  |  |
| What kinds of transportation did they use? |  |  |  |
| Did they migrate or have permanent settlements or cities? |  |  |  |
| What kinds of trade did they engage in with other people? |  |  |  |

*Region 1—North*
# The Tarahumara

The Tarahumara (tar-ah-ou-MAR-ah) lived in the north in what is now the state of Chihuahua (chee-WAH-wah). This area has different ecological regions—the highlands and the lowlands. The Tarahumara lived in the highlands, in the mountains and valleys of the Sierra Madre. To build their houses, they used materials that were available locally, such as pine, clay and branches. Tarahumara people also lived in caves.

The Tarahumara spoke their own language but were linguistically related to other people in the region. They were nomadic and shared hunting and harvesting lands with other people. The Tarahumara raised most of their own food and made most of their clothing from cloth they wove. They grew corn, the staple of their diet, on their mountainous plots of land. They got water for drinking, washing and livestock from the streams in the valleys. In the dry season, water was scarce and the streams often became polluted, causing health problems.

The original name of the Tarahumara was Raramuri (rahr-ah-MOU-ree), which in the Tarahumara language means foot runners. The Tarahumara were known for their great long-distance running abilities. They held competitions that brought together women and men runners from the entire region.

Family groups were the basic structure of these early dwellers of northern Mexico. Basic education took place within the home, as children learned from their elders, other family members and their surroundings.

When the Spanish invaded their region, the Tarahumara fiercely resisted their settlements. They chose to be isolated from the larger culture of Mexico and the changes that took place in the rest of the world.

*Region 2—North Central*
# The Otomí

E vidence of Otomí (oh-toe-ME) settlements in Mexico first appeared around 900 AD, the same time as the rise of the Toltec (TOLL-tek) civilization. For centuries, the Otomí lived in what is now central Mexico. In this dry, rocky region, the Otomí began to cultivate corn, beans and a plant called the maguey (ma-GAY). This plant provided a honey water to drink, fibers for weaving cloth, and leaves used for constructing houses. Though this plant is important to people throughout Mexico, it was of special value to the Otomí, and they referred to it as "Mother." The maguey plant helped the Otomí survive in the arid environment that was their home.

Between the 10th and 14th centuries, the Otomí often were able to resist conquest by the larger, more complex civilizations by frequently moving from place to place. At various times, they were invaded by the Toltecs and Aztecs, but there was very little influence on their culture and customs by these groups. While Toltecs and Aztecs built mammoth stone temples and pyramids, the Otomí made bricks to build huts in which they lived.

The Otomí made paper by pounding bark from trees with rocks. The paper, called *amate* (ah-MAH-tay) was given to a shaman or healer who cut symbolic figures out of paper that were used in sacred rites.

Svien

During the early 14th century, the Otomí people settled along a huge lake, where first Tenochtitlán (ten-o-shteet-LON) and then Mexico City were built. When pressure from neighboring groups mounted, such as from the Aztecs, the Otomí headed north and settled there. Still part of the Aztec territory, many Otomí people were captured and taken as slaves. Other Otomí became soldiers or mercenaries and integrated into other societies.

In 1531, when the Spanish armies moved northwest into the place that is now called Querétaro (care-ATE-tah-ro), Otomí leaders were able to convince the invaders to put down their guns and fight it out with bare fists. For 12 hours they fought, like a vast boxing match, man to man. At sunset, when both sides were exhausted and anxious for the fight to end, there was an omen in the sky that ended the fight. Legend says they embraced each other and joined as brothers. However, later the Spaniards took over the area completely and forced the Otomí people to work on plantations and find gold for them.

## Region 3—South Central
# The Toltec

The Toltec (TOLL-tek) were a complex, multi-ethnic group of people who lived to the north and west of the Valley of Mexico in what is now the state of Hidalgo (he-DAHL-go). Between the 9th and 13th centuries AD, the Toltecs controlled much of central Mexico and developed the site of Tula (TOO-lah), (also called Tollan, "place of the reeds") into a major center. The Toltec's social, artistic and cultural life was influenced by the Olmecs, who traveled and traded throughout central Mexico. When the Olmecs dispersed, it is believed that many joined the Toltecs.

Tula was built in the 10th century. In its pyramids and palaces are many representations of one of the god-kings, Quetzalcóatl (ket-zal-CO-at-el), the Feathered Serpent. Although he was a figure among many groups, the Toltecs' versions portray Quetzalcóatl as a gentle god who disliked violence and human sacrifice. Legends say that Quetzalcóatl was also the name of a Toltec leader who was forced to leave Tula and went somewhere to the east. He said he would return in the Year One of the next 52 year calendar cycle. That happened to be 1519, the year that the Spanish arrived.

Toltec men wore loincloths with tunics or ponchos. The women wore *huipiles* (wee-PEELS) and sarongs, and both men and women wore sandals. The wealthy pierced their noses, cheeks and earlobes and decorated themselves with jewels and feathers. Most people were rural farmers and suburban artisans who lived in stone, earth and adobe brick houses. Families often shared the same occupation and lived together in adjoining houses that shared a common interior courtyard. Farming was done in large fields called *milpas* outside of the villages and in small plots next to the houses. Toltec farmers cultivated maize (corn), beans, chili peppers, amaranth, squash, cotton and the maguey (ma-GAY) plant. Meat was a rare "festival food" rather than a dietary staple.

The name Toltec means "artisan" and indeed, many people were artisans who produced building blocks, pottery, baskets, obsidian tools, textiles, jewelry, and other objects. The Toltec people developed an elaborate market and trade system through which they were able to obtain materials and sell their products. Through this system, they spread their influence all the way to the southwestern part of what is now the US.

Around 1200 AD, political instability and pressure from outside groups helped bring about the decline of Tula and the Toltec civilization. Many Toltecs joined a wave of migration south into the Valley of Mexico where they settled in several communities and assimilated into other cultures. Toltec art, culture and social organization were a profound influence on the Aztecs, who later settled in much of the same territory.

*Region 4—Gulf Coast*
# The Olmec

The Olmec (OHL-mek) civilization flourished between about 1200 BC and 300 AD. The Maya, Zapotec (SAH-po-tek) and Toltec peoples, who are known for their high social, artistic and cultural achievements, most likely drew many ideas from the Olmecs.

The Olmec people lived primarily in the Veracruz area. They traveled and traded across the southern highlands to the Pacific Ocean and south to what are now Guatemala and El Salvador. These are the areas where they found jade, which was extremely valuable to their artwork.

The Olmec people lived in areas of tropical jungle where there was an abundance of rubber. The name Olmec in their language means "rubber people." Whether the Olmec were the people who originally domesticated corn is unknown, but it was their staple food and they ground it and prepared it as tortillas. They also raised beans and squash. The jungle made farming difficult, so to grow these crops they used a "slash and burn" technique. Just before the rains came at the end of May, they burned the plot of land and the remaining ash fertilized the soil. When the rains began, corn seeds were dropped in holes made in the ashes with a digging stick. After about two harvests, they left the plot to lie fallow and recover its fertility. They irrigated the land, using the natural rising and falling pattern of the rivers. The Olmec also ate fish, turtles, shellfish, deer and peccary, a pig-like animal.

The Olmecs lived in houses made of bamboo poles and covered with thatched roofs. Although small villages were most common, larger community centers housed their leaders. In addition, the Olmec built ceremonial centers with pyramids, which were the burial sites of their rulers. Some community centers contained ball fields. The oldest ball game of Mesoamerica was played by the Olmec, using a rubber ball. Spectators lined the walls on each side of the playing field to watch the players try to throw the ball through a hole in a protruding stone in the wall on the side of the field.

Huge stone carvings of the heads of kings are among the artworks of the Olmec. One head weighed 18 tons; it was carved without the help of metal tools and hauled without the aid of the wheel. They also carved miniatures of ordinary people and jaguars; some are molded in clay while others were carved in jade, serpentine and granite. The Olmec had a calendar system which measured time in 52 year increments. At the end of 52 years, the calendar started over.

## Region 5—Pacific Southwest
# The Zapotec

The Zapotecs (SAH-po-tek) lived in what is now the state of Oaxaca (wah-HA-kah) in southern Mexico. During the height of their civilization about 2,500 years ago it is estimated there were 300,000 Zapotecs.

Their main centers were at Monte Albán and Mitla. Monte Albán was not built by the Zapotec people, but it was occupied by them when they moved into the region. It was probably constructed by the Olmec, but the murals that cover the walls of the temples and the pyramids were painted by the Zapotec. Monte Albán was a large and flourishing city built high on a mountain and surrounded by houses built into the terraced slopes that fall away from the mountain.

The Zapotec had a calendar that was central to their religion. The calendar symbols, or glyphs, were painted in temples and on tombs. They also created jaguars and birds out of precious metals. The intricately decorated pottery that the Zapotec made was both for everyday use and for ceremonies.

Zapotecs were primarily farmers. They grew corn that they ground for tortillas, harvested cacao beans for a chocolate beverage, and ate cactus fruits, nuts and avocados. They utilized the maguey (ma-GAY) plant in many different ways, such as for food, syrup, a fermented drink, and fiber for their clothing. Most of the farming was done together on lands that they worked communally.

Hunting was limited to those in the upper class, and their prey included rabbit, turkey and deer. Zapotec houses were usually one-room with no windows and a pitched roof.

For entertainment and sport, Zapotecs played a game that combined aspects of modern-day basketball and soccer. On a large field, players used their bodies to move a ball and push it through a hoop that was on a wall on the side of the field, about four feet off the ground.

The Zapotec people had a highly structured society. The nobles had the most authority, followed by the priests, commoners, serfs and lastly, slaves. In the 14th century, the Mixtec (MIS-tek) people dominated the Zapotecs when they moved into their territory. The Mixtecs added their carvings, pottery, mosaics and statues to the ceremonial site at Monte Albán, and eventually, the Zapotecs adopted many of the Mixtec techniques and customs.

When the Aztecs spread their empire south, Monte Albán was abandoned. By the time the Spanish invaded the region in 1521, Monte Albán was deteriorating.

## Region 6—Southeast
# The Maya Lacandón

The Maya Lacandón (MY-ah-la-cahn-DOAN) people lived in the rainforests of southern Mexico. They used practically every tree, plant and shrub for food, shelter, clothing and medicine. They built canoes from mahogany trees, carved bows and arrows from branches, used the pitch from pine trees for lantern fuel, and made baskets and gourds from vines.

They also grew a variety of colors of cotton from which they wove their clothing. The men wore tunics that hung to their knees and the women wore tunics over their skirts.

Agriculture was the economic base of this Mayan group and corn was the primary crop. The men spear-fished in the river and hunted deer and turkey with bows and arrows. The corn harvest was during the fall of each year. From the corn, women prepared tortillas, corn beverages and other dishes.

Also important was the harvest of squash, tomato, chili peppers and fruits such as avocados, bananas, papaya, lemons and oranges. They grew cocoa beans from which they made a chocolate drink.

In the villages, houses were built in rectangular fashion supported at the base by five or six logs. The roof was made from palm tree branches. Because of the hot climate, they didn't always build walls, but if they did, they used bamboo lashed together with handmade ropes. The cooking area was inside the house. Along the interior walls, they hung hammocks they wove and used for sleeping.

Before the arrival of the Spanish, the Lacandón people lived in villages surrounding ceremonial centers, such as Palenque (pah-LEN-kay). Their art was primarily created for healing ceremonies. The most common art pieces were containers for burning incense.

The Lacandón shared their territory with other Mayan groups. In 1536, the Spanish invaded much of the Mayan territory and tried to convert the people to Christianity. However, their efforts were continuously frustrated by the Lacandón, who moved further into the rainforest, settled there and remained basically untouched by the Spanish. In 1586, a military expedition attacked Lacandón towns, torching them and massacring many people.

*An Exploring the Connections Lesson*

# Exploring Tenochtitlán:
## *Reconstructing Aztec Life*

More information exists about the Aztec people than perhaps any other group of people in the pre-European contact period in the Americas. The information provided in this lesson focuses on the Aztec people and their way of life before the Spanish invasion. The Aztec empire was vast and the organization of the society was complex. Aztec merchants traded throughout what is now central Mexico and with the Mayan people in what is now Guatemala. Aztec warriors engaged other groups in battle, and when victorious, took people for sacrificial ceremonies. They also collected tributes, a form of taxation, throughout their empire. Tenochtitlán was the major Aztec city, built on an island, and designed with a intricate infrastructure of roads, irrigation systems, and neighborhoods. Mexico City currently sits on the site of the grand Tenochtitlán.

In keeping with the theme of *Many Faces of Mexico*, we focus on daily life of the Aztec people, rather than architecture and artifacts. We also do not describe Aztec ceremonies and rituals, despite their importance in Aztec life. Information on these topics can be found in numerous books on the Aztec. The information is presented in short sections, followed by questions that guide students to compare and contrast Aztec life to their own lives.

| | |
|---|---|
| **Learner Objectives** | • To describe important features of Aztec society and daily life in Tenochtitlán. |
| | • To compare and contrast features of Aztec society to the students' surroundings. |
| **Concepts** | • Society |
| | • Custom |
| | • Tribute |
| **Major Questions to be Addressed** | • How did the Aztecs live? |
| | • What was daily life like in an Aztec city? |
| | • How do we know how they lived? |
| **Exploring the Connections** | To help students understand that the ways people lived 1,000 years ago is not all that different from today, students are asked to think about the connections between how the Aztec lived and how they live. They are encouraged to compare and contrast Aztec homes, education, food, shopping, government, etc. with these same aspects of their own lives. |
| **Teaching Strategies** | Reading, writing and small group discussion |
| **Materials Provided** | • Exploring Tenochtitlán (Handout 1) |
| | • A map of Tenochtitlán; suitable for making an overhead (Image 1) |
| | • Living in Tenochtitlán (Handout 2) |
| **Time Required** | 1 class session |
| **Vocabulary** | *(see Glossary for definitions)* |
| | • Aztec |
| | • Tenochtitlán |
| | • Moctezuma |
| | • Codices |
| | • Nahuatl |
| | • Chinampa |
| | • Tribute |
| | • Tlatelolco |
| **Preparation for Lesson** | • Make an overhead of Image 1. |
| | • Make one copy of Handout 1 for each small group. |
| | • Make copies of Handout 2 for homework assignment. |
| | • Write the new vocabulary words on the board so all students can become familiar with them. Refer to glossary for definitions. |
| | • We suggest you find additional illustrations in books about the Aztecs to show during the lesson. |

## Sequence of Lesson

*Anticipatory Set*
*5 minutes*

1. Ask students to imagine a time warp in which people living in the 22nd century return to the present, asking about life at the end of the 20th century. Ask students to consider what they want the future travelers to see and hear about their daily lives? Read aloud the following Aztec poem. You may wish to write it on the board for further discussion.

> *Our house on earth*
> *We do not inhabit*
> *only borrow it*
> *briefly.*
> — Aztec poem

*Body of Lesson*
*30-40 minutes*

2. In this lesson, we look back about 1000 years into the lives of Aztec people living in Tenochtitlán. After reading and answering questions about Aztec life and society, students are asked to describe aspects of their lives and society to the time travelers. Introduce the Aztec city of Tenochtitlán by showing the overhead map and asking students what they think it would be like to live on an island about 1000 years ago.

3. Divide students into groups of three and distribute Handout 1 to the group. Instruct students to divide the nine sections among themselves, so each student has three sections to read silently. After students have completed reading their first section, ask them to explain this section to the other group members and work on the questions together. Use the remaining time for students to read another section and work with others in the group. Continue working until they have completed as many of the sections as time permits.

*Closure*

4. Ask students the following question: if they were to make a time capsule for future generations, what kinds of things would they include in it? What kinds of things are important in their daily lives that they would want others to know about? (If you have time, make a time capsule with your class!)

*Evaluation*

Use the peer evaluation form for students to assess their group's work (see Appendix D).

*Assignment*

Distribute copies of the fictional story, Life in Tenochtitlán, Handout 2. Ask students to think about the story in light of what they have learned during the lesson and to write five new sentences to continue the story. (Lesson 6 about the conquest begins with students reading aloud their continuations of the story.)

# Exploring Tenochtitlán

## THE SETTLING OF TENOCHTITLÁN

The Valley of Mexico was a beautiful fertile plateau with many lakes. The largest of these lakes was fed by the melting snow of surrounding mountains. The Aztec people migrated from the north into the valley in about 1193. When they arrived, the area already was densely populated. For the next hundred years, the Aztecs served as soldiers and servants to their powerful neighbors. Gradually, they absorbed the traditions and customs of these more established communities. The Aztecs finally settled on uninhabited, swampy islands in the middle of a huge lake. According to legend, it was there that they saw an eagle poised upon a cactus eating a serpent—a sign foretold by their war and sun god as a place to settle.

On these swampy lands the Aztec began to build the great city of Tenochtitlán (ten-o-shteet-LON) in about 1325. The city became the center of power for the vast Aztec empire that extended from the Pacific Ocean to the Gulf of Mexico, and from what is now Guatemala to several hundred miles north of Mexico City. Tenochtitlán eventually had as many as 250,000 people, at a time when some historians estimate that perhaps 20 million people lived in central Mexico.

***Directions:*** *Compare the place you live to Tenochtitlán. Fill in the table based on what you just read and what you know about your own city, town, or county.*

| | TENOCHTITLÁN | My city / town / county of: |
|---|---|---|
| How and when did settlement take place? | | |
| What is the symbol of the settlement? | | |

# SOURCES OF INFORMATION ABOUT THE AZTECS

Our knowledge of the Aztec comes from three sources. The first is the ancient Aztec books of drawings, called codices. On paper made from tree bark, the people painted stylized figures and symbols that recorded events and stories. Although the Spanish destroyed many of these codices after the conquest, some did survive and are housed in European and US libraries. Another source is Aztec oral history. The Aztecs told stories and legends about events in their lives as a way of teaching about their past. These stories were passed from generation to generation. Another way we know about their history is through a Spanish friar who talked with the Aztecs shortly after the Spanish invasion in 1519. The Spaniard learned Nahuatl, (NA-hwat-el) the language of the Aztec people. He recorded detailed accounts of Aztec history, religion and daily life by talking with people who had lived in Tenochtitlán.

***Directions***: *Compare the place you live to Tenochtitlán. Fill in the table based on what you just read and what you know about your city, town, or county.*

|  | TENOCHTITLÁN | My city / town / county of: |
|---|---|---|
| How do we know the people who lived here? | | |
| What sources of information do we have? | | |

# THE DESIGN OF TENOCHTITLÁN

Tenochtitlán was an impressive city which was arranged according to a specific pattern. The ceremonial center of the city included huge stone pyramids and temples. The palaces of the nobles were located just outside of this ceremonial district. Farther from the center were the neighborhoods of the common people. These areas had simple houses, along with local temples and houses for the nobility.

Many buildings in the city had walls made of brightly painted. There were also many gardens, giving the city a feeling of openness. Buildings which were used to store grain or weapons occupied strategic locations.

Since the city was on an island, three large "causeways," or raised roads, linked the island with the mainland to the north, west, and south. These causeways were cut at intervals by canals, with wooden drawbridges over the canals for pedestrians. Canals in and around Tenochtitlán were an important part of the transportation system as the Aztecs primarily used canoes to carry their products and transport people They did not have horses, oxen or cattle for transportation, and did not use any vehicles with wheels.

**Directions:** *Compare the place you live to Tenochtitlán. Fill in the table based on what you just read and what you know about your city, town, or county.*

|  | TENOCHTITLÁN | My city / town / county of: |
|---|---|---|
| How is the city / area laid out? |  |  |
| Where is the ceremonial center? |  |  |
| Describe the transportation system. |  |  |

# THE AZTEC ECONOMY

Agriculture was central to the Aztec economy; however, commerce and trade also were important. Traveling merchants engaged in lively trade between towns hundreds of miles apart. The Aztec had highly organized markets based on bartering and on the currency of cacao beans and gold. In addition to agriculture and trading, the Aztec economy depended on taxes, known as tributes, collected from peoples conquered in wars. In the early 1500s, historians estimate that 370 tribes from 33 provinces in the region paid tribute to the Aztecs. Local government administrators were in charge of periodically collecting the tributes from the conquered peoples who lived within the Aztec empire. The tributes were in the form of whatever was produced—jade, gold, food, warrior costumes, animal skins and bird feathers. The Aztecs also accepted or took people as tributes, who they used as slaves or in their sacrificial ceremonies.

**Directions:** *Compare the place you live to Tenochtitlán. Fill in the table based on what you just read and what you know about your city, town, or county.*

|  | TENOCHTITLÁN | My city / town / county of: |
|---|---|---|
| What is the currency? |  |  |
| On what is the economy based? |  |  |

# FARMING AND FOOD

Most people who lived in or around Tenochtitlán were farmers.  Aztec farmers used very simple tools, but developed a  highly productive technique of growing crops in nearby swamps.  *Chinampas* (chin-AHMP-pas), small islands built in the swamps, were created by cutting canals through the swamps. On these small islands the Aztecs piled layers of decaying plants and fertile mud, and then planted willow trees to minimize erosion and anchor them to the lake bottom. Farmers often worked from their canoes, sowing seeds, harvesting crops and transporting them to the mainland. With this efficient system, they harvested as many as seven crops a year.

Corn was the Aztecs' staple food. It was prepared in beverages; eaten as *tamales* (tom-AHL-ees), cornmeal mixed with other ingredients and steamed inside corn husks; or made into *tortillas*, flat cakes of ground corn. The Aztecs also grew beans, squash, chilies, avocados, sweet potatoes and tomatoes. They ate little meat, since there were few large animals to hunt.  Most meat came from the lakes, including fish, geese, turtles, frogs, insects and grubs.  The few chickens, turkeys and dogs which were raised to eat were reserved primarily for the nobility. The lakes also provided an important source of protein: green algae that tasted something like cheese. It was dried into bricks and often carried by warriors into battle.

*Directions*: Compare the place you live to Tenochtitlán. Fill in the table based on what you just read and what you know about your city, town, or county.

| | TENOCHTITLÁN | My city / town / county: |
|---|---|---|
| What do people eat? | | |
| Where is the food from? | | |
| What do farms look like? | | |
| Can farmers raise enough to feed their community? | | |

*Many Faces of Mexico*

# SHOPPING AT THE MARKET

Merchants, artisans and farmers sold their products at Tlatelolco (tlot-el-LOL-co), a large and famous market just north of the center of Tenochtitlán. It is believed that as many as 25,000 people went to this market each day. The quantity and variety of products were impressive: pottery, clothing, building materials, tools, flowers, precious metals, firewood, and all kinds of food were available. Since bartering was the basis of trade, items such as cacao beans, cotton cloaks and turkey quills filled with gold dust were used to make up the difference in value in cases of unequal exchanges. Expensive luxury items brought from faraway places were available for the upper class nobility.

**Directions:** *Compare the place you live to Tenochtitlán. Fill in the table based on what you just read and what you know about your city, town, or county.*

| | TENOCHTITLÁN | My city / town / county of: |
|---|---|---|
| Where is the main marketplace? | | |
| What kinds of things can you buy there? | | |

# AZTEC GOVERNMENT

The basic social, economic and political unit of Aztec society was the local neighborhood. Each neighborhood had temples, markets, schools, land and communal support for the sick and the elderly. Local residents provided labor to build or repair public buildings, temples, bridges and streets, and also served in the army as needed. Each neighborhood was headed by a chief, who represented the common people in community decisions and made up a council which elected the Aztec head of state and commander-in-chief, known as the "Great Speaker."

The Great Speaker, who came from the nobility, was both a great priest and a military captain. He was required to govern the state, and was also expected to expand the power and size of the Aztec empire, and to increase the size of the temple of the sun and war god. Moctezuma II became the Great Speaker in 1502 and continued in this position until 1519.

**Directions:** *Compare the place you live to Tenochtitlán. Fill in the table based on what you just read and what you know about your city, town, or county.*

| | TENOCHTITLÁN | My city / town / county of: |
|---|---|---|
| How are the people organized? | | |
| Who is their leader? | | |
| What is expected of their leader? | | |

# AZTEC SOCIAL SECTORS

Aztec society was divided into two basic groups: the nobility and the common working people. Nobles enjoyed many privileges. They occupied the highest civil and religious positions and lived near the city's ceremonial center. They did not pay taxes, and they were the only ones who could own land. They studied in special schools where they were trained to be priests, warriors or governors. There were special courts for nobles, and men of the nobility could have more than one wife.

The common people lived in neighborhoods that spread out from the city center, or, if they were farmers, on their *chinampas*, the farming islands created in the swamps near the city. Working class craftspeople in the city produced baskets, tools, pottery, reed mats and woven cloth. Goods which were not used by their families were sold in the market. Craftspeople who produced luxury items for the nobility — such as jewelry and brilliantly colored feathered capes and shields — were considered to be of a higher class than ordinary craftspeople.

Aztec society also had slaves. One could sell oneself or one's children into slavery in times of famine or financial difficulty, or fall into slavery for a number of reasons: failing to pay a debt, betting and losing on a ball game, or committing robbery or murder. People accused of serious crimes could become the slaves of the victim or the victim's family. Slaves had certain rights, including the right to buy their freedom. Also, the children of slaves were born as free people.

**Directions**: *Compare the place you live to Tenochtitlán. Fill in the table based on what you just read and what you know about your city, town, or county.*

|  | TENOCHTITLÁN | My city / town / county of: |
|---|---|---|
| What are the different social sectors? |  |  |
| What are the privileges and burdens of each sector? |  |  |
| What are each sector's responsibilities? |  |  |

# HOMES AND EDUCATION

The homes of the nobility, often two stories tall with more than 50 rooms, ringed the inner city. They were usually built on raised platforms and were made of volcanic stone. The walls were covered with limestone cement, which made the outside of the house white. A typical home had a central courtyard which was surrounded by several rooms. Working people lived outside the ring of wealthy homes in small, one-room houses made from branches plastered with mud and covered with thatched roofs. Farmers made their homes in small villages on land surrounding the lake, and some lived on their *chinampas*. All Aztecs, whether wealthy or poor, had little furniture. They sat on straw cushions during the day and slept on mats at night.

Children of noble families went to special temple schools where boys learned the duties of the priests and girls learned to be temple assistants or healers. Most other children did not go to school, but worked with their parents at home and in the field. Most boys learned how to be warriors and most girls learned household. All children were expected to conform to Aztec society and contribute to the needs of the household. Idle or disobedient children were punished, sometimes by being held over the biting smoke of a fire in which red chili peppers were burning.

**Directions:** *Compare the place you live to Tenochtitlán. Fill in the table based on what you just read and what you know about your city, town, or county.*

| | TENOCHTITLÁN | My city / town / county: |
|---|---|---|
| Describe the kinds of homes and the people who live in them. | | |
| What is expected of the children? | | |

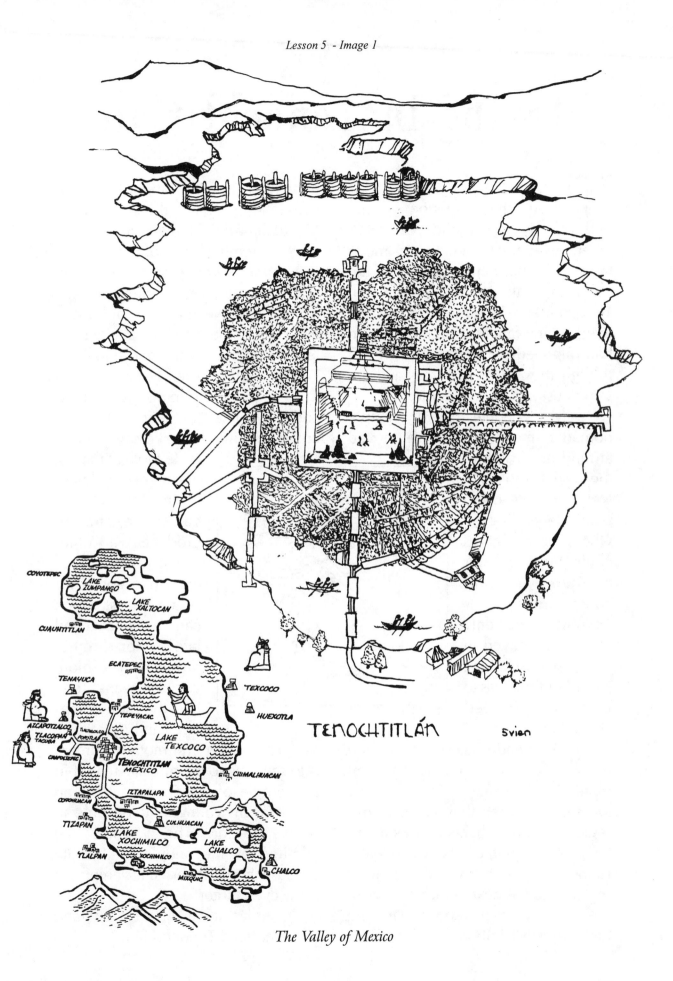

*The Valley of Mexico*

# Living in Tenochtitlán

The story I'm going to tell you is about the migration of my family. It was the year 1441 when my parents decided to move from the northern lands of the Mexican valley to the city of Tenochtitlán where the Aztec people lived. Many families from my region had migrated to the Aztec city, even though the Aztecs did not have the same customs as my people.

My people were mainly nomadic, meaning that we moved around according to the seasons. We went from place to place depending on where our fathers could hunt and our mothers could collect fruits, seeds or roots. The only reason we stayed in one place for a long period of time was to plant and harvest corn.

We had heard about the majestic city of Tenochtitlán from traveling merchants or running messengers when they came to our region. The merchants told us about the greatness of the big city, while the runners, in their hurry to deliver their message to the next runner, told us of the many events in Tenochtitlán. The last and most important event that I remember hearing about was the coronation of the emperor Moctezuma (mock-the-SOO-mah) as the supreme lord of the ever-expanding Aztec empire. The city seemed to be a very exciting place.

I was eleven years old when my father and mother decided to leave the big group and move to Tenochtitlán. My father had learned to make sandals from his grandfather, and if we lived in Tenochtitlán, he could continue to make sandals and trade them at the big market of Tlatelolco. In this market one can exchange products with other merchants or exchange goods for cocoa beans, which can be exchanged later for other products. The more cocoa beans one has, the more things one can buy.

My father and mother's dream is to send me to the military school in the temple of the warriors. It is an honor for any youngster to become an Aztec warrior. The warriors are admired by the people of the city because they help the Aztec empire to grow even larger.

At last it was moving day, and as we entered Tenochtitlán.....

# The Spanish Invasion

The Spanish invasion of Mexico began at Veracruz and continued to Tenochtitlán in 1519. It is one of the most significant events in the history of the Americas. It precipitated changes that immediately affected tens of thousands of people, and continued to have long term, devastating effects on the peoples in the region and in the Americas. One hundred years after the conquest, it is estimated that 19 million of the 20 million Indians in Mexico died from wars, overwork or disease.

This lesson is designed to give the invasion of Mexico a human face. The challenges and dilemmas that people faced are presented, along with sagas of bravery and anguish, indecisiveness and determination, trust and betrayal.

We have included many accounts written by those who were present during the invasion of Tenochtitlán. Through primary sources, we present a variety of perspectives of what occurred. The Spanish sources, from which most history texts are written, come from the letters of Cortés; the diaries of a Spanish soldier, Bernal Díaz del Castillo; and a Catholic Friar, Bartolomé de las Casas. Bernadino de Sahagún, who spoke Nahuatl and Spanish, wrote down stories that Aztec people told him. The Aztecs recorded their history in drawings on paper made of bark and bound them together like books, called codices. For this lesson, we use the Florentine and Lienzo de Tlaxcala codices.

The conquest of Tenochtitlán reveals the vast differences between European and indigenous ways of life. However, the reader will note that both groups took the lives of others to attain their goals: the Aztecs practiced human sacrifice in religious ceremonies to appease their gods and the Spanish indulged in warfare for personal and national gain. In this lesson, we present both Aztec and Spanish points of view.

| | |
|---|---|
| **Learner Objectives** | • To identify the different perspectives of the Spanish and the Aztecs. |
| | • To discuss and explain the values and interests both the Spanish and the Aztecs were trying to achieve/maintain. |
| | • To interpret the codices to understand the Aztecs' recorded history. |
| | • To evaluate the short-term and long-term significance of Spanish invasion and settlement in the Americas. |
| **Concepts** | • Invasion |
| | • Perspective |
| | • Greed |
| **Major Questions to be Addressed** | • What were some of the opposing interests of the Spanish and Aztecs? |
| | • Why are people motivated to invade or conquer others? |
| | • What were some of the short-term and long-term impacts of Spanish settlement in the Americas? |
| **Teaching Strategies** | Oral reading, small group discussion, drawing, writing |
| **Materials Provided** | • Narrative Readings on the Invasion (Handout 1) |
| | • Drawings from Codices, for transparencies |
| | • Key to Drawings (Educator's Background Information) |
| | • The Story of La Llorona (Handout 2) |
| **Additional Materials Needed** | • Plain paper (8 ½" x 11") |
| | • Overhead projector |
| | • Transparencies made from codice drawings |
| | • *Living in Tenochtitlán* (Handout from Lesson 5) |
| **Time Required** | 2- 3 class sessions |
| **Vocabulary** | *(See Glossary for definitions)* |
| | • Codices |
| | • Conquistador |
| | • Quetzal |
| | • Quetzalcóatl |
| | • Tlatelolco |
| **Preparation for this Lesson** | • Copy one set of Handout 1 and cut into sections to distribute among students. Familiarize yourself with the readings and take the role of narrator to direct the flow of the readings. ***Note that statements in italics are excerpts from primary sources; others are written with information from multiple sources.*** |
| | • Make transparencies of the codice drawings and familiarize yourself with the script. The circled numbers correspond to the drawing number, whereas the other numbers indicate the order in which the narratives should be read. At the appropriate place in the reading, place the corresponding drawing on the overhead |

projector to give students a visual image as they are listening to the reader.

- Copy sets of the codex drawings, and cut them apart for small groups. (Optional)
- Instruct students to read *Living in Tenochtitlán* (Lesson 5) and bring to class the sentences they added to the story.
- Copy handout 3 for an extension lesson.

- *Option*: Prearrange with 2 or 3 people (older students, faculty members, etc.) to come into your classroom to simulate an invasion while students are working on their codice project. For details, see Step 6 below in the Sequence of Lesson.

# Sequence of Lesson

*Anticipatory Set*
*10 minutes*

1. Distribute narrative readings from Handout 1 randomly to students. Review the story, *Living in Tenochtitlán*, from Lesson 5. Ask a student to add a new line and, therefore, a new twist, to the story. This serial storytelling should draw upon what students have written in their homework assignment.

*Body of Lesson*
*2-3 class sessions*

2. After a few minutes of this storytelling session, the teacher should interrupt the story with the news that ships have been sighted off the coast. Read the Narrator's Announcement, the first statement in the oral reading.

3. Ask the student with Reading 2 to read his or her narrative aloud to the class. Continue this serial reading through Reading 23, showing the drawings from the codice. Some drawings are close in order, so pause for students to study them. Address any questions and discuss student reactions to the sets of readings, which may take more than one class period.

4. Divide into small groups and distribute copied sets of the codice drawings (Handout 2). Ask students to retell the story of the invasion in their own words using the drawings OR match the drawings to the description on the key OR cut apart the drawings and have students arrange them chronologically while they retell the story. (Optional)

5. Distribute plain paper to each student. Ask them to make a drawing that describes their impressions or feelings about the invasion or a related topic.

6. *Option*: While students are working, have the people with whom you prearranged come into the classroom to simulate the experience of an invasion. Without scaring students, the visitors should tell students the room is now their space. They

can order students to give up their chairs, go to the side of the room, etc. After a few minutes, call off the simulated invasion and do a de-briefing about what happened. Ask the "invaders" to participate with students to talk about how they felt during the exercise.

*Closure*

7. Read Part IV, *The Aftermath,* which begins with narrative reading 24. End with the discussion and individual writing, as noted in the Pause for Closing Discussion.

*Student Assignment*

Ask students to write about the simulated classroom invasion and compare it to the invasion of Tenochtitlán, or write a piece that begins "What if...?" and create a different outcome to the invasion that would have respected the human and cultural rights of the Aztecs and other indigenous people in the region.

# References for Student Handouts

1. Miguel Leon-Portilla, ed. *The Broken Spears: The Aztec Account of the Conquest of Mexico.* (Boston: Beacon Press, 1962), p. 26.
2. Ibid., pp. 30-31.
3. Sophia Coe. *America's First Cuisines.* (Austin: University of Texas Press, 1994), pp. 73-74.
4. Francisco Lopez de Gomara, *Historia de la Conquista de Mexico.* (Mexico City: Editorial Rebredo, 1945), p. 25.
5. Ibid., pp. 72-76.
6. Ibid., pp. 76-77.
7. Rafael López Castro y Felipe Garrido, *Escenas de la Conquista.* (Ediciones del Ermitaño, 1984), p
8. Ibid., p 149)
9. Bernal Diaz del Castillo, *True History of the Conquest of New Spain.* (London: Penguin Books, 1966), p. 413.
10. Bartolome de las Casas, *History of the Indians.* (Mexico City: FCE, 1951), pp. 5-6.
12. Gioconda Belli, *The Inhabited Woman.* Translated by Kathleen March. (Willimantic, CT: Curbstone Press, 1989), p. 106.

# NARRATIVE READINGS ON THE INVASION

---

## 1.  Narrator's Announcement

Attention!  Attention! I am an Aztec scout who watches over the ocean. Large boats that look like floating mountains have been cited off the coast of our land. Strange people with light skin and long beards have been seen from a distance. Our leader, Moctezuma, has sent a scouting party to the coast to find out who these strange looking people are.

---

# THE AZTECS

---

## 2.  Reader

My name is Moctezuma (mock-the-SOO-mah). I am the king of the valley of Mexico and the city of Tenochtitlán (ten-o-shteet-LON). Terrible omens tell us that danger is coming to our land. First we saw a comet that seemed to bleed fire, like a wound in the sky. At night we hear cries of a weeping woman, warning that her children must flee. We have heard the crane sing, telling us something is about to happen. Do these signs mean the end of the world is coming? Or is a great event going to take place? When I heard about the ships and the strangers near the coast, I sent my most trusted messengers to the Gulf coast to find out what was happening. My people are frightened and confused. What am I to do? I must protect my people, for I am their leader. **[Codex A]**

---

## 3.  Reader

I am a messenger sent by Moctezuma to bring gifts to the strangers on their ship; that is our custom. We gave them our most divine gifts that included a fine cloak made of *quetzal* (ket-ZAL) feathers and shells. After we had given the strangers many beautiful things, their captain asked us, *"And is this all? Is this your gift of welcome? Is this how you greet people?"* We replied, *"This is all, our lord. This is what we have brought you."*

*Then the Captain gave orders, and we were chained by the feet and by the neck. When this had been done, the great cannon was fired off. We lost our senses and fainted away. We fell down side by side and lay there. But the Spaniards quickly revived us: they lifted us up, gave us wine to drink and then offered us food.*[1]   **[Codices B, C, D]**

## 4. Reader

This is what we told Moctezuma after returning from the strangers' ships: *The strangers' bodies are completely covered, so that only their faces can be seen. Their skin is white, as if it were made of lime...As for their food...It is large and white, and not heavy. It is something like straw, but with taste of a cornstalk...Their dogs are enormous, with flat ears and long, dangling tongues....Their deer carry them on their backs wherever they wish to go. These deer, our lord, are as tall as the roof of a house...*

*And they have a thing called a cannon that shoots a ball of stone out of its entrails; it comes out shooting sparks and raining fire...If the cannon is aimed against a mountain, the mountain splits and cracks open. If it is aimed against a tree, it shatters the tree into splinters...The strangers dress in iron. Their swords are iron; their bows are iron; their shields are iron; their spears are iron.*

*When Moctezuma heard this report, he was filled with terror. It was as if his heart had fainted, as if it had shriveled. It was as if he were conquered by despair.*[2]

## 5. Narrator

Why do you think the great Aztec leader Moctezuma was so afraid and confused? He was having dreams about ominous events. There was a legend about the Aztec's great god Quetzalcóatl (ket-zal-CO-aht-el), who was supposed to return from the East to visit his people. Moctezuma perhaps thought the strangers were bringing back Quetzalcóatl. He also had heard stories about the power of the Spaniards and their leader, Hernando Cortés. Although there were only 350 Spanish soldiers, Moctezuma was totally awed when he heard about their weapons, horses and armor.

## 6. Reader

*They [the Aztecs] sent Cortés (kor-TEZ) five slaves, incense, domestic fowl, and cakes, so that if he was, as they had heard, a fearsome god, he could feed on the slaves; if he was a benevolent god, he would be content with the incense; and if he was human and mortal, he would use the fowl, fruit and cakes that had been prepared for him.*[3]

## *PAUSE FOR DISCUSSION*

Imagine that a space ship lands near you and brings people who look unusual and act strangely. They carry large machines that look like vacuum cleaners. You don't know if these machines might clean up polluted land, air and water here on Planet Earth or they might be weapons that could destroy the people. What do you think your response would be? Apply this analogy to the Aztecs and Moctezuma. What do you imagine the Aztec reactions were to the Spaniards? If you were a messenger and advisor to Moctezuma, what advice would you give him about the strangers?

# PEOPLE OF THE INVADING PARTIES

## 7. Reader

My name is Cortés, Hernando Cortés. I was born in Spain. In 1504, at age 19, I sailed to the West Indies to the island where Christopher Columbus landed. I have a natural military gift, so when I was asked to put down an uprising on the nearby island of Cuba, it was an easy task. In return, the governor gave me land and Indians to work on it. When the Spanish wanted a soldier to lead an expedition to new lands, I was selected. I often wrote to King Charles I of Spain and told him what happened during my first seven years in New Spain. This is what I told those interested in joining the expedition: *I offer you great rewards, although they will be wrapped about you with great hardships... and if you do not abandon me, as I shall not abandon you, I shall make you in a very short time the richest of all men who have crossed the seas.* [4] **[Codex E]**

## 8. Reader

I am one of the Spanish soldiers who joined Cortés on his first expedition. Most of us soldiers had settled in the Indies, but we were unhappy because we were not given the land and slaves that had been promised. We call ourselves *conquistadors*, but so far we have found no lands to conquer. When we heard about the expedition to New Spain we saw an opportunity to get gold, silver and jewels. We also want land and slaves to work the land for us.

## 9. Reader

My name is Beatriz Palacus, but I am called "La Parda," meaning "the black," because my mother was African. I am one of 12 women who accompanied our husbands from Spain in the 1519 invasion of Mexico. We cooked and nursed our men, stood guard, and in some instances, we fought alongside Spanish soldiers. One of our women was so blessed with a gift for healing that the Spanish crown honored her with the title "Doctor" and she received permission to practice medicine in New Spain.

## 10. Reader

My people are the Tlaxcalans (tla-SCAL-ans). We live in villages three days toward the sun from Tenochtitlán. The Aztecs have been our enemies for many years. They make us pay taxes, or tributes to them. They demand that our daughters serve in their houses and our sons work on their plantations. Sometimes they take our people for their ceremonial sacrifices. When the strangers with skin the color of the sun first came to our village, we fled in fear. Thousands of our warriors fought these Spanish soldiers and their allies, but our bows and arrows were no match against their muskets and cannons. Our leader finally made peace with the strangers. They promised they would help us stop the Aztecs' crimes against us if we provided 2000 men for their first expedition to Tenochtitlán. **[Codex F]**

## 11. Reader

I am called Doña Marina now. That is the name the Spanish gave me after I became Christian. When they landed near my village in the Yucatán (you-ka-TAN), the Spaniards took me with them since I know two languages, Maya and Nahuatl (NA-hwat-el). There is a Spaniard here who speaks Maya, and together, we are the interpreters for Cortés.

When I was a girl, my parents sold me as a slave. My new owner gave me as a gift to Captain Cortés. Eventually there were 19 other Mayan women who were given as gifts to cook for and serve the Spanish. When the Spaniards got us they said our ways of worship and sacrifice were evil. There is only one true God, they said, and they showed us an image of their God. We had to bow and kiss their holy cross. Then they said we were Christians, and we became the first women Christians in New Spain. After that, we were given to each of the captains on the Spanish ships. **[Codex G]**

---

# *PAUSE FOR DISCUSSION*

Imagine today that you had the opportunity to go to an unfamiler land that was known to be beautiful and prosperous, but perhaps dangerous for newcomers like you.
What would motivate you to go? What values would you want to uphold when meeting people in this new land? What do you think the Spanish hoped to gain from their expedition to the land that was new to them? What values did they uphold?

---

# THE INVASION

---

## 12. Narrator

Cortés was disobeying orders when he decided to do more than trade with the Aztecs. Therefore, when the Spanish left their eleven ships off the Gulf coast, Cortés had all but one ship dismantled so his men wouldn't be able to leave the expedition. The Spaniards began the 200 mile journey, over mountains and through valleys, and finally arrived at the Valley of Mexico. From the pass between spectacular volcanic peaks, they viewed an amazing sight: the city of Tenochtitlán.

On November 8, 1519, the Spanish and their Tlaxcalan allies entered the Aztec stronghold and stayed until the following May, 1520. The inhabitants of the valley flocked to observe the newcomers who entered the city and who were received by Moctezuma. Under a canopy they exchanged gifts and greeted each other. Moctezuma offered a palace where Cortés and his companions could stay.

For several days the Spaniards wandered, in a tourist-like fashion, and admired the city. The city of Tenochtitlán was well organized with long avenues, markets, gardens, canals and temples. The city of Tenochtitlán even had a zoo.

But Cortés knew his people were surrounded by the Aztecs who could attack and kill them in an instant if they so desired. Due to the suspicion that the Aztec may be planning an ambush, Cortés took Moctezuma hostage inside his own palace.
**[Codex H]**

## 13. Reader

*When the Spaniards were settled in the palace, they asked Moctezuma about the city's resources and reserves... They questioned him closely and then demanded gold... The riches of gold and feathers were brought out to them: ornaments made of quetzal feathers, shields made from disks of gold... and gold nose rings, gold bracelets and crowns. The Spaniards immediately stripped the feathers from the gold shields and ensigns. They gathered all the gold into a great mound and set fire to everything else, regardless of its value [to the Aztecs]. Then they melted down the gold into ingots. As for the precious green stones, they took only the best of them; the rest were snatched up by the Tlaxcalans.[5] [Codex I]*

## 14. Narrator

During their six months at Tenochtitlán, the Spaniards collected huge amounts of gold. One fifth of all they took was sent to the Spanish King and Queen. Other portions of the gold went to Cortés, the Captains and the Spanish priests. The soldiers divided the rest.

Meanwhile, the governor of Cuba, who had dispatched Cortés' voyage, tried to suspend the expedition. He had become distrustful of Cortés and wanted to replace him. He sent a fleet of 15 ships and 900 men to arrest Cortés and bring him back.

Cortés heard about the plans to bring him back to Cuba. He decided to go back to Veracruz to encounter the expedition, but left some soldiers behind to guard Tenochtitlán. Cortés made a surprise attack on the new Spanish forces, and their leader surrendered. Cortés told the soldiers about all the gold at Tenochtitlán and offered them part of the loot if they joined him, which they did. The two armies began their return to Tenochtitlán. Along the way, 2000 Tlaxcalan warriors also joined the Spanish forces.

Meanwhile, at Tenochtitlán, the Aztecs prepared to celebrate an important holiday in honor of their sun and war god. Rumors spread among the Spaniards that during the celebration in the temple the Aztecs would attack the Spaniards. The acting Spanish commander reacted by blocking the four entrances of the temple during the celebration.

## PAUSE FOR DISCUSSION
What do you think happened?

## 15. Reader

*All the young warriors were eager for the fiesta to begin. They had sworn to dance and sing with all their hearts, so that the Spaniards would marvel at the beauty of the rituals... At this moment in the fiesta, when the dance was the loveliest and when song was linked to song, the Spaniards were seized with an urge to kill the celebrants. They all ran forward, armed as if for battle. They closed the entrances and passageways, all the gates of the patio...they posted guards so that no one could escape.*

*They ran in among the dancers, forcing their way to the place where the drums were played. They attacked the man who was drumming and cut off his arms. Then they cut off his head, and it rolled across the floor. They attacked all the celebrants, stabbing them, spearing them, striking them with their swords.[6] [Codex J]*

## 16 Narrator

In retaliation for their 600 warriors who were killed that day, the Aztecs launched an attack. They drove the Spaniards back to their quarters and held them captive.

## 17. Reader

*When the news of this massacre was heard outside the Sacred Patio, a great cry went up: 'Aztecs, come running! Bring your spears and shields! The strangers have murdered our warriors!'*

*This cry was answered with a roar of grief and anger: the people shouted and wailed and beat their palms against their mouths...Then the battle began. The Aztecs attacked with javelins and arrows, even with the light spears that are used for hunting birds. They hurled their javelins with all their strength.*

*The Spaniards immediately took refuge in the palace. They began to shoot at the Aztecs with their iron arrows and to fire their cannons. And they shackled Moctezuma in chains.*[7]

## PAUSE FOR DISCUSSION

It was into this scene that Cortés, the Spanish, and the additional 2,000 Tlaxcalan warriors entered Tenochtitlán after the trip from Veracruz. What do you think happened next?

## 18. Narrator

The Aztecs allowed Cortés and his soldiers to enter Tenochtitlán, but then they cut them off from all their supplies, food and water. The Aztecs intended to weaken the Spaniards and then to attack them. Realizing this plan, Cortés persuaded Doña Marina to intervene on behalf of the Spaniards. He thought the Aztecs would listen to her, since she was Indian and spoke the Aztecs' language.

## 19. Reader

*Doña Marina called the nobles together. She climbed up to the palace roof and cried: "Aztecans, come forward! The Spaniards need your help! Bring them food and pure water. They are tired and hungry; they are almost fainting from exhaustion! Why do you not come forward? Are you angry with them?"*

*The Aztecs were too frightened to approach. They were crushed by terror and would not risk coming forward. They shied away as if the Spaniards were wild beasts, as if the hour were midnight on the blackest night of the year. Yet they did not abandon the Spaniards to hunger and thirst. They brought them whatever they needed, but shook with fear as they did so. They delivered the supplies to the Spaniards with trembling hands, then turned and hurried away.*[8]

## *Pause for Discussion*

Why do you think Doña Marina asked the Aztecs to help the Spanish? Why do you think the Aztecs brought food and water to the Spanish? What would you do?

---

# THE SECOND ATTACK

---

### 20. Narrator

After feeding the Spanish, the Aztecs began to attack. Thousands of warriors threw stones, followed by spears, bows and arrows. The Spanish fought back with their reinforced army and a cavalry of eighty horses. They burned houses, but the canals of Tenochtitlán stopped the fires from spreading. On the 23rd day of the battle, the Spanish captured the Aztec temple and destroyed the Aztec's sacred statues. The Aztecs became so enraged that they screamed for revenge. Knowing they were doomed, Cortés persuaded Moctezuma to appeal to the Aztecs to allow the Spanish to leave Tenochtitlán. As Moctezuma climbed to a rooftop to make the appeal, he was killed. The Spanish claim he was murdered by his own people; the Aztecs said the Spanish were responsible for the killing.

---

### 21. Reader

On a dark night, Cortés and the Spanish tried to escape over a causeway. But the heavy fog and the rain did not protect them from Aztec eyes. A woman who was getting water at one of the canals saw them and called out an alarm. Aztec warriors came out of the shadows. They blocked the causeway, boarded canoes and shot their bows and spears at the fleeing Spanish. Confusion overwhelmed the Spanish, and many drowned in the canal weighted down with their armor and the jewelry and gold they had stolen.

Cortés himself escaped, crossing the causeway and reaching the mainland. 870 Spanish and 1,200 Tlaxcalans died that night. The swampy grounds and the canals were full with bodies of soldiers and horses. This was the Sad Night, *La Noche Triste* (la NO-chay TREE-stay). **[Codex K]**

---

### 22. Narrator

For a while, the Aztecs in Tenochtitlán enjoyed their triumph. But soon small pox appeared, and in a matter of months, it devastated the population of Tenochtitlán. The Aztecs were not immune to this European disease and thousands of Aztec corpses lay decomposing on the streets and in the temples.

The Spanish who survived *La Noche Triste* regrouped not far from the city. Spurred by their desire for gold, they made plans to retake the city. Cortés brought his dismantled ships from the Gulf Coast and rebuilt them on the lake that surrounded Tenochtitlán. By chance, ships from Spanish settlements in the Caribbean arrived during this time at Veracruz, bringing soldiers, horses and guns. Cortés promised the men a percentage of the loot if they joined him.

After a year, with more than 80,000 men, the invasion of Tenochtitlán began. Of that number, fewer than 600 were Spanish; most were Tlaxcalans and warriors from the neighboring region. The offensive on Tenochtitlán lasted for about 80 days. Aztec warriors who had not been struck with small pox fiercely defended their city. The Spanish cut off supplies to Tenochtitlán with their ships, and the Aztecs had to eat worms and the bark of trees to survive. Despite the Aztec efforts, the city of Tenochtitlán fell into Spanish hands on August 21, 1521. The Aztecs never surrendered; to take the city, Cortés had to ravage it. No temple, palace or idol remained. **[Codices L, M]**

## 23. Reader

*Nothing but flowers and songs of sorrow*
*are left in Mexico and Tlateloco (tlot-el-LOL-co),*
*where once we saw warriors and wise men.*

*We know it is true*
*that we must perish,*
*for we are mortal men...*

*We wander here and there*
*in our desolate poverty.*
*We are mortal men.*

*We have seen bloodshed and pain*
*where once we saw beauty and valor.*

*We are crushed to the ground;*
*we lie in ruins.*
*There is nothing but grief and suffering*
*in Mexico and Tlateloco,*
*where once we saw beauty and valor.*[9]

**[Codices N, O]**

## *Pause for reflection and discussion*

Distribute copies of the codices. See instructions 4-6 under Body of Lesson.

# THE AFTERMATH

## 24. Reader

My name is Bernal Díaz. I was a soldier with the Spanish expedition. When Cortés was chosen to lead the exploration of New Spain, I quickly joined. Later in my life, I wrote an account about the conquest of New Spain. Reflecting about that time, I wrote: *Many interested readers have asked me why the true Conquistadors who won...the great and strong city of Mexico did not stay there to settle, but went on to other provinces...We had realized from Moctezuma's account books that there were no gold or mines or cotton in the towns around Tenochtitlán, only a lot of maize [corn] and the maguey (ma-GAY) plantations from which they obtained their wine. For this reason we thought of it as a poor land, and went off to colonize other provinces. But we were thoroughly deceived.*[10]

## 25. Reader

My name is Bartolomé de las Casas. I was a Dominican Friar in the Catholic Church. I came to New Spain originally because I saw great opportunity to gain land and to convert the Indians to Christianity. *As I look back on my 40 years here, I am appalled at the wickedness, injustice and violence which the Christians have done in the Indies. I am very certain that during the years from 1502 to 1542 more than 12 million souls, men, women and children perished unjustly and tyrannically. It would have been better for the Indians to go to hell with their heresies than to be saved by the Christians. The Christians killed and destroyed such an infinite number of souls so they could acquire gold and riches. In a word, the cause of the demise of the Indians has been the Christians' unending ambition.*[11]

## 26. Reader

I am an Aztec woman and I write this many years after the invasion of Mexico: *The Spanish said they had discovered a new world. But our world was not new to us. Many generations had flourished in these lands.... We cultivated the land, we lived in great settlements beside the lakes, we hunted and spun, we had schools and sacred festivals. The Spanish said they had to make us 'civilized,' made us give up our 'barbarianism.' Yet they defeated us, they decimated us barbarously. In just a few years they made more human sacrifices than we had ever made in all the history of our festivals.*[12]

## *Pause for Closing Discussion*

What do you think is meant by the statements by Bartolome de las Casas, Bernal Díaz and the Aztec woman? If you were asked to make a statement of the conquest, what would you say? Write a paragraph in your journal.

A

B

C

D

E

F

G

H

I

**J**

**K**

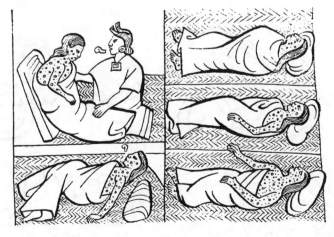

**L**

M

N

O

# AZTEC CODICES

*The Aztecs recorded their history in codices, or manuscripts, that included symbols and drawings portraying their actions, concepts and emotions. Most of the drawings used in this lesson to describe the conquest are from Book Twelve of the Florentine Codex and the Lienzo de Tlaxcala Codex.*

A. Ten years before the Spanish came, the Aztec people saw a comet that looked like a flaming ear of corn that seemed to bleed fire. When they saw this strange wonder, they were amazed and frightened, and they spoke of it constantly, trying to interpret its meaning. It was seen as a bad omen.

B. The Aztec messengers brought gifts of welcome to the Spanish on board their ships.

C. After receiving the gifts, the messengers were chained, and a cannon was fired. The Aztecs fainted away in fear.

D. The Spanish helped revive the Aztec messengers by giving them wine to drink and then some food.

E. The Spanish followed this route from Veracruz through Tlaxcala to Tenochtitlán.

F. The Spanish marched toward Tenochtitlán, past the volcano of Popocatépetl. On their journey they recruited allies from Tlaxcala.

G. Doña Marina was sold as a slave and given to Cortés.

H. At a meeting between Cortés, Moctezuma and the Aztec chieftains, gifts of food, flowers, and gold necklaces were given to Cortés. Doña Marina is the interpreter.

I. The Spanish gathered all the gifts of gold and melted them down into ingots.

J. The Spanish massacre of the Aztecs during their holiday celebration, the Toxcatl, in honor of their god Huitzilopochtli.

K. The Spanish and their allies fled across the causeway to the mainland while being attacked by the Aztec warriors. This is known as The Sad Night, or *La Noche Triste*.

L. A terrible plague of smallpox spread through Tenochtitlán, killing or debilitating thousands of men, women and children.

M. The Spanish returned. They rebuilt their ships on the lake surrounding Tenochtitlán, and captured the city in 80 days.

N. The Aztecs never surrendered, but more than 240,000 were killed.

O. The remaining Aztecs fled Tenochtitlán while the Spanish searched for gold.

## Facts and Legends:

# The Story of La Llorona

The story of La Llorona
(yore-OWN-a), or
The Weeping Woman,
has been told throughout Mexico
for many centuries. She can be traced back
to Aztec drawings, called codices, where she
was portrayed as a goddess who was
half woman and half snake.

*La Llorona was a beautiful but poor woman who
passionately loved a stranger. She had two sons by
him, but he would not marry her or support the
children. One day he left her, and in despair, she killed
her children and herself. At night, the ghost of La
Llorona wanders about, with wind blowing in her hair,
weeping for her lost children.*

One interpretation of this legend associates La Llorona with Doña Marina, the Mayan woman
from the Yucatán area of Mexico who became Cortés' translator. Through Doña Marina, who
spoke Mayan and Nahuatl, the Aztec language, Cortés could communicate with the Aztecs.
Dona Marina traveled with Cortés throughout Mexico and bore him a son, Martin. When
Cortés' Spanish wife joined him in Mexico, Doña Marina and her son were cast aside.

Some people think La Llorona weeps because of the way Cortés treated her; others believe she
weeps for all the Indian people whom she betrayed when she became the voice for Cortés.
What do you think?

*From <u>The Hungry Woman: Myths and Legends of the Aztecs</u> by John Bierhorst. New York:
Wm. Morrow. 1984.*

*An Exploring the Connections Lesson*

# Colonizing the Americas
## *Analyzing the Legacy*

This lesson is intended to give students a basic understanding of the effects of colonialism on the land and people of the Americas, especially focusing on the outcome of the colonial system for indigenous people throughout the hemisphere. The lesson compares and contrasts several aspects of British and Spanish colonialism, giving students the tools to understand important differences and similarities between the two systems. It helps students understand the rationale for the imposition of the colonial system, the means that colonial powers and colonizers used to establish control in the Americas, and the effects of colonialism in the areas controlled by the British and the Spanish. Lesson Eight expands on these same themes by exploring the impact of Spanish colonialism specifically in Mexico.

This lesson also asks students to begin to question the ongoing legacy of colonialism in the thoughts and practices of people in contemporary society. A strong element of the colonial system was a firm belief on the part of the colonizer in their superiority to the indigenous people and cultures which they dominated. The result was the assimilation, manipulation, and/or destruction of indigenous cultures. The legacy of this process continues in the struggle to recover the rich cultural heritage of all the people of the Americas and in the need to challenge racist assumptions today.

| | |
|---|---|
| **Learner Objectives** | • To demonstrate an understanding of the European struggle for control in the Americas by analyzing the similarities and differences between Spanish and British colonization. |
| | • To analyze the cultural and economic impact of colonization on both the colonizers and Indian peoples. |
| **Concepts** | • Colonialism, colonizer, colonized |
| | • Indentured servitude |
| | • Slavery |
| **Major Questions to be Addressed** | • How were British and Spanish colonialism similar and different? Why does this matter? |
| | • How did British and Spanish colonialism shape the future development of land tenure, labor systems and relationships with Indians in the Americas? |
| **Exploring the Connections** | • This lesson compares and contrasts the effects of British and Spanish colonization on the land and people in the Americas. |
| **Teaching Strategies** | Reading, Inquiry, Writing |
| **Materials Provided** | Effects of Colonialism on the Land and the People (Handout 1) |
| **Additional Materials Needed** | • Large map of American hemisphere |
| | • Student Journals |
| | • Large sheet of newsprint or poster board (optional) |
| **Time Required** | 1 class session |
| **Preparation for this Lesson** | Make one copy of Handout 1 for each student . |

# Sequence of Lesson

| | |
|---|---|
| *Anticipatory Set* *10 minutes* | 1. In a large class discussion, ask students the following questions and write their responses on the board or overhead. (Possible responses in italics.) |
| | • What is a colony? |
| | • What is colonialism? *(A system by which a country maintains foreign colonies, especially for economic exploitation, Webster's New World Dictionary)* |
| | • Who is a colonizer? |
| *Body of Lesson* *40 minutes* | 2. Distribute Handout 1 for students to read in class. Discuss the material in the handout, as well as the questions below. Use a large map to identify areas or countries: |

- Who were the early colonial powers? *(Spain, England, France, Portugal, Germany, Belgium, Holland, later the US).*
- Who were the colonized, or what areas were colonized? *(Africa, Asia, the Americas).*
- What does it mean to be colonized?
- What conditions enable one group of people to colonize another group of people? What kinds of tactics were used by colonizers? *(Trading, force, negotiation, laws.)*
- What were some of the advantages of colonialism for the colonizers? *(Access to land, resources, cheap labor; political power and religious freedom; etc.)*
- What were some of the disadvantages of colonialism for the colonizers? *(Uprisings by Indians, slaves; forced to pay taxes to European powers; loss of own cultural traditions, etc.)*
- What were some of the advantages of colonialism for the colonized? *(Access to European goods, trade; Christianity; etc.)*
- What were some of the disadvantages of colonialism for the colonized? *(Loss of land, culture, language and freedom; disease; hunger; Christianity; forced subjugation; genocide; etc.)*

3. Work in small groups to answer the questions accompanying the reading in Handout 1.

**Closure**

4. With the time remaining, discuss with students the following question: "are there circumstances that justify colonization?" (Alternatively, this question could be assigned as homework.)

*Assignment*

- Ask students to copy the following question in their journals and then to write their reaction to it.

  *Some people argue that colonialism still exists in the form of neo-colonialism, which is defined as the policy of a strong nation seeking political and economic power or dominance over an independent nation without necessarily reducing the subordinate area to the legal status of a colony.* (Adapted from Random House College Dictionary, 1982.)

- Based on this definition, do you think neo-colonialism exists? Why or why not? In your answer, try to give one or more examples of a neo-colonial relationship between countries today.

# The Effects of Colonialism on Land and People

## Pre-colonial Societies

Before the invasion and colonization by the Europeans, many indigenous societies in the Americas were highly developed and self-sufficient. Several had advanced trade and agricultural systems, as well as complex social, legal and religious structures. The more powerful and highly organized societies, such as the Aztecs and Incas, frequently dominated and controlled other people through military conquest, occupation, and a system of tribute and taxation. By and large, however, the dominated peoples were allowed to practice their own beliefs, maintain their language, and continue systems of internal economic organization. This was to change dramatically with the arrival of the Europeans in 1492.

Beginning in the 15th century, European colonialism reached its height in the 18th and 19th centuries, with the expansion of control in the Americas, Africa and Asia. Europeans used colonies as a source of land, food, and other raw materials; as a market for European manufactured goods; and as a source of slave or cheap labor. Colonization brought extraordinary wealth to Europe, and was the foundation for the Renaissance and Industrial Revolution. For indigenous people, colonization brought death and destruction. Traditional ways of life on the land were forever altered by the colonizers' desire for resources and land. Millions of people died—from overwork, disease and wars of conquest and resistance.

European colonialism in North America can be simplified into four major forms:

| | |
|---|---|
| **Large territorial empires** | (Spanish empire in Central America) |
| **Trading-post empires** | (French trading-post empire in Great Lakes region) |
| **Plantation colonies** | (British slave plantation colonies in the Caribbean and the southern United States) |
| **Settler colonies** | (British settler colonies along Atlantic coast) |

This reading compares and contrasts the first and last forms of colonization — Spanish territorial empires and British settler colonies. The British also had plantation colonies in the South, but for the purposes of this lesson, we will only examine the settler colonies of New England. As you read, consider the effects that colonialism had on the land and the people in the region who were dominated.

## British Colonization in the Americas

Much of the British colonial system in the Americas relied on settler colonies. In settler colonies, whole groups of people, including men, women and children, left England and moved to the new territory in search of land, economic resources, and/or religious and political freedom. They established new communities, displacing the original inhabitants of the land by whatever means necessary. While there was some interaction between Native and English people, in general a strong separation existed between the two groups. The British considered the Indians outsiders, a people apart from their own society.

Settler colonies were often connected to economic ventures carried out by individual companies that acquired charters from the British crown. A charter granted a company the right to trade and exploit resources within a certain territory. Generally the companies exercised little direct control over the daily lives of the colonists or the Indian people in the territory. Some British colonists found Indian people to be useful trading partners. However, in the main, they considered Indians to be competitors for the land, and therefore, enemies to be dealt with harshly. In the latter case, they removed the Indians from the land they wished to occupy by military force.

The land systems set up by the British varied, of course, between the slave plantations of the South and the system of smaller private land holdings of the northern colonies. In either case, the land which the colonists came to own and control originally was the territory of various Indian nations. Whole nations of Indian people were *removed* by force, coercion, and deception so the Europeans could establish their farms and communities in the New World.

# Spanish Colonization in the Americas

The Spanish relied on a different system to organize and maintain authority over the vast lands gained during the invasion of the Americas. In general, the lands brought under Spanish control were *not* settler colonies, made up of whole communities who had moved across the ocean to establish themselves in the new land. Rather, the lands under control of the Spanish were governed by direct representatives of the Spanish crown, assisted by representatives of the Catholic Church. These people were overwhelmingly men, living without families in the new land. The result was more ethnic mixing between the colonizers and the colonized.

In general, the Spanish exerted more direct control over their colonial holdings, including the lives of the people who lived on the land. When land grants were given to representatives of the Spanish crown, the Indian people living in the area were included as property of the new owners. Rather than removing the Indians as was done in the British system, the Spanish used Indian labor to work their vast holdings. The land holding system established by the Spanish had many characteristics of feudalism, with Indian people acting as servants or serfs to the large land holders.

In addition, in the Spanish system, it was considered the responsibility of the colonial power to "civilize" the Indians by converting them to Catholicism. This meant outlawing cultural and religious practices of the indigenous people and often destroying traditional ways of life. Despite the fact that Indians were legally recognized as "human beings" and were protected by law, Indians were regularly abused, mistreated, and held virtually as slaves. The Spanish considered Indians to be a conquered people and, as such exploited them and their labor to build the colonial economy. In contrast, British colonists relied on their own labor, that of indentured servants or African slaves.

# Comparing the Effects of Colonialism

Although the methods of the British and Spanish differed, the result of colonization was largely the same for the indigenous communities they encountered. Millions of Indian people died. In the areas controlled by the British, they died from war, diseases brought from Europe, and from the loss of their land and livelihood. Many Indians were killed in battles over land and resources, while others were forcibly relocated.

In the areas controlled by the Spanish, millions of Indians also died due to military conquest, disease, and loss of agricultural land. In addition, hundreds of thousands of Indian people died from overwork, as they were used to clear forests, work the mines, and build the infrastructure of Spanish colonial society.

Most of those who survived under either system of colonization suffered the destruction of the way of life that had sustained their societies for generations. Despite this legacy, Indian people struggled to keep their cultures and traditions alive. They developed ingenious ways of resisting the dominant society and maintaining cultural practices, often done secretly and under adverse conditions. An example is religious practices, which have the features of Christianity but may incorporate hidden meanings known only to the Indian people. Moreover, Indian groups who lived on the frontier of colonial society throughout the Americas (in the deserts, mountains and rainforests) were able to retain much of their cultural heritage, despite repeated attempts to conquer or integrate them.

### *Respond to the following questions...*

What differences existed between the British and Spanish systems of land ownership? Why is that important today?

What differences were there between the British and Spanish view of Indian people? In the ways they treated Indian people? Does this effect present day society? How?

Describe how you think present-day Mexico, US and Canada have been shaped by their unique colonial heritages.

# Colonizing the Mind and Spirit

Identity is the spirit of a person. Dominating that spirit affects a person's entire sense of being. Colonization, regardless of the approach or process, greatly affects the human spirit and mind. The process of colonization therefore has meant not only control of the land and resources of the conquered people, but control of the minds and cultures of the colonized people as well.

Colonization also produces a sense of superiority and inferiority. In order to colonize the Americas successfully, the colonizers maintained certain belief systems which supported that process. The Europeans believed their culture, their society, their religion, and their way of life was superior to that of the people they eventually were able to dominate. An example of the regard for Indians is reflected in a 1881 report on United States Indian Policy:

> *To domesticate and civilize wild Indians is a noble work, the accomplishment of which should be a crown of glory to any nation. But to allow them to drag along year after year, generation after generation, in their old superstitions, laziness, and filth, when we have the power to elevate them in the scale of humanity, would be a lasting disgrace of our government...If the Indians are to be civilized...they must learn our language and adopt our modes of life.*
>
> ( <u>Annual Report of the Commissioner of Indian Affairs</u>, 1881, edited by Francis Paul Prucha, *Documents of United States Indian Policy*, p. 156.)

## The Legacy of Colonialism

The legacy continues today in the attitudes that some people are inferior or superior to others, which is the foundation of racism. Native American philosopher, John Mohawk writes,

> *Even modern scholars identify the period of the conquest as the birth of racism in the modern world. It was the first time that arguments were seriously put forward in courts of Spain...arguing that the Indians were biologically inferior beings, that they were not even human beings at all...All those arguments still go on right to the present day, certainly in places like Guatemala and Peru and Mexico where the conquest, I say, is not ended.*
>
> (Mohawk, John. "The Indian Way Is a Thinking Tradition", *Northeast Indian Quarterly*. Fall 1990, p. 15.)

## For further reflection...

If colonization relies on the notion of the superiority and inferiority of people, how do we begin to challenge the racist legacy of the colonial system? How is the colonial legacy a part of our own lives and society?

How do people who have been colonized for centuries become "decolonized"? How do we begin to heal the mind and spirit?

# Colonizing New Spain
## *The New Economic & Social System*

This lesson is designed to help students develop an understanding of Mexico during the 300 years of Spanish colonization, 1521—1810. The first part is a reading that describes three of the most important sectors of the colonial economy—manufacturing, mining and plantations. It looks at the effects of labor practices on workers and the complex social system that developed. The lesson then describes the ways in which ordinary people resisted oppression in colonial Mexican society.

Providing a concise overview of 300 years of Mexican history is a difficult task. We think it is important for students to gain some insight into the difficult living and working conditions most people faced. It is also important for students to recognize the subtle forms of everyday resistance that peasants waged against their oppressors. To accomplish these goals, we have included excerpts about the impact colonization had on ordinary people. These brief accounts run down the left-hand column of each page of Handout 1, while a more general history runs down the right-hand side of each page. Since history is more than one story told in chronological order, this reading provides students with several entry points. In this lesson, students gain insight into the social and economic relationships which formed during the colonial era and then assess how these relationships might have shaped contemporary Mexico.

The second part of the lesson is a role play. Through the role play, students can creatively express and analyze the economic, political and social relationships among these sectors.

*Note: You may wish to use the stories from Lesson 9 before Part 2 so that students have people's names and lives to draw from.*

| | |
|---|---|
| **Learner Objectives** | • To assess the historical processes which have shaped modern Mexico, focusing on Spanish colonization and Indian peoples' resistance to colonialism. |
| | • To identify methods the Spanish used to incorporate Indian and African labor into the colonial system. |
| | • To analyze the economic, political and social relationships among the major sectors during the colonial era. |
| **Major Questions to be Addressed by Lesson** | • How did the Spanish exploit the land and peoples of Mexico? |
| | • What were the repercussions of this exploitation? |
| | • What were the goals of the major sectors during the colonial period, and how did they pursue their interests? |
| | • To what extent does modern Mexico reflect the systems established during colonialism? |
| | • Is colonization ever justified? |
| **Concepts** | • Colonialism |
| | • Exploitation |
| | • Resistance |
| | • Social stratification |
| **Teaching Strategies** | • Reading/Small Group Discussion |
| | • Role play/socio-drama |
| **Materials Provided** | • Understanding Colonial Mexico (Handout 1) |
| | • Forecasting the Future: The Consequences of Colonialism (Handout 2) |
| | • Social Stratification Chart and Role Cards (Handout 3) |
| | • Did You Know? (Handout 4) |
| | • Evaluation Form (See Appendix D) |
| **Additional Materials Needed** | • Paper and markers for name tags |
| | • Props for role play (optional) |
| **Time Required** | 3-4 class sessions |
| **Vocabulary** | *(See Glossary for definitions)* |
| | • *Criollo* |
| | • *Ejido* |
| | • *Hacienda* |
| | • Maroon society |
| | • *Mestizo* |
| | • Mulatto |
| | • *Obraje* |
| | • Subjugation |
| | • *Zambo* |
| **Preparation for this Lesson** | • Make one copy of Handout 1 for each student. |
| | • Make enough copies of Handout 2 so each small group will have two scenarios. |

- Copy and cut apart a set of the role cards (Handout 3) for each group of 12-15 students.
- Make an overhead or large reproduction on newsprint of the *Social Stratification Chart*, which shows the estimated percentage of the population in each sector in New Spain in 1810.
- Select and make copies of *Evaluation Form* from Appendix D.

# Sequence of Lesson

*Anticipatory Set*
*5 minutes*

1. Ask students to brainstorm words or ideas they associate with colonialism and write the words on the board. Do not erase until after this lesson.

*Body of Lesson*
*Part 1*
*45 minutes*

2. Distribute one copy of Handout 1 to each student. Indicate to students the design layout of the pages, with excerpts of people's lives running down the left-hand column of the page, and a more general history running down the right-hand side of the page.

3. Introduce students to the main concepts and vocabulary they will encounter in this lesson (see glossary for vocabulary terms). Emphasize the important economic sectors and the rigid social stratification that characterized colonial Mexico. Ask students to read the handout individually or in groups.

4. When students have finished reading Handout 1, ask them to form small groups of not more than 5 students. Distribute two sections from Handout 2 to each group. Each group should read the statement and brainstorm possible answers to the question. Encourage them to be creative! After students have had an opportunity to work on these questions, ask a group representative to report to the entire class that group's statement, question, and response. If more than one group responded to the same question, discuss differences in the responses each group gave.

*Closure and Evaluation*
*Part 1*

5. Refer to the board where you listed what students knew about colonialism. Did their readings today confirm what they wrote on the board? What questions do they still have? Indicate to students that the "answers" will become clearer as they learn more about contemporary Mexico because the roots of colonialism are still in place. You may wish to pause here to read the stories from Lesson 9. The stories may help students personalize the next part of the lesson.

*Body of Lesson*
*Part 11*
*2 class periods*

6. Explain and discuss the purpose of the particular type of role play used in this lesson, called a socio-drama. The socio-drama is a technique which encourages the participation of all students to act out a situation using words, creative movement, mime, gestures, songs, props or human sculpture. A socio-drama can help participants to identify and work with a real

situation, to help them understand the dynamics and relationships of a given issue or situation, and to illustrate different perceptions about a situation. The ideal group size for this socio-drama is 12-15 participants.

7.  Divide the class into groups of 12-15 students, separated in space as much as possible. Place the Social Stratification Chart in view of all groups. This chart provides students with a guideline as to the proportion of "characters" to include from each social class in their socio-drama.

8.  Ask the groups to brainstorm a list of ideas for a setting, such as a *hacienda* or the mines, and an issue or circumstance that involves all of the socio-economic sectors. After the groups have selected a setting, distribute a set of role cards to each group. Each card represents a social group and includes a short description. Tell the class that you represent the Spanish Crown and read aloud the description on your card. In their small groups, students should read aloud the descriptions on each of the cards. They should then divide the group into five smaller groups that represent the role cards using the Social Stratification Chart to decide how many people should represent each social class. Then have the students prepare a role play illustrating the needs and interests of the five sectors based on the issue or circumstance they chose earlier. Encourage the students to draw on the stories they read in Handout 1 for story ideas. Once the scenes are plotted, the group can find and/or make props to help illustrate the story. Each character should be clearly identified with name cards. The group should rehearse its socio-drama before presenting it to the class. Encourage them to keep it simple. Allow about 45 minutes (1 class period) to prepare the socio-drama.,

9.  Each group presents its socio-drama, taking no more than 15 minutes (per group).

*Closure*
*20 minutes*

10. Debrief the students by discussing the role plays. This is the most important part of the socio-drama process. The discussion is designed to ensure that students understand the issues and concepts presented. Begin the discussion using straightforward questions and then move to more complex, analytical questions (see the list of suggested questions). If you have two groups, let them question each other about their presentations. Synthesize the main points emerging from the discussion. Be sure to raise any points which were reflected in the socio-drama, but were not articulated in the class discussion.

*Some suggested questions:*

*   Why were certain sectors of people represented as they were?
*   What assumptions do you think the various sectors made

about each other; for example, what assumptions did the Spanish make about the Indians and the African slaves (and vice-versa)?

- What were some of the conflicts, or potential conflicts, between various social and racial sectors during three hundred years of colonial control?
- How do you think the Indians perceived their relationship to the Spanish, *Criollos*, and *Mestizos*?
- Do you think the relationships presented in this socio-drama are accurate? Were there any gaps where more information was needed?

*Evaluation*

Distribute the Self-Evaluation Form to each student to complete and hand in.

*Extra Credit*

Students should be encouraged to do additional reading and writing about colonial Mexico. (See bibliography for suggested readings.)

The information about the socio-drama is adapted from *A Popular Education Handbook* (Ottawa, Ontario: CUSO Development Education and Ontario Institute for Studies in Education) and *Basics and Tools: A Collection of Population Education Resources and Activities* (Ottawa, Ontario: CUSO Education Department, 1985). The materials for Handout 2, Forecasting the Future: The Consequences of Colonialism, was adapted from *Colonialism in the Americas: A Critical Look* (Victoria, B.C.: Victoria International Development Education Association, 1991).

# Understanding Colonial Mexico

*As early as 1544, the Spanish crown forbade the use of Indian labor in sugar cane mills "because one [sugar] plantation is sufficient to kill two thousand of them in one year." This argument was used by colonists to increase the number of Africans brought for slavery. [1]*

*The less fortunate lived for the service of others, bound by the debts that they had accumulated. These men and women labored in fields and workshops for two or three pesos each month. With debts that might approach 100 pesos, such people normally faced years of servitude. [2]*

*Disease and accidents were common in colonial times. In mining areas, "workers were often crushed by collapsing roofs of mineshafts, and the 12 hour shifts led to fatigue and decrease in resistance to disease. Mine laborers contracted lung ailments by breathing foul air and fumes from candles and smoke from fire setting." [3]*

## COLONIAL LABOR SYSTEMS

After Cortés conquered Tenochtitlán, the Spanish continued to invade and settle surrounding territory. Over the next 300 years, the colony of New Spain grew to include large parts of what is now the US, including Texas, New Mexico, Utah, Arizona, California and part of Colorado.

This territorial expansion generated wealth for the Spanish who lived in New Spain as well as for the Spanish crown. Spanish colonizers gained enormous power and wealth through three principle economic activities: large farms known as *haciendas* (ah-see-EN-dahs), silver and gold mining, and the manufacturing of goods in workshops, called *obrajes* (o-BRA-hays).

### Haciendas (Farms and Ranches)

Spanish colonists bought or laid claim to large pieces of Indian land and formed vast farms and ranches known as *haciendas*. The *hacienda* workers produced food and other goods for urban markets in New Spain, as well as goods for export to Spain.

The Spanish brought domesticated animals with them to New Spain, including horses, cattle, sheep, chickens and pigs. Since most Spanish colonists were not farmers, they often forced Indians to work the land. The growth of *haciendas* forced many Indians, who originally had lived in these areas, to migrate in search of work or land to farm.

### Mining

Striking it rich in a mine made Spanish and *Criollo* owners wealthy overnight. Mines were also an important source of wealth for Spain, as the Spanish crown automatically received one-fifth of any silver ore.

Mining contributed to the rapid growth of towns and cities in remote areas, since people moved to areas surrounding mines to provide goods and services to miners. In turn, nearby agricultural areas increased production in order to supply these urban areas with food. Many Indians left their communal lands to find work in these growing urban areas.

## Obrajes

Although colonists in New Spain imported many goods from Spain, over time Spanish colonists began manufacturing goods in New Spain. *Obrajes* were textile workshops producing cloth and other goods. *Obrajes* were known for their harsh working conditions and low pay.

## Effect of the Labor Systems

The large profits made through the mines, *haciendas*, and *obrajes* were possible through the exploitation of Indian and African labor. The Spanish devised a number of ways to force the Indians to work for them. After the conquest, Cortés made grants of as many as 20,000 Indians to Spanish officials. These officials forced Indians to pay tribute (similar to taxes) and to provide free labor. In return, owners were obligated to Christianize and "civilize" their charges. In later years, workers were paid wages, which were extremely low, and forced to work a certain number of days each year for the Spanish colonizers. Workers were forced to labor from dawn to dusk, and they often were beaten and unpaid.

The impact of Spanish colonization was devastating to Indian peoples. Studies indicate that the population of Indian peoples in central Mexico alone to be about twenty million before contact with the Spanish. In less than one hundred years, this population had declined to a little more than one million people. The Spanish carried germs for diseases such as smallpox, measles, and yellow fever to peoples who had never been exposed to such deadly diseases. The Spanish also killed hundreds of thousands of Indians in wars, conflicts, and through exploitative labor practices. The forced relocation of Indian peoples off their native land and the ecological changes caused by Spanish settlement further contributed to the devastation of the indigenous population.

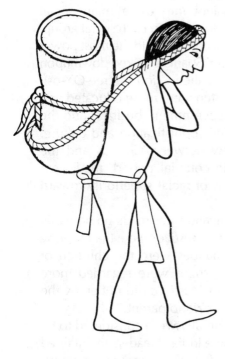

1. Palmer, Colin A., *Slaves of the White God: Blacks in Mexico, 1570-1650.* Cambridge, MA: Harvard University Press, 1976, p. 70.

2. Super, John, "Miguel Hernandez, Master of Mule Trains, " in *Struggle and Survival in Colonial America,* ed. Sweet and Nash. Berkeley: University of California Press, 1981, p. 301.

3. Palmer, p 82.

# SOCIAL STRATIFICATION IN NEW SPAIN

*Many Spanish and Criollos held great contempt for non-white peoples, calling those of African and Indian descent names such as "parrot," "donkey," "dirty," or "pig."*

*These insults, heaped on top of brutal working conditions, often resulted in acts of resistance and rebellion. Historians have recorded more than 140 village revolts that occurred from 1700 to 1820.*

*At the sound of a commonly understood signal, such as the ringing of church bells, villagers assembled in certain locations with whatever weapons were at hand—machetes, rocks, household tools, etc. Women played an especially important role in the rebellions, perhaps because men were often working outside the community. Many of these uprisings were targeted at officials or official institutions that symbolized Spanish authority, such as a local jail. For instance, a jail might be attacked in order to release someone, and then set aflame. The violence usually ended with the villagers achieving their goal of freeing someone from jail, getting a promise from a colonial official that a grievance would be acted upon, or driving off an intruder.*

After the conquest, the Spanish developed a rigid race/class system in New Spain. Three different racial groups made up colonial Mexican society. The first group, Indians, lived in the territory before the Spanish invasion. The second group was made up of the Spanish and others who followed to seek riches. Finally, there were Africans, brought by the Spanish to work as slaves to fill labor demands not met by the Indian population.

The Spanish created a society in colonial Mexico in which each individual was aware of his or her place in the social order. Over time, racial distinctions were more difficult to make because of the many racial categories that resulted from the intermixing of Indians, Africans and Spanish. Race remained an important determinant of an individual's position in society, although family background, occupation, and personal and political contacts also played an important role.

One can divide colonial society into three main social categories, although there were divisions within each social group. European-born Spanish and their descendants held the most power and prestige in society. European-born Spanish looked down upon Spanish born in Mexico, who were called *Criollos* (cree-OY-os). The European-born Spanish, who often were more educated and occupied the highest positions in government, business and the church, thought that *Criollos* lacked sophistication and culture. Although important divisions grew between *Criollos* and the European-born Spanish during the colonial period, they were united by their culture and feelings of racial superiority toward Indians and Africans.

The second rung in social classification was made up primarily by *Mestizos*, but also some Mulattoes. *Mestizos* were the offspring of Spanish and Indians, while Mulattoes were the children of Spanish and Africans. Although *Mestizos* were regarded more highly than Indians or Africans, most *Mestizos* did not enjoy the same advantages as their Spanish or *Criollo* parent.

Finally, Indians and Africans generally were considered to be at the bottom of the social scale. Some Indians leaders maintained their elite status and privileges after the conquest. Spanish colonists relied on cooperation with Indian leaders to maintain control of the surviving Indian population. The majority of Indians, however, were considered lowly commoners by the Spanish and were forced to serve the upper classes and pay them taxes, known as tributes. Indians living in urban areas and *haciendas* often became integrated into Spanish society. They learned Spanish, wore European clothes, and ate Spanish food. In many rural areas, however, Indians lived separated from the Spanish in Indian

*(Indians) believe that the roots of oppression are to be found in the loss of tradition and memory, because that loss is always accompanied by a loss of a positive sense of self. In short, Indians think it is important to remember, while Americans think it is important to forget.* [4]

*I am part of this creation as you are, no more and no less than each and every one of you within the sound of my voice. I am the generation of generations before me and the generations to come.* [5]

communities called *pueblos* and farmed communally. In these instances, people retained much of their traditional life, preserving family structure and language. The Maya, Mixtecs, Tarahumara, Otomí and Zapotecs were largely successful in retaining their cultural ties. Although the Spanish imported Africans for slave labor, Africans never comprised more than 2 percent of the population. The children of Africans and Indians were called Zambos.

## The Role of the Catholic Church

The Catholic church played a crucial role in the process of "incorporating" Indians into colonial Spanish society through their conversion to Christianity. Numerous Catholic religious orders followed the conquistadors to New Spain, seeking to convert Indians to Christianity and abolish Indian religious practices.

These priests played an important role in extending Spanish authority to rural areas. Priests had substantial influence in local affairs, reporting to government officials and at times serving as judges and tax collectors. The church wielded a great deal of influence in colonial Mexico, in part because it was able to acquire large tracts of land. Many Indians complained of ill-treatment by local priests. However, there were some priests who were compassionate in their care for Indians and attempted to protect them from abusive treatment by the Spanish.

4.  Allen, Paula Gunn, *Dangerous Memories*. Chicago Religious Task Force on Central America, 1991. p. 209.

5.  Aquash, Anna Mae Pictou. *In The Spirit of Crazy Horse* by Peter Matthiessen. New York, Viking. p. 252.

# SLAVERY AND REBELLION IN COLONIAL MÉXICO

*Juan de Morga was a young mulatto slave born in New Spain in 1627. He was purchased by a Mestizo man named Mr. Arratia, an entrepreneur in the mining industry. When Morga arrived at Arratia's house, Morga was placed in chains and his face was branded with the letter "s" to signify his permanent status as a slave. When Morga tried to escape, Arratia beat him severely, leaving him with deep scars. Morga became seriously ill from the beatings, but this did not stop Arratia from having him branded again—this time with a mark that extended from ear to ear.*

*One morning, when Morga was getting off late to work, Arratia tied him behind his horse and dragged him around the encampment over rocks and gullies and spiny plants until he was horribly wounded; and then he sent him to get about his duties as well.*

*Slave owners also treated girls and women harshly. Girls not born into slavery in colonial Mexico had two choices for their lives. They either could marry and remain in the home or they could become nuns.*

*Gertrudis de Escobar, born a free mulatta, began working as a small child in the convents of Mexico City. One day, a nun punished Gertrudis for misbehaving. In response, Gertrudis repeated some words she had probably heard on the street, was convicted of blasphemy and ordered to pay a fine. Since her family could not pay the fine, a relative sold her into slavery on a sugar plantation. A glimpse of her life story follows:*

*"...Gertrudis was sent out to help with the backbreaking work of cutting cane. Each adult worker was expected to cut twenty-five rows of cane in a working day; the youthful and inexperienced Gertrudis was expected to do just the same. After two weeks she was punished with fifty lashes one evening for having failed to fulfill her quota. For a time she was put back to work in the harvest; and later she was sent to feed cane into the dangerous rollers of the grinding mill. This was heavy and dangerous night work, beginning at 8:00 in the evening and finishing in the morning.... Many of those assigned to this work, which was reserved for women, lost hands or arms when they got them caught between the rollers. All of this...was being demanded of a girl who was still only fourteen."* [6]

6. The stories of Juan de Morga and Gertrudis de Escobar are told by Solange Alberro in "Juan de Morga and Gertrudis de Escobar: Rebellious Slaves," in *Struggle and Survival in Colonial America*, ed. Sweet and Nash, University of California Press, 1981.

Africans were concentrated in four areas of New Spain. Thousands of Africans lived in the eastern coastal lowlands around Veracruz, working as dock hands in the ports or on sugar plantations or cattle ranches. In the area north and west of Mexico City, more than 15,000 slaves worked in silver mines and on cattle, mule, and sheep ranches. Several thousand also worked on sugar plantations, ranches, and mines along the southwest coast and in the port of Acapulco. Certainly, the largest concentration was in and around Mexico City, where Africans, both free and slave, worked in urban occupations.

Slaves resisted harsh working conditions and cruel treatment. Some escaped, and slave owners had to pay military troops or local vigilantes to recapture them. Indians often assisted slave revolts, which made the revolts difficult to prevent and control.

New Spain's rugged terrain made it fairly easy for slaves to find hideaways. In some cases the escaped slaves formed self-sufficient communities on the frontier called maroon societies. Maroons used extensive fortifications such as booby traps and false paths to protect themselves. They also developed sophisticated guerrilla warfare tactics to raid ranches or wagons and to free other slaves. Some maroon communities became so powerful that Spanish officials deemed the passage between Mexico City and Veracruz unsafe for both travelers and commerce in 1609. This prompted Spanish officials to commission an armed force to "pacify the area." To do this, the Spanish had to negotiate with the maroons and sign a truce.

# 1. Forecasting the Future: The Consequences of Colonialism
# THE LAND GRAB

DIRECTIONS: In your small group, read the paragraph below along with the *Consider This!*
question. Choose a group recorder, and then brainstorm some answers to the question.
The recorder should write down all of the ideas. Boil down your ideas to
one "educated guess" which you will share with the class.

One of the most important goals of the Spanish invaders was to acquire as much wealth as possible. This meant exploiting the land for mineral resources and for its agricultural productivity. In order to exploit the natural resources, they needed a large amount of human labor. Spanish settlers forced *Mestizos*, Indians and Africans to be part of this labor force. It also meant taking land from the people who lived there, even though these people felt connected to the land in a spiritual sense. The Indians did not think about the land as "property" or an exploitable "resource," but as a source of life.

## Consider This!
The creation of huge plantations and mines owned by just a few people
might have some future effects. What do you think these effects might be?

----------------------------------------------------------------------------------------

# 2. Forecasting the Future: The Consequences of Colonialism
# EUROPEAN EXPANSION

DIRECTIONS: In your small group, read the paragraph below along with the *Consider This!*
question. Choose a group recorder, and then brainstorm some answers to the question.
The recorder should write down all of the ideas. Boil down your ideas to
one "educated guess" which you will share with the class.

Most of the crops and minerals produced in New Spain by Indian labor were loaded on ships bound for Spain and other European countries. The Spanish crown automatically took one-fifth of all of the gold and silver mined! Much of the wealth of New Spain was used to develop Europe, instead of providing for the well being of the workers and peasants who produced it.

## Consider This!
How might things be different today if these resources
had been used to develop Mexico?

## 3. Forecasting the Future: The Consequences of Colonialism
# COLONIAL CONSUMERS

DIRECTIONS: In your small group, read the paragraph below along with the *Consider This!*
question. Choose a group recorder, and then brainstorm some answers to the question.
The recorder should write down all of the ideas.  Boil down your ideas to
one "educated guess" which you will share with the class.

Spain's purpose for colonizing Mexico was both to provide raw materials for use in
Spain and to create and enlarge the market for products manufactured and
processed in Spain. For the most part, Spain did not encourage the development or
growth of local industries in New Spain.

### Consider This!
How might the lack of industries in colonial times affect Mexico today?

------------------------------------------------------------------------

## 4. Forecasting the Future: The Consequences of Colonialism
# SOCIAL STRATIFICATION

DIRECTIONS: In your small group, read the paragraph below along with the *Consider This!*
question. Choose a group recorder, and then brainstorm some answers to the question.
The recorder should write down all of the ideas.  Boil down your ideas to
one "educated guess" which you will share with the class.

When you think about the effect that colonization had on Mexican society, imagine
a pyramid. The system of colonization depended upon a small number of wealthy
Spanish and *Criollos* at the top of the pyramid (the élite), and large masses of people
(*Mestizos*, Indians and Africans) at the base of the pyramid.

### Consider This!
What effect do you think this "élite" class had on the development of Mexico?
Do you think an élite class still exists?

## 5. Forecasting the Future: The Consequences of Colonialism
# CULTURAL DESTRUCTION

DIRECTIONS: In your small group, read the paragraph below along with the *Consider This!*
question. Choose a group recorder, and then brainstorm some answers to the question.
The recorder should write down all of the ideas.  Boil down your ideas to
one "educated guess" which you will share with the class.

---

Although there were few Spanish settlers compared to the number of Indian people,
they forced Indians to learn their language, converted people (often with threats) to
their religion and outlawed much of the culture and traditions of the Indian people.

### *Consider This!*
What effect might these policies have on the way
Indians feel about themselves and their culture?

## Social Stratification in New Spain in 1810

**Percentage of Population**
1 percent Spaniards
14 percent *Criollos*
30 percent *Mestizos* / Mulattoes
55 percent Indians / Africans

**For a Group of 12 Students**
1 Spaniard
2 *Criollos*
3 *Mestizos* / Mulattoes
6 Indians / Africans

* There are exceptions to these class distinctions. Although there were not large numbers of Mulattoes or Africans, they would join the *Mestizos* and Indians in economic / social levels.

# Spanish Crown

I represent the Spanish Crown. During the past 50 years, my country has been involved in numerous wars, especially against England and France. In 1808, just two years ago, Napoleon Bonaparte of France invaded Spain, and his brother Joseph is now our ruler. To pay for these wars, we count on the profits from our colony, New Spain. We have invested millions in the gold and silver mines there. These could make us the richest country in Europe. However, our officials who oversee New Spain and collect taxes aren't very good administrators. Some of them are even corrupt and keep profits for themselves. We protect New Spain from other foreign countries and provide a market for all their exports, like animal hides, tobacco, dyes, cacao, sugar, cotton and wool. To protect our economic interests we don't allow New Spain to produce anything that may compete with our products, like wine, silk or olive oil.

# The Spanish

Although we are less than 2 percent of the population, we are the most privileged people in New Spain. That is because we were born in Spain. Most of us live in mansions in the large cities like Mexico City and Guadalajara. We own many mines and have investments in shipping businesses that link New Spain to Spain. Our people have been given the most prestigious jobs in the colonial government. We are the governors and judges in the cities, generals in the military, and bishops in the Catholic Church. Life is very good here in New Spain.

# The Indians

Before the invasion, we Indians lived communally and shared all the land. It provided everything we needed. We still maintain our traditional ways, but we no longer have much land. Many of our families have been divided by the Spanish. We have been forced onto meager plots where we can't raise enough corn and beans for our own families. For part of the year we must work for the *Criollos* on their *haciendas* where we are treated like animals. What we produce is then taken as "tribute," a payment for the privilege of just staying alive and living on the land that was ours originally.

# The Mestizos

We are known as the *Mestizos*, or "intermediate" class. Many of us have *Criollo* fathers and Indian mothers. Don't ask how that happened. Because of us, the *Criollos* and Spanish are rich. They can have shops and export things to Spain because we produce the goods. We are the workers in New Spain. In factories in the cities, we make cloth, cigarettes and cigars that are exported to Spain. In the rural areas, we are the laborers on the cattle ranches and in the fields. We also work deep down in the silver mines. We want land so we can have ranches and farms of our own, but the *Criollos* have the best land and they are unwilling to sell it. The Indians' land is used communally and they guard it closely, even though it isn't very good land.

# The Criollos

Our parents and grandparents were from Spain but we were born in New Spain. No matter how well educated we are, we will never have the privileges of the Spanish. That is because we are *Criollos*. However, we do have good jobs as government workers, teachers, storekeepers, merchants and priests. Many of us own land and live quite well. But the Spanish block our way to having real political and social clout. Simón Bolívar recently came to Mexico and told us that Argentina had declared independence from Spain. He urged us to unite in order to bring freedom to all the Americas, to expel the Spaniards and establish a free government.

## Did You Know?

# The Story of Sor Juana

One of the great poets of Mexico lived and wrote during the Colonial era, despite the censure she received. Juana Inés de Asbaje was born in 1651 near Mexico City. She taught herself to read, which was quite unusual for girls of that time, especially since she was only three years old. By age nine, Juana was writing poetry. At that time, she convinced her parents to send her to Mexico City to further her education.

Women like Juana had few options during the 1600s—they either married and stayed in the home, or they joined a convent to become a nun. The latter was her choice, and Sor Juana, as she was now called, was able to pursue her passion for reading and writing, in addition to scientific experimentation and music.

With her broad range of knowledge, Sor Juana wrote poems and plays about love, history and politics. She soon was in trouble with the Catholic Church hierarchy because she had strayed from the topics reserved for women, such as the family, home and religion. In 1691, Sor Juana was ordered to confine her writings to "appropriate" topics. In response, Sor Juana wrote a letter to the bishop in which she tried to camouflage her belief in women's rights by writing about cooking. While she appeared to accept the bishop's order, Sor Juana challenged the unfairness of society's rules in this excerpt:

> *What couldn't I tell you of the secrets of nature that I have discovered while cooking? Do you know how or why an egg unites and fries in hot oil, but falls apart in hot syrup? How sugar can be kept in liquid form by adding a tiny bit of water in which a citrus fruit has been soaking? Have you discovered the differences between the white and the yolk of an egg? I don't want to continue with these examples, which probably only make you laugh, but, after all, what can we women know other than kitchen philosophy?*

Pressure from the church authorities increased, and in 1693, Sor Juana was forced to submit. With her own blood she signed a confession that her writings were worldly and irreligious. She gave away her books and withdrew from all contact with the outside world. Two years later at age 44, Sor Juana died while caring for sister nuns during an epidemic.

Today, Sor Juana's poems have been translated into many languages. She is recognized as an important poet and also as a pioneer of women's rights.

# Bringing History to Life

*Stories from the Colonial Era*

One of the objectives of *Many Faces of Mexico* is to bring a human face to the complex issues of Mexico. To do this, we incorporate stories about people who represent different social and economic sectors and who live in different regions of the country. In this unit, we introduce several individuals and show how the concerns and events of the Colonial Era are interwoven into their lives. Descendants of these people will appear again during *The Mexican Revolution*, Lesson 15, and *Contemporary Mexico*, Lesson 22. The stories, written by Octavio Ruiz, are based on historical memory, imagination and research.

*Stories from the Colonial Era* introduces six people who live in each of the six regions presented in Lesson 4. Of the six, two are Spanish, three are Indian and one is African. The African woman and the Spanish man recount similar experiences on the ship coming to New Spain. However, their views differ, as the one is "above deck" and the other is "below". All of them are affected by the new systems that the colonizers have established, whether through their work, where they live, or how they interact with one another. The Spanish influence was greater in some areas, especially around cities and administrative centers.

Students work in the same regional group for the first part of the lesson while they read and discuss their story. They then "jigsaw" and form new groups made up of one representative from each region. Each person tells his or her story to others while they take notes about the experiences.

| | |
|---|---|
| **Learner Objectives** | • To describe important events that occurred during the Colonial era. |
| | • To assess the impact these events had by identifying ways in which people's lives changed due to Spain's colonization of Mexico. |
| | • To develop an understanding of different perspectives about changes in Mexico during the Colonial era. |
| **Concepts** | • Customs |
| | • Social change |
| | • Continuity |
| **Major Question to be Addressed** | How did economic, social and political changes affect people's lives in Colonial Mexico? |
| **Teaching Strategies** | • Reading and discussion in small groups |
| | • "Jig-sawing" and teaching others |
| **Materials Provided** | • Six Stories from the Colonial Era (Handouts 1a-1f) |
| | • Family Time-line (Handout 2) |
| | • Note-taking Grid (Handout 3) |
| **Additional Materials Needed** | • Map of Mexico |
| | • Student journals |
| **Time Required** | 1 class period |
| **Preparation for this Lesson** | • Make copies of the six stories from Handout 1 (one story per small group with enough copies for each student in the small group). |
| | • Make one copy of Handouts 2 (*Family Time-line)* and 3 (*Note-taking Grid)* for each student. |

# Sequence of Lesson

*Anticipatory Set*
*10 minutes*

1. Divide students into the same regional small groups as in Lesson 4, *Historical Imagining*. Instruct students to jot down on plain paper all they can recall about their region, such as the topography, the people's housing, food, clothing and customs.

*Body of Lesson*
*40 minutes*

2. Give each student the story from his/her region to read and a copy of Handout 2 to write down key points about the story in the column for the colonial era. They should work with the story enough so they are able to retell it to other students.

3. After about 15 minutes, do a "jigsaw" in which students number off in each group, beginning with 1. The "1s" will make a new group with a representative from each region, etc. (For example, if there are 24 students in the class, there were 4

students in each of 6 regional small groups. After this jigsaw, there should be 6 students in the 4 new teaching groups.)

4. Distribute a copy of Handout 3 to each student. In the new groups, each student should tell about the person's life, referring to his or her notes from Handout 2. Other students should take notes for each region on Handout 3. When all the stories are retold, ask students to compare and contrast how each family was affected by issues or events of the era in which they lived. If there is time, ask students to imagine a conversation between the six story characters as if all of the people in the story met. Role play the conversation.

*Closure*

5. Instruct students to write in their journals a dialogue poem between at least two characters, and continue the writing for homework. At the beginning of the next class period, ask students to read aloud their poems. Suggest using the form of a dialogue poem in which two people speak about their lives in parallel columns, such as these lines from *Rich Woman, Poor Woman*, a dialogue poem:

"I am a woman.

> *I am a woman.*

I am a woman born of a woman whose man owned a factory.

> *I am a woman born of a woman whose man labored in a factory.*

I am a woman whose man wore silk suits, who constantly watched his weight.

> *I am a woman whose man wore tattered clothing, whose heart was constantly strangled by hunger.*

I am a woman who watched two babies grow into beautiful children.

> *I am a woman who watched two babies die because there was no milk..."*

*Evaluation*

- Look at the students' grids. Each one should have essentially the same information.
- Ask for volunteers to read their dialogue or do a role play with their dialogue.
- During the next class, collect and read the journal assignment, or ask students to read aloud their dialogue.

## Story from Region 1 — North

# COLONIAL ERA

In the 16th and 17th centuries, the Spanish continued to move north of Tenochtitlán. This venture north was mostly due to the Spaniards' belief that there was an *el dorado*, or a city of gold. Several expeditions set off with dreams of becoming rich by finding this enchanted city. They reached as far as the current US states of New Mexico, Arizona, Texas and Oklahoma. Becoming rich was not easy for the Spanish, however, as they encountered resistance from the inhabitants of the areas through which they traveled.

The Spaniards attacked and massacred Indian people that were in their way. After their armed expeditions, Catholic missions followed. The Catholic priests were concerned about the "souls" of the Indian people and converted many of them to Catholicism. This story is the account of Ochaván, (oach-a-BAN) a Tarahumara (tar-ah-ou-MAR-ah) Indian, born in the area now known as the state of Chihuahua (chee-WHA-wha), Mexico.

Times are changing very fast for my people, the Tarahumara, and the peoples around us. Strange soldiers have arrived with new ways. The sky doesn't look the same since they arrived. The birds don't sing the same way anymore. The owl at night announces the death of many of my people.

My name is Diego Rodriguez. That's the name the strangers gave me when they arrived in this land, but my real name is Ochaván. I like the name Ochaván best since it is the name that my people gave me. Recently, most of my people escaped to the mountains, because Spanish soldiers took a group of my people as prisoners. The soldiers wanted to know the way to *el dorado*, the legendary "city of gold." I don't understand why these people want this metal

so much. When the strangers saw that some of our elders had gold ornaments in their ears, they went crazy. They pulled the ornaments off, making their ears bleed. Other men from my group were taken by the soldiers to build what they call a church in honor of their god.

The same thing is happening all around us. Almost all our neighbors have been fighting against the strangers, who have powerful weapons and animals that help them win battles against our warriors who use bows and spears. The animals they ride seem to be from a bad dream, from a different world. I never saw such beasts in my entire life. Their god is good to them because their god helps them win battles and kill my people.

Before they came, everything was so different around here. That does not mean that our life was always peaceful. We had wars with some of our neighbors when they came into our territory to hunt without the agreement of our elders. But my people hunted and collected plants that we could eat and our life never changed very much. The desert was a peaceful place and the mountain was disturbed only when there were the strong northern winds.

I am what is called a medicine man or Shaman. Before the arrival of the strangers, I had an important function among my people. I was the man who could read the night sky and then predict a good rainy season or a cold winter. I was the one who cared for and healed the sick. I was the one who called the elders together to decide whether or not to start a war.

Those were the times when my people were united. Now we are mixed with people from several other groups and scattered all over the region. Here on the mountain, the only time we all come together is to defend ourselves from our common enemy. When we hear rumors that the strangers are coming, mounted on their animals, we all come together.

Now this has become a forlorn place....

## Story from Region 2 — North Central
# COLONIAL ERA

After the fall of Tenochtitlán, Spanish armies continued their invasion to the north and south, claiming lands for what would become New Spain. Although there was fierce resistance by the Indians, such as the Otomís (oh-toe-MEES), the Spanish took the Indian lands for what would become the colony of New Spain. The soldiers were followed by Catholic missionaries, and soon, people from all regions of Spain began to cross the ocean and settle in New Spain. The Spanish founded new cities and new Spanish migrants arrived to manage these administrative centers. The account of one of these settlers follows.

It is 1580 and my name is Francisco Alvarado de Ojeda. I am 42 years old and my father came from Spain. I am what the people of this land call a *Criollo*. That's because my mother and father were born in Spain but I was born in New Spain. My father and mother came from the city of Madrid and were proud of their Spanish heritage. Their families were rich and they held high administrative positions in the government of Spain. But my father thought he would have better opportunities in New Spain. Here there were mines and land that needed developing and my father was the person to do this. My father had a wise administrative mind, so he traveled to New Spain to look for a more promising future.

I was born in the newly-founded city of Querétaro (care-ATE-tear-o), northwest of Mexico City. At that time it was the last civilized northern frontier. As new Spanish settlers arrived and as the Indians surrendered to the power of the Spanish crown, other cities were founded farther north.

My father died three years ago and my mother two years ago. From my father I inherited the title to one silver mine, and ownership of land that he had been awarded because of his services to the Spanish crown.

Now I live in the city of Guadalajara (wah-da-la-HAR-ah). This is a Spanish city where most of the rich Spanish and *Criollo* people live. Many of the *Criollos* have large houses and travel about the city in grand carriages. The main social events are festive parties, which we take turns hosting.

Indians also live here, and those who have received the word of the Lord can work in our homes as servants. They also can work in mines not far from here. I own three homes—one in Querétaro and two in Guadalajara. I am married and we have two daughters. My wife stays at home and supervises our Indian servants and two African maids. She also makes sure that our daughters receive the right education and are prepared to marry into a good family.

Guadalajara is the government center of this region of New Spain. The city has been improving since new mines farther north have been opened. More Spanish people have been moving here. The most difficult problem we face is with the Indians who live north of here. They have attacked several of our soldiers in the area. We hope that our army will be able to protect us. With the help of God we hope that these Indians will be converted and adopt our more civilized Spanish customs.

## Story from Region 3 — South Central
# COLONIAL ERA

Hundreds of years after the era of the Toltec civilization and immediately after the fall of the Aztec city of Tenochtitlán, Spanish soldiers and settlers began to colonize the land that belonged to the Indians. Many people from Spain pursued their dream of coming to the Americas in search of wealth and fortune. Such is the case of Martín de Muñoz, who was originally from southern Spain.

My name is Martín de Muñoz. I was born in Spain 62 years ago. I never thought I actually would live in New Spain — it always seemed like a dream to go to that land of opportunity. As a young boy, I remember sitting by the docks in a Spanish port city, watching the sailing ships depart and waiting until their top flags disappeared over the horizon. I knew about Christopher Columbus, who believed he had found his way around the world to India. Then Señor Magellan left from here to go south across the ocean to lands of mystery and wealth and to go around the world. Even though four of his five ships were wrecked and most of the sailors died, including Señor Magellan, I knew that was what I wanted. Like the other sailors, I wanted to explore the world!

I remember the sacred war in 1492 against the Muslims who had invaded our land and taken possession of most of it. Our Catholic majesties not only wanted to recover that land, but also convert the people to Catholicism. How I wish I could have served in King Ferdinand and Queen Isabel's army!

In 1522, we received news about the heroic conquests of the Spanish army over the Indians in America. By then I had achieved a high rank in the army and was really anxious to go to New Spain. After the long trip across the ocean from Spain, I finally arrived at the port of Veracruz. It was a relief to reach America because pirates were in the Caribbean Sea, attacking our ships and trying to take our cargo. Many Spanish ships were sunk by the pirates' cannons and many people died in those attacks.

I was in disbelief when I saw the new land and its people. I felt I had entered a totally different world. I was assigned first to the port of Veracruz and then to the newly-founded Mexico City. At times, I was lonely for my family and friends back in Spain.

In my only battle, I fought Indians who refused to become subjects of the Spanish crown. It was a fierce battle but we finally subdued the Indians and forced them to submit to our authority. We sold some of them as slaves while others were given to us as a reward for our heroism. I still have two of the six Indians who were given to me to be my servants. The other four died from some kind of disease.

Now I live in Mexico City and I work with the treasury. I am responsible for keeping account of the gold that is sent to our Majesties in Spain. Here in New Spain I have the opportunity to succeed, because this is a land of plenty. The Indians have not learned the value of the wealth that is under their feet. There is gold and silver in the north, and to the south the land is good for sugar cane and other crops. If the Indians do not know how to take advantage of all this, we Spanish people will.

# Story from Region 4 — Gulf Coast
# COLONIAL ERA

The early history of African people in the Americas is a dramatic one. African people were forcibly brought to all parts of the Americas. They suffered or died on the trip from Africa, and once on the continent, they suffered or died from overwork. African people originally were brought to replace the Indian people who had been killed or had died as a result of the Spanish invasion. Africans were brought to the same area where the Olmecs had settled, around the Gulf of Mexico, and later, when they were bought or traded, went to work in other regions of the country. When the Spanish took over Indian lands they needed people to work, mainly in mining, manufacturing of textiles and dyes, and agriculture. This is the account of Josefina Silva, an African woman brought by the Spaniards to work in the sugar cane fields in what is now the state of Veracruz, Mexico.

My name is Josefina Silva. That's the name the Spanish gave me after I was brought to an island in the Caribbean and they baptized me. I was put to work serving a Spanish soldier. I was traded several times. Finally I was brought here to New Spain.

But back to the beginning. I was captured along the African coast by Portuguese soldiers and sold to Spanish slave traders. I was put with a large group of men and women from different tribes. I know that because we spoke different languages. The trip was a nightmare. We were crowded into the lower deck of a cargo ship. We didn't have enough air and could hardly lie down. We didn't have enough food or water. The conditions were so bad that we were glad the rats ate the excrement around us.

Not long after we started the trip some of the people committed suicide. They used their ankle chains to strangle themselves or refused to eat or drink. One day pirates attacked us. I think that they wanted to capture the Spanish cargo and steal the merchandise, which was us. For hours we could hear the shouts and the explosions of the cannons. We didn't know if the ship was sinking or if the pirates had taken control. Some of us lost our minds and started pulling ourselves from our ankle chains until we bled. The struggle ended many hours later.

A few days later we landed on an island. Most of the Africans who had begun this nightmarish journey had died. Only twenty of us survived.

Eventually I was traded to a Spanish soldier and he brought me here to New Spain. He actually gave me good treatment in comparison to other slaves, as long as I took good care of his house. Other slaves built a church while they waited to be traded again. They received really bad treatment. Some were whipped and some were hanged because they refused to work or weren't able to work anymore. Some tried to run away, but they were almost always captured, returned to their owner and beaten.

After my first owner, I ran out of luck. My next owner hit me or punished me almost every day. I was traded several times until I came here to the sugar plantation. I must have been very young, maybe 17 years old. Now I am around 40 years old. I married a man who works here in the field. We hardly see each other because I work in the big house with our owners. We have two children and they work on the plantation.

In the fields my husband and children work together with people the Spanish call Indians. I think they already were here when the Spanish came. We don't talk very much because we speak different languages and live apart from one another. The other day I offered water to an Indian and he gracefully accepted it. They seem to be nice people.

I don't understand why we have been brought here to work for these people. I hope my children have better luck and get better treatment. I hope they are not traded and taken away from me.

## Story from Region 5 — Pacific South
# COLONIAL ERA

In the 1400s, before the Spanish arrived, the Aztecs occupied vast areas of Mexico, and Aztec soldiers and merchants influenced the culture and traditions of several groups. In the Oaxaca (wah-HA-kah) region, the Aztecs had a profound effect on the daily lives of the Zapotec and Mixtec people. The Aztecs in Tenochtitlán were able to thrive as the dominant culture before 1521 because of the tribute system, a system in which the people under their rule had to give the Aztecs a portion of all that they made or grew. This is the story of a young woman who lived in the state of Oaxaca in 1528. She lived in a village close to the ancient ceremonial site of Monte Alban.

My name is Xochitl (zoe- CHEET-el) and I am 16 years old. I am a weaver. I make cloth from cotton plants and sew clothes for my family. I also help my mother with the cooking and the care of our house. Every morning we arise before the sun to make corn tortillas.

When I was 13 years old, I was initiated as a woman. The women in my family accompanied me to a gathering of the most respected women in my village. We cooked and ate together at a sacred place. After that time, I was looked upon as a woman. Soon I will marry a merchant's son and we will live with my parents and grandparents. My husband will work with my father and they will build a home for us and the children we hope to have.

I live in a beautiful, old village that existed when my ancestors lived. In those days they went to the ceremonial center of Monte Alban.

Now most of our villages have disappeared. After the Spanish came, they made people move to new communities to split us up. They said they could rule us better if we lived apart. But I think they did this so we couldn't organize to fight them. In some villages, the Spanish tore down ceremonial sites and built churches in the same place. But my village remains, and for that we give thanks to the river that runs through it.

We are Zapotecs, but we live close to the Mixtecs. When I was a child, we both had trouble with the Aztecs. Their merchants often crossed our territory when they went south to sell their products, and returned north with new products. They got permission to cross from our elders, who are the authorities of our village. The merchants traveled as far as the Mayan lands to trade with people there. One time when the merchants came they were

followed by Aztec warriors. While the warriors waited in the distance, a special Aztec envoy came to our village to speak with the elders. The meeting went all through the night while we waited to hear if we were going to be attacked.

The next morning the Aztec messenger left hastily without receiving a special farewell from the elders. This meant there could be war. In the next hours, women, children and the elders went to the rain forest while our armies assembled. Zapotecs from other villages joined our army, and surprisingly, hundreds from the Mixtec villages came also. As night fell, I hid with the children in the rain forest. In the morning, we were awakened by shouting and screaming in the village. The Aztec armies had launched an attack.

We were very anxious for several hours. By the afternoon the battle was over, and by dawn we were told to come out from hiding. In our village, the bodies of our warriors were scattered everywhere. The Zapotec and Mixtec armies had surrendered to the Aztecs. As a result, my village had to pay tribute to Tenochtitlán.

Now we have the Spaniards. Before they came, we heard that strange people with skin the color of the sun and hair on their bodies had invaded Tenochtitlán. When they came, a new wind blew through the mountains, and there was a different color in the sky. Several villages welcomed the Spaniards and became their allies. We wanted to be free from both Aztecs and Spaniards, but the Spaniards subdued us with their guns and horses. Now instead of paying tribute to the Aztecs, we pay it to the Spanish. Maybe things will continue to change as fast as they have been changing. Maybe the Spaniards are the new wind.

## Story from Region 6 — Southeast

# COLONIAL ERA

This is the account of Ana Santiago, a Tzeltal (zel-TALL) Mayan Indian. She lived in the mid-1500s in the southern highlands of Mexico, in what is now the state of Chiapas. Spanish soldiers built the city of San Cristobal de las Casas in 1524 when they invaded southern Mexico. They took Mayan lands and built San Cristobal as a center of commerce and administration. In order to control the Indians and suppress possible resistance, the Spaniards developed military strongholds in the region. Priests came with the soldiers to convert Indians to Christianity.

My name is Ana Santiago. This is not my birth name, but it is the name by which most people know me. This is a Christian name, given to me by Spanish priests when they baptized me. You see, when the Spaniards arrived, they came with their armies and their priests. Their soldiers fought against our people. Our armies finally lost the battles against the powerful Spaniards with their firing sticks, fast horses and powerful crossbows. There are some Indians who fled to the mountains and still live there because they refuse to become the subjects of these people.

I was born in the outskirts of the city that the Spaniards recently founded; San Cristobal is what they call it. We, the Indian people, know it as Jovel (HO-vel).

The Spanish priests who came with the soldiers say that if we believe in their god on a cross, we will go to heaven. I don't understand this. They say their god is a compassionate one, but why, then, are Spanish soldiers killing my people?

I am 20 years old. I have learned Spanish in the house where I work for a Spanish family, the Gonzalez family. My mother gave me to them when I was only seven years old. They came to our neighborhood to look for a servant. My mother knew they were coming, so she offered me to them. Maybe she did the right thing, maybe she didn't. Since my father died fighting the Spaniards, my mother had a hard time taking care of my two sisters and me. It has been a while since I saw my mother and sister.

One of my sisters died recently from a strange disease that never was here until the Spaniards came. It is called small pox. My other sister was taken by a Spanish man to work in another city not far from here. I miss my mother and sister very much.

The Gonzalez family treats me well. They say I am an obedient Indian. I clean their home and wash their clothes. I wash their clothes in the river with other servant women, and I always look forward to hearing about what is happening in my village. I also like the Gonzalez family. I am very faithful to them and I take good care of their children. I walk with them to their church and sometimes I sit with the Gonzalez family. I am allowed to do this because I have lived with them for a long time. Most other Indians who have been converted to this new religion are not allowed to sit down in church with the Spanish people. They must stand in the very back. I pay attention to what their priest says, although I don't understand many things. I repeat what the priest tells us to say during the mass, although I usually don't understand the meaning of the words.

A long time ago, I learned to speak the Gonzalez's language and I dressed with the clothes from Spain they told me to wear. My life now belongs to the Gonzalez family. Señor Gonzalez says that he is going to let me go in one or two years because I will be ready to get married. I think they want a younger servant. I don't know what I am going to do next.

# FAMILY TIME-LINE

|  | COLONIAL ERA 1521-1810 | REVOLUTION 1910-1920 | CONTEMPORARY 1990s |
|---|---|---|---|
| Who is your story about? Where does s/he live? |  |  |  |
| What happened to the family between eras? |  |  |  |
| Describe her/his lifestyle. |  |  |  |
| How do events in Mexico affect her/him? |  |  |  |

# NOTE-TAKING GRID for the COLONIAL ERA

*Use this grid to fill in the information about the five other regions*

| | Who is the story about? Describe the person and their way of life. | How do events in New Spain / Mexico affect her / him? |
|---|---|---|
| REGION _____ | | |
| REGION _____ | | |
| REGION _____ | | |
| REGION _____ | | |
| REGION _____ | | |

# The Struggle for Independence

## *Analyzing Interests and Alliances*

In 1810, Mexico gained its independence from Spain after 300 years of colonialism. Thirty-five years before, people in Haiti gained their freedom from France and colonists in what is now the United States won their independence from England. The Spanish colonial system was deeply embedded in Mexico and for many people, this system provided a secure way of life. Others, mainly the *Criollos*, wanted to end Spain's rule so they could establish themselves in power.

This lesson looks at the reasons why Mexican people fought for independence from Spain, or joined the loyalists and resisted the move to independence. We provide students with a reading to give them some background about the independence movement. We also include an excerpt from Father Higalgo's famous speech in 1810 in which he called for independence from Spain and rallied others to join the struggle. We ask students to consider the alliances between groups of people, as well as what groups had to gain or lose by becoming a self-governing republic. Finally, we consider some of the consequences of Mexico's independence on future generations.

| | |
|---|---|
| **Learner Objectives** | • To assess the causes of the independence movement through primary source materials. |
| | • To analyze the political, economic and ideological objectives of the independence movement. |
| | • To make inferences about the impact Mexican independence had on different groups of people and on future generations. |
| **Concepts** | • Independence |
| | • Cause and effect |
| **Major Questions to be Addressed** | • What were the conditions and factors that precipitated the struggle for independence? |
| | • Who fought for or resisted independence? Why? |
| | • What were some of the consequences of independence? |
| **Teaching Strategies** | Reading and discussion in small groups |
| **Materials Provided** | • The Call to Rebellion (Educator's Background Information) |
| | • The Struggle for Independence (Handout 1) |
| | • Discussion Grid (Handout 2) |
| | • Our Lady of Guadalupe (Handout 3 Extension Idea) |
| **Time Required** | 1 class session |
| **Preparation for this Lesson** | • Make one copy of Handouts 1 & 2 for each student. Distribute Handout 1 as homework to prepare for this lesson. |
| | • Make an overhead of Handout 2 (optional). |
| | • Make a classroom set of Handout 3 for Extension Lesson. |
| | • Collect pictures and stories about Our Lady of Guadalupe. |

**Sequence of Lesson**

*Anticipatory Set*
*5 minutes*

1. Write the word INDEPENDENCE on the board and ask students what that term means to them. Begin with a personal concept, such as freedom from parents, and expand to a political concept.

*Body of Lesson*
*40 minutes*

2. Review the homework reading, *The Struggle for Independence* (Handout 1). Ask students to list the main points. If they have any questions about the information, ask students to respond to one another's questions.

3. Read aloud *The Call to Rebellion* (Educator's Background Information) which rallied people to revolt against Spanish rule. When finished reading, ask students to imagine what changes might take place as a result of independence.

4. Discuss the following questions:

   • Who was Father Hidalgo? What did he say?
   • What do you think were Hidalgo's goals when he called the people to rebel against Spain?
   • What alliances do you think might form among the Spanish, *Criollos*, *Mestizos* and Indians to fight for independence or resist independence?

5. Divide the class into 5 small groups of equal size that represent each of the following: the Spanish Crown; Spanish living in Mexico; *Criollos*; *Mestizos*; Indians and Africans. Distribute copies of Handout 2 to each student. Allow students about 10-15 minutes to prepare responses to the questions on Handout 2 from the perspective of the group they represent. Students should take notes on Handout 2.

6. Bring the class back together. Ask each group to report back with its responses. Use a grid on an overhead or on the board such as Handout 2 to organize the discussion and responses to the following questions. Students should take notes on Handout 2 to fill in the rest of the grid.

   • What do you think were the motives for the Spanish Crown and the four major sectors to support or resist independence?

   • What do you think the Spanish Crown and the four sectors gained and/or lost through independence? What remained essentially the same?

   • Overall, what do you think changed as a result of independence? How did life change for people in the four social classes: the Spanish; *Criollos*; *Mestizos*; Indians and Africans?

**Closure**

7. End the class with the question, how do you think Mexico would have been different if Hidalgo's vision had been realized and the rights of the poor and oppressed had been defended?

**Assignment**

The United States also fought a war of independence in the 18th century. Ask students to write a reflection piece addressing the following questions: what was similar and what was different between the Mexican and U.S. wars of independence? What changed and what remained the same in the United States as a result of the Revolutionary War?

**Extension Idea**

Read *Our Lady of Guadalupe*, Handout 3, and answer questions.

Read and do a report on the Mexican War of Independence. See bibliography for suggested books.

# The Call to Rebellion
## *El Grito de Dolores*

The year is 1810. Since 1808, there has been a drought with no rain day after dry day. Food is scarce and prices are high. Discontent is widespread among many people in New Spain, but especially among *Criollos*. In the central part of the country, *Criollos* have been planning a rebellion against the Spanish Crown and the Spanish people who run New Spain. The *Criollos* want to run the government themselves. They know they do not have the fighting power to defeat the Spanish Crown, but with the help of the *Mestizos* and Indians, they think they can win. But how are they to appeal to these people to convince them to join the revolt?

Father Miguel Hidalgo is a *Criollo* priest in the small village of Dolores, near Guanajuato (wah-nah-WAH-toe). His parish is composed of poor people, namely Indians and *Mestizos*. Hidalgo is sympathetic to their plight and he blames their unjust treatment on the Spanish people and the Crown. Hidalgo is also realistic; he wants to be part of the *Criollo* crusade and perhaps he will gain something, too.

On the night of September 15, 1810, the bell begins to toll in the Dolores church. Father Hidalgo calls together his parishioners. He begins:

*I have been your priest and your protector for seven long years. Together we have made a community of which we all have a right to be proud. Together we planted mulberry trees and grapevines, raised silkworms, and made wine, in spite of the Spaniards' opposition. Together we put up our factory where pottery and leather goods are produced. Always, as you well know, I have been your friend. Always I have zealously defended the poor and the oppressed. When the Spaniards came and uprooted our trees, because of the competition, I protested with all my might, but it was in vain. Finally the time has come for us to unite and rise up against our oppressors, both yours and mine. So now in the name of our beautiful land, and in the name of our beloved Virgin of Guadalupe, let us take back the lands that were stolen from Mexico three centuries ago.*

*Viva la Virgen de Guadalupe! Viva Mexico! Long live the Virgin of Guadalupe! Long live Mexico!*

Then with the banner of the Virgin of Guadalupe, Hidalgo and his parishioners begin to march toward Guanajuato. After a few hours, tens of thousands join the dissident crowd. They often are unruly, looting, raping and killing those who do not join. By the time they reach Guanajuato, there are 100,000 furious sympathizers who destroy the city in a few hours. Five hundred Spaniards die at Guanajuato, along with nearly two thousand of Hidalgo's allies. Eventually Hidalgo is captured, imprisoned and killed by a firing squad in 1811. His head is put on a pole in a public place in Guanajuato to remind others about the penalty for treason. Hidalgo, the martyr, incited a rebellion that lasted until the year 1821.

# THE STRUGGLE FOR INDEPENDENCE

New Spain was the richest colony held by any European country during the 17th and 18th centuries. Spain needed New Spain's wealth because it had huge expenses trying to maintain its powerful position in Europe. To manage the resource-rich colony, the Spanish exerted strong social, political and economic control over New Spain. But as Spain increased its demands, more and more people began demanding independence from Spain.

## Social Stratification in New Spain

In order to keep social and political control, the Spanish developed a caste system in New Spain. This classified people by skin color and determined their status during their lifetime. Those born in Spain were given high positions in the government and church. *Criollos* got less powerful positions in the government and the church, but the Spanish Crown gave them high positions in the army. Although *Mestizos* and Indians were the majority, neither had a voice in governing New Spain, except when they organized themselves to rebel against the authorities. Most Africans in New Spain were forced to be slaves, whereas most Indians were obligated to give labor and products to the crown as "tribute."

## Imports and Exports

Since the time the Spanish set foot in New Spain, raw materials such as gold and silver were taken back to Spain and other European countries to decorate cathedrals and palaces. Spanish colonizers had developed the economy of New Spain by encouraging and subsidizing the production of cloth, animal hides and dyes. These new industries stimulated the growth of sweatshop-type factories, that exploited the cheap, plentiful labor in New Spain. (These are a prototype of the *maquiladoras* of modern Mexico.) However, the profits from these industries were not re-invested in New Spain or given back to the workers in the form of decent wages. Instead, most of the profits went back to Spain.

Spain also determined which goods could be produced, exported and imported in New Spain. New Spain could not sell silver, textiles, dyes or other products except through Spain. New Spain was forbidden to produce some goods such as wine, olive oil and silk; they had to be imported from Spain. In addition, Spain imposed tariffs, duties and taxes on New Spain.

## Working Conditions in New Spain

From 1800-1810, some of the specific factors that increased discontent among the working classes in New Spain were difficult labor conditions and food shortages. For example, labor conditions in the gold and silver mines were extremely dangerous. To increase productivity, owners forced African, Indian and *Mestizo* laborers to carry up to 300 pounds of ore on their backs. In addition, the price of basic foods grown in New Spain doubled during these years because of poor harvests as a result of droughts and frost. Consequently, large numbers of people became desperately hungry.

## The Decision to Revolt

The *Criollos* became especially frustrated during these years. They could own businesses and have some political power, but they paid high taxes and had little control over their markets. Due to these economic and political factors, many *Criollos* decided to revolt against Spanish domination.

Other external influences fueled the desire for independence. Napoleon conquered Spain in 1808, and *Criollos* believed Spain would be in a weak position to fight a war. The French Revolution, the revolt by the settlers in the thirteen colonies of North America, and the drive for independence in Haiti increased interest in revolution as a solution to their problems.

*Criollos* who followed these events noticed that all these revolts involved small populations fighting against world powers, namely England and France. The *Criollos* faced a similar situation with Spain.

Although *Criollos* organized the revolt, *Mestizos*, Indians and Africans were united in the desire to end colonialism if that would end their oppression. *Criollos* and a few well-educated Mestizos led the struggle for independence, but the poorer *Mestizos*, Indians and Africans made it a reality. The Spanish colonists remained loyal to Spain, their country of birth. They had little to gain from independence.

## The War for Independence

On September 16, 1810, independence from Spain was declared. Miguel Hidalgo y Costilla, a *Criollo* priest, gave a speech this day in the town of Dolores, near

Father Hidalgo

Guanajuato (wah-nah-WAH-toe), and his "Grito de Dolores" is repeated throughout Mexico every independence day. Father Hidalgo urged Indians, *Mestizos* and *Criollos* to band together to revolt against the oppression of the Spanish Crown.

The war for independence ended in 1821 when a *Criollo* leader crowned himself emperor. A peace accord, called the *Plan de Iguala*, was signed on September 9, 1821, and in 1824, Mexico became an independent constitutional republic.

## Consequences of the War

The newly liberated colony paid dearly for independence. Thousands of people died, many of them Indians who had fought with the dream of becoming free again. Power simply changed hands from the Spanish elite to the *Criollo* elite. The destiny of the majority, the Indians, was still in the hands of the privileged minority. The "freedoms" gained by the war most benefited *Criollos* and *Mestizos*. Most of the Spanish living in Mexico returned to their place of birth.

After the war, Mexico opened its borders so free trade could take place. Merchants from the US and European countries scrambled to invest in businesses and trade with the Mexicans. Open borders also meant that people from countries other than Spain began to move to Mexico.

After 1821, Mexico was no longer a colony, but the social, economic and political systems that had existed under Spain were not reformed. Poverty and illness continued to be widespread, especially among Indians and Africans. The ideals of Hidalgo were cast aside. For many, the only thing that changed were the names and faces of the leaders. The social, political and economic systems that had been in place for 300 years remained essentially the same for the majority of people. However, Mexico now was an independent republic and by 1824, Mexico had its own constitution.

The war campaigns produced a number of military heroes, and soon the military was the only group capable of maintaining order. The new leadership and the political parties were weak and inexperienced. They continued to follow the Spanish mode of undemocratic, authoritarian rule. Consequently, the ground was fertile for dictatorships, political corruption and violence.

# DISCUSSION GRID

Answer these questions from your group's perspective,
then fill in the grid during class discussion.

1. Did you resist or support independence? Why? What was your motive for your position?
2. What did you gain or lose? What might remain the same with independence?

| | Your Motive | Gain | Lose | Remain the Same |
|---|---|---|---|---|
| Spanish Crown | | | | |
| Spanish living in Mexico | | | | |
| Criollos | | | | |
| Mestizos | | | | |
| Indians and Africans | | | | |

# *Did you know?*

# *Our Lady of Guadalupe*

Our Lady of Guadalupe, also known as the Virgin of Guadalupe, has been revered and worshiped by millions of Mexicans for more than four centuries. She is the patron saint of Mexico. Her image was on the banner that Father Hidalgo carried when he rallied Indian and Mestizo people to fight against Spain.

According to tradition, a newly converted Indian peasant named Juan Diego had a vision of the Virgin in 1531. The virgin was dark-skinned with Indian features. She asked Juan Diego to have a shrine built in her honor on the place she appeared, which was the site where Indians had worshiped Tonantzin, mother of gods.

Juan Diego went to the bishop of the Catholic Church, who was skeptical, but the Virgin appeared to him again, this time with roses wrapped in a cloak. Juan Diego took the roses to the bishop who was then convinced of her appearance. A church was built on the site where she appeared and has been the destination for religious pilgrimages ever since.

## *Questions to think about:*

* What do you think is the importance of a Catholic saint with Indian features?

* What do you think is the importance of the fact that she appeared before an Indian peasant?

* How do you think this symbol helped convert Indians to Catholicism?

*An Exploring the Connections Lesson*

# Mexico's Loss of Land

## *Perspectives from Mexico and the United States*

This lesson examines an important time in both US and Mexican history. In the early-mid 1800s, the US acquired vast new territories while Mexico lost almost half of its territory. How did this happen? How did people in the US and Mexico feel about the critical decisions that changed their borders? The period of time which includes the annexation of Texas and the Mexican-American War is often given little coverage in US history courses, but merits much greater attention. The history of these conflicts is crucial for understanding US-Mexico relations today. In particular, reconsider the argument made by many in the current immigration debate that Mexicans entering California, Arizona, New Mexico and Texas are "illegals."

The lesson begins by exploring the attempts of US citizens living in Texas to secede from Mexico, and the US government's later acquisition of Mexican territory. Students learn about the Mexican-American War and the concept of Manifest Destiny using a number of primary sources representing different perspectives. These documents will help students to examine their own and others' interpretations of and biases about important ideas and historical events. This period of history is important for understanding contemporary US-Mexico relations, the use of ideology to justify expansion, and an individual's responsibility to society.

| | |
|---|---|
| **Learner Objectives** | • To explain the economic and racial roots of Manifest Destiny and analyze how the concept influenced the westward expansion of the country. |
| | • To explain the causes of the Mexican-American War, the sequence of events leading to the outbreak of war, and the consequences of the Treaty of Guadalupe Hidalgo. |
| | • To analyze the Mexican-American War from different perspectives. |
| **Concepts** | • Annexation |
| | • Manifest Destiny |
| **Major Questions to be Addressed** | • What arguments were used to justify US expansion and to oppose Mexico's loss of land? |
| | • How did the Mexican-US relationship change in the mid-nineteenth century? |
| **Exploring the Connections** | In Mexico the conflict with the United States is known as the American Intervention in Mexico, while in the US it is referred to as the Mexican-American War or the Mexican War. The war of 1846 was a conflict between two countries over land on which many Mexican people lived and whose descendants continue to live today. |
| **Teaching Strategies** | Reading, writing, group discussion and image analysis |
| **Materials Provided** | • Mexico After Independence (Handout 1) |
| | • Examining Perspectives (Handouts 2a, b & c) |
| | • Examining Perspectives Question Sheet (Handout 3) |
| | • Map of Mexican Territory Acquired by US (Image) |
| **Time Required** | 1 class session |
| **Preparation for Lesson** | • Make one copy of each Handout for each student. |
| | • Ask students to read Handout 1 before coming to class. Students should think about their responses to the reflection questions raised in the text and write their responses in their journals. |
| | • Make an overhead of the map. |

# Sequence of Lesson

*Anticipatory Set*
*5 minutes*

1. Introduce the day's lesson by asking provocative questions about the reading, such as, "Was the Mexican-American War really nothing more than a border skirmish?" and "What was at stake for both Mexico and the US?"

*Body of Lesson*
*45 minutes*

2. Ask students if they have any questions about the reading and try to clarify any questions. Place the overhead of the map

showing Mexico's loss of land to the US on the projector. Ask students to briefly summarize the various conflicts which led to Mexico's loss of land (the fight over Texas and the Mexican-American War).

For a more dramatic display of the vast amount of territory Mexico lost, make a photocopy of the map and cut apart the Texas annexations, the land acquired under the Treaty of Guadalupe Hidalgo, and the contemporary map of Mexico. Then, place the pieces of territory lost over the contemporary map of Mexico and compare the size of the territories.

3.  Distribute one copy of Handouts 2a-2c to each student to read individually during class.

4.  Divide students into pairs or small groups. Students should reflect upon what they read in the handouts and discuss their responses to the questions on Handout 3. Students may write one group response or individual responses to the questions on Handout 3. (Students should finish as homework any questions not answered.) Alternatively, the instructor may wish to use the questions on the handout as discussion questions for a discussion with the entire class.

*Closure*                5.  Ask students to imagine how they might have felt about Mexico's loss of land if they had lived in that era. Do a quick straw poll of those in support of, or in opposition to, the war. Ask students to briefly share their reasons for supporting their position.

*Evaluation*             Evaluate student responses on the *Question Sheet* (Handout 3).

*Assignment*             Think about the arguments both in support of, and in opposition to, US expansion. Write about how you think those arguments pertain to US foreign policy today (e.g., US actions in Panama, Iraq, Somalia, and Haiti).

*Extension Lesson*       A painting by John Gast expressed many Americans' feelings about westward expansion in the early to middle 1800s. The painting of "Manifest Destiny" helped to shape people's vision of a modern empire filling a continent. Obtain a reproduction or enlarged photocopy of the painting (included in many social studies textbooks, or in history books at the library). Ask students to analyze the painting and to answer the following:
*   What images does John Gast use to depict the concept of Manifest Destiny?
*   Does Gast's depiction of East and West reveal his biases?
*   Based on this painting, how do you think Gast and others who believed in Manifest Destiny felt about Indians?

This lesson is adapted from "Opposition to the Mexican War of 1846," *OAH Magazine of History*, Spring 1994.

# Mexico After Independence

In 1824, the Estados Unidos Mexicanos (United States of Mexico) was formed. The new country was a federal republic, consisting of 19 states and 4 territories. It had a constitution which called for the separation of legislative, judicial and executive powers, and which established both a senate and a chamber of deputies.

After the war of independence from Spain (1810-1821), the process of creating a new nation was difficult. People disagreed about which type of government to create. Some favored a centralist model with a strong national government, while others favored a federalist model with more independence for the regions. All were concerned that the model chosen should restore order and be respected by people both within and outside of Mexico. Mexicans had a long history of foreign domination, and wanted to establish a governmental system that would protect their land and people from domination by the United States and European countries.

The early years of the republic were turbulent ones. The leadership of the country changed hands several times. General Santa Anna, who had been a prominent military officer in the war with Spain, was President eleven different times between 1832 and 1855. While the Mexican people were focused on resolving internal issues, a new problem was developing in Mexico's northern territories from Texas to the Pacific Ocean.

## The Texas Territory

The US government's purchase of the Louisiana Territory from France in 1803 nearly doubled the size of the United States. By 1819, the US had added eight new states in addition to the Missouri and Arkansas territories, which bordered Mexico. US citizens began to move into these territories, and from there, they began to enter the Mexican territories of California, New Mexico and Texas. Although officials from Spain and Mexico gave some US citizens the permission to settle on land in Texas, the majority of people settled on the land illegally, in part because the land in Texas cost only one-tenth as much as land in the United States.

Increasing numbers of US citizens entered the Texas territory and ignored Mexican laws and customs. For instance, slavery was illegal in Mexico—it had been outlawed since 1829. Mexican officials objected to settlers who brought slaves from the US. Many settlers ignored the decree and kept their slaves. Mexico also required those settling in Texas to convert to Catholicism, which many people resisted. Mexican leaders became increasingly frustrated by the people living in Texas, but the unstable government could do little to enforce its laws in the distant Texas territory.

**Pause for Reflection: Why did people want to settle in the Texas territory?**

## The Alamo

As the Mexican Republic became more established after gaining independence from Spain, Mexican leaders paid more attention to what was happening in Texas. The Mexican government was concerned the US government would use the settlements in Texas as an excuse to claim that territory. General Santa Anna came to power in 1832, reinforced the Mexican army in Texas, and ordered more strict law enforcement in the region. The Texans rebelled, and Santa Anna mobilized troops in Texas to put down the rebellion. His troops arrived outside of San Antonio in 1836, and the rebels abandoned the city and barricaded themselves in a mission fort called the Alamo outside of the town. Santa Anna was determined to crush the rebellion, and killed all but a few women.

What Santa Anna did not know was that other resisters met and declared Texas an independent state on March 2, 1836. The Texans organized reinforcements and eventually defeated Santa Anna's forces. Mexico continued to view Texas as a rebellious state, but its attempt to crush the rebellion failed.

---

**Pause for Reflection: Why was Mexico concerned about settlements in Texas?**

---

## Texas' Bid to US for Statehood

The US government recognized Texas as an independent government, nicknamed the Lone Star State. However, the US government refused its petition for admission as a state into the United States. From 1836 to 1845, the possible annexation of Texas was a controversial political issue in the US. At stake was Texas' admittance as a free or slave state. Many Northerners in the US objected to admitting another slave state, whereas many Southerners favored admitting a slave state. If Texas had been admitted as a slave state, it would have changed the balance of power between slave and non-slave states.

The 1844 presidential election was pivotal in determining Texas' future. Henry Clay, who opposed Texas' annexation, ran against James Polk, an expansionist who favored annexing Texas. Polk won the election, and Congress passed the proposal for Texas' annexation on March 1, 1845. From the perspective of the US government, Texas had achieved statehood. The Mexicans, however, maintained the US had illegally acquired Mexican territory. Although Mexican leaders wanted to stop the US government from taking Texas, they did not want to enter into a costly and damaging war with the United States.

Polk sent a negotiator to Mexico with orders to offer the Mexicans $5 million for New Mexico and $25 million for California. In return, Mexico would agree to recognize the Rio Grande as the official border between the two countries. Polk hoped to almost double the size of the US. He especially wanted California, because its ports would give the US access to the Pacific Ocean and valuable trade routes to Asia. The Mexicans refused to even meet with Polk's negotiator, which made Polk furious. In retaliation, he began looking for a way to provoke the Mexicans into war. Polk knew that war with Mexico would be controversial, but he also believed many US citizens were eager to expand to the Pacific coast even if it meant war.

---

**Pause for Reflection: Why did the US originally refuse to admit Texas as a state? What do you think US officials' motives were for annexing Texas? What was Mexico's response?**

---

## Manifest Destiny

Although many US citizens rejected expansionism, a majority embraced the idea. In the summer of 1845, John O'Sullivan, editor of the newspaper *Democratic Review*, wrote that it was "Our manifest destiny to overspread the continent allotted by Providence for the free development of our yearly multiplying millions." In other words, it was the "manifest destiny," or God-given right and ultimate fate, of the United States to gain control of the entire North American continent. The ideology of Manifest Destiny suggested that since God intended the US to control the continent, there must be something special about the white people who populated the country. Manifest Destiny provided the justification for invading lands already being used by Indians and Mexicans, whom many Whites considered to be lazy, inferior and unworthy.

---

**Pause for Reflection: Using your own words, how would you explain the concept of Manifest Destiny to someone who didn't know what the term meant?**

---

## War with Mexico

General Zachary Taylor led US troops to a piece of land between the Nueces and Rio Grande rivers, which was claimed by both Mexico and the US. Although it is unclear who fired first, there were casualties on both sides. Taylor sent a message to Polk, telling him that the Mexicans had caused American blood to be shed on American soil. Polk drafted a declaration of war on May 11, 1846, which the House of Representatives passed 173 to 14. The Senate passed it the following day.

During the next two years, the US and Mexican armies battled one another. The US army, however, had superior firepower and advanced quickly toward the Mexican interior. The US army captured Mexico City in the autumn of 1847, leaving the countryside in disarray and the government in shambles. Some members of the Mexican Congress wanted to stop the bloody war with the US, while others argued that Mexico should resist the US occupation.

Polk and other US leaders were reluctant to make Mexico a part of the US, in part because it would be difficult to control a group of people who spoke a different language and had a different culture. In 1848, US and Mexican officials signed the Treaty of Guadalupe Hidalgo. It established the Rio Grande as the southern border of Texas and allowed the US to purchase the California and New Mexico territories for $15 million. This vast territory included all or parts of the future states of Colorado, Wyoming, Utah, Arizona, New Mexico, Nevada, and California. This vast region contained bountiful natural resources and strategic ports, which allowed the United States government and businesses to acquire important resources. The land acquisition was not complete, however. The US government also wanted the Mesilla Valley (today Southern New Mexico and Arizona) because it offered the best location for building a railroad to newly-acquired California. In 1853, the US government purchased a strip of land in the Gadsden Purchase. The US defeat of Mexico and the acquisition of Mexican territory was an important factor in the rise of the US to a world superpower.

---

**Pause for Reflection: How do you think the Mexicans living in Arizona, California, Colorado, New Mexico, Texas and Utah felt about living in US-controlled territories after the war with Mexico? What do you think some of the advantages and disadvantages were?**

---

# Examining Perspectives: Mexican Perspective

*The following selection is excerpted from a Mexican textbook on the annexation of Texas and the US Intervention in Mexico, as presented in a book titled* <u>As Others See Us</u>. *This book gives students and teachers the opportunity to understand US history from a different perspective. Note: this is not the only perspective which Mexican people hold about the war.*

Texas was annexed to the United States by the treaty of April 12, 1844, despite the protests of our [the Mexican] government and even though the treaty was rejected by the American Congress. Thereupon the annexation of the territory [Texas] was proposed in the House and approved on March 1, 1845, which forced our Minister in Washington to withdraw. The Texans, backed by the American government, claimed that its boundaries extended to the Rio Bravo del Norte [Rio Grande], whereas in fact the true limits had never passed the Nueces River. From this [boundary dispute] a long controversy developed [during which negotiations were carried on] in bad faith by the Americans.

They ordered troops to invade places within our territory, operating with the greatest treachery, and pretended that it was Mexico which had invaded their territory, making [Mexico] appear as the aggressor. What they were really seeking was to provoke a war, a war in which the southern states of the Union were greatly interested, in order to acquire new territories which they could convert into states dominated by the slavery interests. But since the majority of the people of the United States were not pro-slavery nor favorable of a war of conquest, President Polk tried to give a defensive character to his first military moves, foreseeing the opposition which he would otherwise encounter. Once he obtained a declaration of war, Polk made it appear that he wanted nothing more than peaceful possession of the annexed territory. When at last the city of Mexico was

captured, he made his fellow countrymen understand that they would receive no other indemnity for the expenses of war and the blood spilled than a cession of territory. Thus Polk would achieve the goal he sought from the outset....

The Mexican War was a brilliant move astutely planned by the United States. The magnificent lands of Texas and California with their ports on both oceans, the gold deposits soon to be discovered in the latter state, and the increase in territory which made possible the growth of slave states compensated [the United States] many times over the costs in men and money of the unjust acquisition....

Mexican Territory Acquired
by the United States, 1848

# Examining Perspectives: Support for War

In 1845, the *Washington Union*, a newspaper that supported the position of President Polk, insisted that westward expansion into Mexican lands was inevitable. An editorial in the paper asked: *Let the great measure of annexation be accomplished, and with it the questions of boundary and claims. For who can arrest the torrent that will pour onward to the West? The road to California will be open to us. Who will stay the march of our western people?*

The influential *American Review* said that Mexico should bow before "a superior population, insensibly oozing into her territories, changing her customs, and out-living, out-trading, exterminating her weaker blood."

The New York *Herald* said in 1847, "The universal Yankee nation can regenerate and disenthrall the people of Mexico in a few years; and we believe it is a part of our destiny to civilize that beautiful country."

The Reverend Theodore Parker of Boston criticized war with Mexico, arguing that the US should expand not by war but by the power of ideas. He referred to the Mexicans as "a wretched people; wretched in their origin, history and character." He viewed US expansion as the "steady advance of a superior race, with superior ideas and a better civilization."

An editorial in the *Congressional Globe* echoed this sentiment, stating, "We must march from Texas straight to the Pacific Ocean....It is the destiny of the white race."
Many leaders shared these attitudes. Ohio Congressman Delano described Mexicans as an inferior people who "embrace all shades of color...a sad compound of Spanish, English, Indian and Negro bloods...and resulting, it is said, in the production of a slothful, ignorant race of beings."

On May 9, even before Polk had received news of any battles between US and Mexican troops, Polk held a cabinet meeting. He recorded in his diary what he said at the meeting.

*I stated...that up to this time, as we knew, we had heard of no open act of aggression by the Mexican army, but that the danger was imminent that such acts would be committed. I said that in my opinion we had ample cause of war, and that it was impossible...that I could remain silent much longer...that the country was excited and impatient on the subject....*

When Polk heard the news of US casualties, he and his cabinet decided to declare war. The declaration of war contained the following text:

*After reiterated menaces, Mexico has passed the boundary of the United States, has invaded our territory and shed American blood upon the American soil.... The cup of forbearance has been exhausted, even before the recent information from the frontier of the [Rio Grande]. But now, after reiterated menaces, Mexico has passed the boundary of the United States, has invaded our territory, and shed American blood upon American soil. She has proclaimed that hostilities have commenced, and that the two nations are now at war.*

*As war, notwithstanding all our efforts to avoid it, by the act of Mexico herself, we are called upon by every consideration of duty and patriotism to vindicate with decision and honor, the rights, and the interests of our country.*

The US House passed the war resolution by a vote of 174 to 14. Senators debated the measure, which was limited to one day, and approved the measure by a vote of 40 to 2. The poet Walt Whitman reacted to the declaration of war against Mexico by writing in the *Brooklyn Eagle*, "Yes: Mexico must be thoroughly chastised!...Let our arms now be carried with a spirit which shall teach the world that, while we are not forward for a quarrel, America knows how to crush, as well as how to expand!"

# Examining Perspectives: Opposition to War

Colonel Ethan Allen Hitchcock, an aide to General Taylor, wrote the following in his diary:

*I have said from the first that the United States are the aggressors....We have not one particle of right to be here... It looks as if the government sent a small force on purpose to bring on a war, so as to have a pretext for taking California and as much of this country as it chooses, for, whatever becomes of this army, there is no doubt of a war between the United States and Mexico....My heart is not in this business...but, as a military man, I am bound to execute orders.*

Some newspapers protested the war from the very beginning. Horace Greeley wrote in the *New York Tribune* on May 12, 1846:

*We can easily defeat the armies of Mexico, slaughter them by the thousands, and pursue them perhaps to their capital; we can conquer and "annex" their territory; but what then? Who believes that a score of victories over Mexico... will give us more liberty, a purer Morality?*

Congressman Joshua Giddings, one of a small number of war dissenters in Washington, wrote:

*In the murder of Mexicans upon their own soil, or in robbing them of their country, I can take no part either now or hereafter. The guilt of these crimes must rest on others—I will not participate in them.*

Other political leaders shared Giddings' views. A Massachusetts Protest of the Mexican War, written in 1847, made the following claim:

*Resolved, That the present war with Mexico has its primary origin in the unconstitutional annexation to the United States of the foreign state of Texas while the same was still at war with Mexico; that it was unconstitutionally commenced by the order of the President, to General Taylor, to take military possession of territory in dispute between the United States and Mexico, and in the occupation of Mexico; and that it is now waged ingloriously—by a powerful nation against a weak neighbor—unnecessarily and without just cause, at the immense cost of treasure and life, for the dismemberment of Mexico, and for the conquest, of a portion of her territory, from which slavery has already been excluded....*

Abraham Lincoln was a first term member of the US House of Representatives elected in 1846. On January 12, 1848, he delivered one of the few speeches he made while in Congress. He challenged President Polk's war against Mexico:

*The President sent the army into the midst of a settlement of Mexican people who had never submitted, by consent or by force, to the authority of Texas or of the United States, and...thereby the first blood of the war was shed....*

*[If] he can show that the soil was ours where the first blood of war was shed—that it was not within an inhabited country, or, if within such, that the inhabitants had submitted themselves to the civil authority of Texas or of the United States,... then I am with him....But if he can not or will not do this,...then I shall be fully convinced of what I more than suspect already—that he is deeply conscious of being in the wrong; that he feels the blood of this war....As I have before said, he knows not where he is. He is a bewildered, confounded, and miserably perplexed man.*

The war had just begun when a writer named Henry David Thoreau refused to pay taxes to support the war. While he was in jail, his friend Ralph Waldo Emerson visited him. Emerson agreed with Thoreau's position against the war, but thought his protest was in vain. When Emerson visited Thoreau, he asked, "Henry David, what are you doing in there?" Thoreau reportedly replied, "Ralph Waldo, what are you doing out there?"

Two years later, Thoreau gave a lecture entitled "Resistance to Civil Government," later printed in an essay, "Civil Disobedience."

*It is not desirable to cultivate a respect for the law, so much as for the right. The only obligation which I have a right to assume is to do at any time what I think is right....Law never made men a whit more just; and, by means of their respect for it, even the well-disposed are daily made the agents of injustice.*

# Examining Perspectives: Question Sheet

1.  What perspective did the Mexican textbook authors have on the war with the United States?

2.  What are some of the arguments that political leaders, journalists and others made supporting US expansion?

3.  What are some of the reasons that President Polk gave for asking Congress for a Declaration of War? Do you think he had the support of the majority of US citizens? Why or why not?

4.  What are some of the arguments that political leaders, journalists and others made opposing US expansion and the Mexican-American War?

5. Why do you think there was so much opposition to the Mexican-American War?

6. Think about how Hitchcock, Lincoln, Thoreau and Emerson responded to government policies. How did their approaches differ? What role do *you* think individuals have in taking responsibility for government policies with which they disagree?

7. Do you think the war against Mexico was a "just" war? Explain.

# Mexican Territory Acquired
# by the United States, 1848

*An Exploring the Connections Lesson*

# Taking a Stand

## *Research & Debate on the Mexican Revolution*

I n *The Wind That Swept Mexico*, Anita Brenner writes that the Mexican Revolution "is a living story underneath what happens in Mexico now and tomorrow." These words, written in 1943, ring true in Mexico today. The ideals of justice and equality that spurred the revolution are unrealized for the majority of Mexicans, who remain disenfranchised and marginalized.

The story of the Mexican Revolution is complex. The revolution was not a single event, but a process of change. Alliances across classes and regions were formed and broken according to what the parties considered their most immediate advantage. To help students understand the nuances of the revolution, we have included a background reading that looks at the causes of the war and its various phases.

The focus of this lesson, however, is student research and analysis. To assist students, we have identified four factions of people involved in the revolution: Conservatives, Reformers, Revolutionaries and Outside Interests. Students form small groups, research one of the above factions and then write a position paper. After they have completed their research, students make a poster or banner and hold a mock rally, presenting their faction's position.

Many sources of information on the Revolution are available from libraries, including books, films, newspapers, magazines, and cartoons. Encourage students to use at least one reference written by a Mexican. A bibliography is provided at the end of this lesson.

**Learner Objectives**
- To make inferences about the causes and effects of the Mexican Revolution.
- To develop research skills by locating, organizing and analyzing information about the Mexican Revolution.
- To write a research paper that demonstrates an understanding of one faction's perspective on the Mexican Revolution.
- To assess various perspectives on the Mexican Revolution and develop a personal position on the conflict.

**Concepts**
- Revolution (social vs. political)
- Dictatorship
- Land reform
- Outside Interests

**Major Questions**
- What were some of the factions involved in the Mexican Revolution, and what were the goals of each?
- What were some of the strategies used to achieve these goals?
- What were some of the alliances that formed among various factions?
- What changed in Mexico as a result of the Revolution?

**Exploring the Connections**

The causes of the Mexican Revolution, while rooted in long-standing economic, social, cultural and political patterns established during the colonial era, did not develop in a vacuum. US and other outside interests played a role in the festering conflict that erupted into revolution. In this lesson, we look at the interests and responses of foreign business leaders, labor unions and governments to the Mexican Revolution.

**Teaching Strategies**

Research, Writing, Role-play and Discussion

**Materials Provided**
- School Board Recommendations (Image 1)
- Factions During the Mexican Revolution (Handout 1)
- Seeds of Revolution (Handout 2)
- Going to The Sources (Handouts 3a -3d)

**Materials Needed**
- Books on the Mexican Revolution (check the library)
- Paper (poster board and/or rolls of paper)
- Markers

**Time Required**

At least 2 class sessions, plus time for research and group work

**Preparation for this Lesson**
- Make one copy of Handouts 1 & 2 for each student.
- Make copies of Handout 3 — one faction per small group, with enough copies for each student in the small group.
- Make signs on 4 sheets of 8 x 11 paper. Each sheet should have one of the following words/phrases written on it: Conservatives; Reformers; Revolutionaries; Outside Interests. Place these signs

in four different parts of the room.
- Make an overhead from Image 1.

# Sequence of Lesson

*Anticipatory Set*
*20-30 minutes*

1. Divide students into four groups and ask each to form near one of the signs posted around the room. Place the transparency of Image 1 on the overhead and indicate to students that some members of the community have been complaining to the school board about the low level of academic achievement and about the amount of crime and vandalism being committed by young people. The school board is committed to doing something about these problems, but doesn't have the funds necessary to implement many new programs. After months of work and a lot of debate, the school board announced the following reforms at a recent meeting.

   Review the reforms with students, asking them to save their comments. Indicate that each group will be asked to role play how to respond to these reforms based on their group's, or faction's, position. The positions are as follows:

## Conservatives
*Our schools have a duty to teach responsibility. These reforms will help students understand that there is no "free lunch," that education is a privilege, and that they have responsibilities to society. Besides, these reforms may save the school district some money.*

## Reformers
*Students are in school to learn how to be productive members of society. These reforms are a step in the right direction, but are a little drastic. Things definitely need to change, but maybe there's some middle ground that can be reached.*

## Revolutionaries
*The school board members have it all wrong! What students need is not more rules and restrictions, but more freedom... freedom to make decisions themselves about what they should learn and when they should be in school. If students make the rules, they will follow them.*

## Outside Interests
*As part of a task force from another school district that has implemented similar reforms, we want to help you implement the reforms here. After all, these reforms have had a really positive impact in our community!*

Give students 10-15 minutes to discuss what actions each group would take based on its position. Debrief and discuss how groups of people sometimes have different perspectives on issues and different ideas on how to respond. Indicate to

<table>
<tr>
<td>

*Body of Lesson*
*15 minutes*

</td>
<td>
</td>
<td>

students that the same was true during the time of the Mexican Revolution.

</td>
</tr>
<tr>
<td></td>
<td>2.</td>
<td>

Students should remain in the same groups. Explain that they will research the history of the Mexican Revolution from the perspective of one the following different factions — Conservatives, Reformers, Revolutionaries and Outside Interests. Distribute Handout 1 and review each of the factions, identifying key leaders and explaining the positions and strategies each faction took. Explain that students will be writing a research paper focusing only on the faction they were assigned. Refer to the questions on Handout 1, and indicate that all students will be answering these questions. The names of the leaders listed on Handout 1 should help students with their library research.

</td>
</tr>
</table>

3.  Introduce the concepts of political and social revolutions. In *States and Social Revolutions*, Sociologist Theda Skocpol distinguishes between the two:

### Social Revolution
Social revolutions are rapid, basic transformations of a society's state and class structures; in other words, old social, political and economic patterns are destroyed in favor of newer ones. She identifies three stages in this process: first, the collapse of the old state or governing system; second, peasant insurrection and revolt; and third, the consolidation of power and process of state building by a new elite.

*Examples: French Revolution (1787–early 1800s), Russian Revolution (1917–1930s), and Chinese Revolution (1911–1960s).*

### Political Revolution
Political revolutions bring about less fundamental change than social revolutions. They usually transform state structures but not social structures, and they are not necessarily accomplished through class conflict.

*Examples: the US Revolution (1776–1789), Russian Revolution of 1990-1992.*

4.  Distribute a copy of Handout 2 to each student to read. This provides an overview of the people, ideas and events involved in the Mexican Revolution. As students read, ask them to reflect on whether they would consider the Mexican Revolution to be a social revolution or a political revolution.

<table>
<tr>
<td>

*Succeeding Days*

</td>
<td>5.</td>
<td>

Allow time for students to do research based on the questions in Handout 1. Students may wish to divide the work among themselves to achieve wider coverage of important people, issues, and events. Students then can share information within

</td>
</tr>
</table>

their small groups, but should answer individually the
questions on Handout 1.

Suggest resources to students, and make available some of
the resources included at the end of this lesson. Students
should develop the position of their faction and write a
position paper, including at least five sources of information.

- Show students examples of primary, secondary, and tertiary
  resource materials. In a large-group discussion, help
  students to understand the nature and shortcomings of
  primary, secondary and tertiary sources. Make available
  copies of Handouts 3a-3d, which are primary source
  documents that give students greater insights into each
  faction's positions. Although these documents may be
  written in a style that is not familiar to students, they
  provide important insights into the actions, thoughts and
  feelings of people actually involved in the Revolution.

- In order to help students work with these rather difficult
  documents, suggest that students circle what they think are
  the five most important words or concepts are. Then ask
  them to discuss these choices with others in their group.
  Alternatively, students could write a 3-5 sentence summary
  of the document to ensure that they understand the main
  points. This part of the research process will need a fair
  amount of guidance, but the rewards can be great!

- Have each student prepare an outline of her or his research
  paper, including the primary and secondary sources for
  information. Have students discuss their outlines and
  sources with other group members for suggestions and
  support.

- Arrange progress checks with students as often as possible.
  Ascertain how or where they are having problems collecting
  data.

- Have students prepare drafts of their papers, and ask each
  student to have at least one other student in his or her
  group read the draft copy of the paper for clarity,
  grammatical corrections, and general help and support.
  Have students make corrections based on this help.
  Ask students to edit their papers and submit the final copy.

6. When the research is complete (*at least* 3-5 days recommended
   for research and writing), reconvene into the same small
   groups. Ask students to assume the role of a person supporting
   the faction that they have researched. Working within these
   small groups, ask students to create a poster or banner that
   reflects their position on the Revolution. Some groups may
   wish to include their slogans from Handout 1 and any reforms

they are demanding. Some groups may wish to create more than one poster or banner.

7.  When groups have finished their posters/banners, ask them to imagine that a political candidate is traveling around Mexico on a train, making campaign stops. The person is stopping for an hour in your area, and a rally is planned at the train station. Each group, or faction, is expected to be there to voice its demands. Ask each group to make a brief presentation to the other groups, covering the main points raised in the questions on Handout 1. Decide upon the format for the Whistle Stop Rally. You may wish to structure this as a 4-way debate. To be more democratic, ask students how they think the debate should be structured: in what order should the factions be allowed to present their viewpoints? How much time should be allowed for rebuttal? Should there be a brief time allocated at the end for a summation of points?

8.  When each of the groups is ready, announce that the Whistle Stop Rally has begun. When the debate is complete, ask students to reflect upon the role play/debate. Ask them questions such as:

    Reflection questions
    •   What were some of your thoughts, impressions and feelings during the role play/debate?
    •   Did the role play help you to learn more about perspectives other than those of your own group? What did you learn?

    Analysis questions
    •   Who do you think had most of the power in the time of the Mexican Revolution?
    •   Who "won"? Who "lost"? Why?
    •   What is your own point of view on the Mexican Revolution?

*Closure*

9.  To conclude, ask students to complete the following sentence: "If I had been living during the time of the Mexican Revolution, I would have supported (faction x) because ......"

*Assessment*

Collect and evaluate students' research papers and group's posters or banners. Use small group evaluation for peer review.

*Journal Assignment*

What similarities do you find between Mexico during this period and contemporary United States? What changes do you support in the US today? Who would benefit most? Explain.

**Extension Lesson**

Use the 1952 film, *Viva Zapata!*, on the Mexican Revolution (110 minutes).

The Mexican Revolution has been a topic of great interest to writers and film makers in Mexico and the United States. *Viva Zapata!* is the story of the popular Mexican hero, Emiliano Zapata. The script for this classic film was written by John Steinbeck, and Elia Kazan was the director. Marlon Brando, who was at the height of his career, played the role of Zapata, and Anthony Quinn was Zapata's brother. The film follows the historical events during the Mexican Revolution. To make the film "work", it emphasizes or omits certain aspects. Typical of films of its era, characters lack complexity and often are portrayed as stereotypical good or weak women and men.

To help students understand some of the events in the film, you may want to list names and events between 1909 and 1919 when Zapata was assassinated. Historical persons who are portrayed are Emiliano Zapata and his brother, Eufemio; Josefa, wife of Emiliano Zapata; Blanco the horse; Porfirio Diáz; Francisco Madero; Victoriano Huerta; and Pancho Villa.

Sequence of historical events between 1909-1919: Emiliano Zapata and his army in Morelos fight to overthrow President Porfirio Diáz. Diáz leaves Mexico for France. Francisco Madero becomes president and retains General Vistoriano Huerta, who regards Zapata as an enemy. General Huerta betrays Madero, takes him prisoner and has him killed. Huerta becomes president; Zapata and his army continue to fight . Huerta is forced to resign and goes to the US. Pancho Villa and Zapata meet in Mexico City. Venustiano Carranza becomes president; his supporters trick Zapata and kill him.

While you show the film, you may want to pause the film occasionally to answer any questions or clarify the situation. After the film, ask questions such as: who was Zapata fighting during different points in the film? What did he say he was fighting for? Do you think Zapata and others had alternative ways to voice their grievances? What was historically accurate and what was inserted in the film for dramatic effect? What clues are there to support your assumptions? Why did the film maker choose non-Mexicans to play the lead roles? What were the key issues that led the peasants to take up arms?

**Closure**

Ask students to write in their journal an hypothesis about what happened to Zapata's followers after his death and reflect on this statement, taken from the end of the film, "sometimes a dead man can be a terrible enemy."

# RECOMMENDED BOOKS

## *Non-fiction*

*Contemporary Mexican Paintings in a Time of Change* by Shifra M. Goldman. (Austin: University of Texas Press, 1981.)

*The Course of Mexican History* by Michael C. Meyer & William Sherman. (New York: Oxford University Press, 1991.)

*Independence and Revolution in Mexico, 1810-1940* by Rebecca Stefoff. (New York: Facts on File, 1993.)

*Insurgent Mexico* by John Reed. (New York: Simon & Schuster, 1914. Reissued 1969.)

*Mexican American Heritage* by Carlos Jiménez. (Berkeley: TQS Publications, 1993.)

*Mexico in Crisis* by Judith Adler Hellman. (New York: Holmes and Meier Publishers, Inc., 1978.)

*Revolution in Mexico: Years of Upheaval, 1910-1940* by James W. Wilkie & Albert L. Michaels. (Tucson: University of Arizona Press, 1969.)

*Triumphs and Tragedies: A History of the Mexican People* by Ramón Eduardo Ruiz. (New York: W.W. Norton & Company, 1992.)

*Zapata and the Mexican Revolution* by John Womack. (New York: Knopf, 1968.)

## *Fiction*

*The Carreta* or other books from *The Jungle Novels* by B. Traven. (New York: Hill and Wang, 1970.)

*The Death of Artemio Cruz* by Carlos Fuentes. (New York: Farrar, Straus & Giroux, 1964.)

*The Eagle and the Serpent* by Martín Luis Guzmán. (New York: Dolphin, 1965.)

*The Underdogs* by Mariano Azuela. (New York: New American Library, 1963.)

# New School Board Recommendations

*Beginning next week, the following reforms
will be put into effect:*

1. To offset the costs of the reforms, the price of the school lunch will double, regardless of a student's ability to pay. Sports and Arts programs will be cut to save money.

2. Parents and business leaders have been complaining that students are not learning enough in school. Therefore, the school day will be extended to allow for more school work. Classes will begin at 7 am. and conclude at 5 pm.

3. As part of the school day, students will begin working on organized work and cleanup crews around the school. Failure to do so will result in a doubling of the duty time.

4. Anyone challenging the authority to make and enforce these rules will be punished severely.

# Factions During the Mexican Revolution

## The Conservatives

**Leaders:** President Porfirio Díaz and General Victoriano Huerta

**Position:** Porfirio Díaz and his followers strove for progress, which to them meant economic growth and modernization. Progress could be attained through private enterprise and large investments of foreign capital and business.

**Strategy:** To attract foreign investments, corporations needed to be assured that there would be order and stability in Mexico. This was guaranteed through increasing police protection and military strength.

**Slogan:** "Order, followed by Progress."

## The Reformers

**Leaders:** Francisco Madero, Venustiano Carranza, Alvaro Obregón

**Position:** The goal of these reformers was political reform that would restore democracy. They wanted to create a multiple party system with free elections. Their goals were expressed in the *Plan de San Luis Potosí.*

**Strategy:** They wanted to manage change so it would be slow and orderly, and not cause armed conflict.

**Slogan:** "Liberty will give you bread."

## The Revolutionaries

**Leaders:** Emiliano Zapata, Pascual Orozco, Pancho Villa, Flores Magón brothers, Lázaro Cárdenas

**Position:** The revolutionaries wanted social justice and an entirely new social order for peasants and workers. This required that land be redistributed, and that there be better working conditions and fair pay for workers. Their goals were expressed in the *Plan de Ayala.*

**Strategy:** Their strategy included organizing workers and peasants to form unions that would use strikes and boycotts. Zapata, Villa and Orozco also led large armies to fight for a more just society.

**Slogan:** "Land and Liberty."

## The Outsiders

**Leaders:** Political representatives, business leaders and labor organizers from the United States and European countries

**Position:** Protect their interests, including the lives and property of their citizens.

**Strategy:** Support whichever administration would best protect these interests.

# Position Paper Questions
# to be Addressed by each Faction

- How would you describe your faction? Who are the leaders of your faction? Are there disagreements or divisions among members of your faction? Explain.

- What are your faction's short-term goals and strategies for meeting these goals?

- What is your relationship to the other factions? Who are your allies? Who is likely to support your goals? Who is likely to oppose your goals?

- What kind of power does your faction have? How can you use it? What can your faction do to bring about your goals?

- According to your faction, who has (or should have) the right to the land and its resources? Does your faction support a land reform program? If so, what are some of the elements of the proposed reform? Who would benefit from the reform? How?

- What is your faction's vision for the future? What changes, if any, does your faction want to see come about as a result of the revolution?

# Seeds of Revolution

## Mexico Under Díaz

Long-standing economic, social, cultural and political patterns that were established during the colonial period led to the Mexican Revolution. Elites, including military generals, wealthy urban industrialists, *hacienda* owners, and foreigners, controlled political and economic life in Mexico.

General Porfirio Díaz, who aligned himself with these elites, seized power in a military coup in 1876 and ruled Mexico as a dictator for more than thirty years. These elites believed in a form of "progress" that would help Mexico become an international economic power. Little did they know that their desire for progress would become a seed of revolution and destruction.

During Díaz's dictatorship, some Mexicans and foreign business leaders prospered. Foreign investment in mines, ranches, iron and steelworks, and breweries skyrocketed in Mexico during Díaz's regime. French, German, British and US millionaires soon dominated Mexican business and industry, especially in the northern part of the country. With foreign money, the government built railroads and modernized port facilities in order to increase foreign trade and investments. Parts of Mexico City were transformed into a beautiful modern city with statues and wide avenues. During the first ten years of the 20th century, Mexico was a major producer of petroleum, pumped by US and British companies from oil fields near the Gulf Coast.

Díaz and his advisors welcomed the burst of economic growth ushered in by foreign investment, but many Mexicans did not share in the prosperity. An editorial appearing in a Mexican newspaper in June 1908 stated:

> *The Yankees [from the US] enjoy all the influence, the dominant position, all the power, all the land, all the large businesses, all the wealth. The Mexicans are left with submission, poverty, second class jobs and even worse salaries. There is prosperity in Mexico but it is Yankee prosperity; there is poverty and misery in Mexico and that belongs totally to the Mexicans.* [1]

Fearful of unrest among the masses, Díaz and his supporters believed it was necessary to keep order and stability in Mexico to maintain foreign investment. The military provided the order necessary for economic development, and this development provided the revenues necessary to keep the military and local political bosses loyal to Díaz.

## Seeds of Revolution

The Revolution of 1910 began as a protest against Díaz's 34 year dictatorship. During this time, he manipulated elections in his favor, censored the press, and supported a countrywide system of local political bosses who used promises and threats to make sure that the common people did what the government wanted them to do. These political bosses used three main methods to reduce discontent among the people: first, an offer of a job or bribe; second, blackmail; and finally, as a Díaz telegram ordered, "Catch in the act; kill on the spot."

Economic growth came at a heavy price to the vast majority of Mexico's population. During Díaz's regime, the disparity between rich and poor grew. By 1910, fewer than 200 families owned one-quarter of the land, while foreigners owned another quarter. Workers with little or no land of their own often migrated to other parts of Mexico to find work. A business person who was working for the British government and traveling in a prosperous agricultural area in north-central Mexico, made the following comment about the workers in that region.

> *...[T]he labor has to be imported to a very large extent, and in no other part of the country have I seen such a great predominance of "half castes" over true Mexicans. This "mongrel" race is less settled and more ready to move where employment is to be found. They seem a sturdier and stronger race than in the south but, by universal consent, they combine the vices of both the Indians and the Spaniards without possessing any of their redeeming qualities.* [2]

As the upper classes and foreigners benefited from Mexico's progress, the poor lived in squalid conditions. They often worked six days a week for twelve hours a day. There were no labor unions or child labor laws; benefits such as pensions, health care and insurance were non-existent.

The rural population barely survived under the semi-feudal conditions on the *haciendas*. *Hacienda* owners controlled almost all aspect of workers' lives. Most workers had very little contact with the owners of the *hacienda*, even if the owners lived there. The owner's children usually were not allowed to associate with the workers' children. The owner maintained control by planting spies who reported any unrest among the workers. Most *haciendas* also had armed guards to settle any problems. Many large plantations had uniformed police forces and jails. On some *haciendas*, administrators had the authority to jail troublesome workers or ship them off to the army.

Owners also tied workers to *haciendas* through debt. Instead of paying wages, owners paid workers with vouchers for credit for goods at the *hacienda* store. As a result, workers' wages ended up back in the hands of the *hacienda* owner. The workers accumulated debt and owed so much to the *hacienda* store that it could take generations for the family to pay its debt. This was called debt peonage. If a worker tried to flee his or her debts, the owner tried to trace the worker to his or her new employer. If a worker acted up or committed a crime, word spread throughout the region, and he or she often could not find another job.

Following leaders who began to call for social justice and democracy, workers and peasants began to formulate their own ideas about changed based on their experiences and needs. Workers were concerned with winning the right to organize and form labor unions, guarantees of decent working conditions, greater job security, and other basic labor rights. Peasants had demands that varied according to their relationship to the land. Sharecroppers and renters wanted land of their own. Laborers who worked for wages on large estates had grievances similar to those of the workers such as higher pay, better working conditions, and so forth. Peasants tied to *haciendas* sought relief from heavy debts to the owners.

# Phases of the Mexican Revolution

The Mexican Revolution was not a single event, but a process of change. The revolution was not a single civil war, but a series of struggles and blows against the old order that took place in different places at different times. To simplify this complex story, one can divide the revolutionary process into four phases. The first phase was the overthrow of Díaz's dictatorship and attempts at modest reforms. The second phase is a return to the conservative politics characteristic of Díaz's regime. The third phase is one of competing radical and moderate ideologies, culminating in the 1917 Constitution. Finally, the fourth phase is one in which actual progress was made through the Presidency of Lazaro Cárdenas.

## *Phase 1*

In the first phase, individuals throughout Mexico began calling for and end to Díaz's dictatorship. In addition to sporadic outbreaks of violence, protests and strikes all over Mexico, this phase was precipitated when three brothers with the last name of Flores Magón began to write and distribute a weekly newspaper to protest the injustices perpetrated by Díaz. The brothers were thrown in jail, and then went into exile in the United States where they, and other dissidents continued to attack Díaz and call for revolution.

On October 5, 1910, Francisco Madero, a wealthy landowner from northern Mexico, called for the resignation of Díaz, coupled with election reform and land distribution. This was written in his *Plan de San Luis Potosí* which drew together people from all ranks of society with its appeal for change. His goal was a political revolution to restore democracy through fair elections and the rule of law. Madero felt that the country should progress slowly and carefully. He feared that if his government pushed the conservatives too hard, they would fight back and try to regain control. Therefore, he proposed gradual changes in education and land and labor laws.

In the north, Pascual Orozco and Francisco "Pancho" Villa became military commanders of large armies. In the state of Morelos in central Mexico, a farmer named Emiliano Zapata led 70,000 landless men and women to overthrow Díaz so they could redistribute land. Zapata used the mountains and forests of Morelos as his base of operations. His followers formed small, highly mobile guerrilla bands, which struck swiftly at the federal forces sent in to the region to suppress the rebellion. They then returned to their villages, buried their rifles under the dirt floors of their houses, and resumed their everyday lives. When federal troops arrived, they found peasants quietly tending to their small plots of land.

After seven months of armed uprising, Díaz left Mexico for France and Madero was elected president in November 1911. Madero faced a country in turmoil when he took office. Don Zefernio Dominguez, an agricultural expert in Mexico, commented on the conditions in Mexico in 1911. He wrote,

*There are 6,000,000 persons hungry and the land of Mexico is in the hands of only 300 families. When men are hungry it is easy to start a revolution. Madero was only an incident of the last revolution. He promised the people of Mexico a division of these vast estates. If he brings this about his administration will be a success and peace will reign in Mexico. If he does not there will be an uprising. The people are fighting for food for themselves and their families, for a right to own a home. If Madero can give them this he will be a great benefactor and the Savior of Mexico. If he does not then there will be no peace.* [3]

The *Zapatistas* and *Villistas*, or the people who followed Zapata and Villa, at first were sympathetic to Madero because he talked of a land reform plan that would return some land to the peasants. Once in office, however, Madero became indecisive and procrastinated on implementing reforms. When he selected many of Díaz's supporters to remain in his government and asked Zapata to disarm his troops, Zapata and Villa broke with him and fought against him. The *Zapatistas* drew up their own land reform proposal called the *Plan de Ayala*. This plan called for the restoration of land taken from the peasants: one-third of the lands of the *haciendas* would become *ejido* lands in keeping with the traditional communal system of the Indians. All those owners and politicians who opposed this redistribution would have their land taken without compensation.

## Phase 2

In the second phase of the Revolution, Victoriano Huerta, formerly a general under Díaz, was now the leader of Madero's armed forces. He led a military coup in February 1913 and ordered the assassination of Madero and his vice-president. Major opposition to the new government of General Huerta followed. During this time, Villa, Zapata, Venustiano Carranza and Alvaro Obregón led an armed revolt against Huerta, and in 1914, he resigned as president.

## Phase 3

Phase three of the Revolution encompasses the struggle between the ideologies of Villa and Zapata with those of Carranza and Obregón. Villa and Zapata represented the more radical interests for social reform to benefit the lower classes while Carranza and Obregón represented the interest in political reform for the more moderate middle-class. Carranza became president in late 1915 and tried to bring order to the country by organizing a conference to draw up a new constitution. To avoid conflict, he excluded all *Villistas* and *Zapatistas*. Even so, his moderate position was outvoted, and the resulting Constitution of 1917 was based on the principles of social revolution, education, redistribution of land, and the right of workers to form unions and to strike. It also limited the president to a single term of six years and limited the role of the church in society.

The writers of the Constitution also responded to demands to reduce the influence of foreign and national elites and to defend the interests of the subordinate classes. Article 27 of the Constitution established national control over Mexican territory and resources, including oil. The article also outlined the conditions under which the government could take land, in order to redistribute it more equally. A key passage follows:

> *The nation shall at times have the right to establish regulations for private property which the public interest may dictate, such as those regulating the use of natural resources for conservation purposes or ensuring a more equitable distribution of public wealth. With this end in view, the necessary measures shall be taken to break up the large estates.*

Although this provision for land reform was written into the Constitution, Carranza refused to implement substantial land redistribution and other social reforms. After a short period of peace, Zapata and Villa once again began fighting for what they believed was the real revolution. By the end of 1917, more than one million people had died in seven years of fighting. Many of the victims were non-combatants, killed in pointless acts of violence committed by all sides in the conflict.

Thousands of women, who were called *soldaderas*, were involved in the war. The armies did not provide food or lodging, but gave money to the soldiers for their basic needs. As a result, many women followed their fathers, husbands, lovers or sons to provide food, wash clothing and nurse the wounded. Some women were abducted, while others joined voluntarily for idealistic reasons, or for adventure. Often the *soldaderas* served as spies or couriers; occasionally, they fought alongside the men, usually disguised as men. Sometimes the *soldaderas* organized themselves into bands of fighters.

In 1919, President Carranza had one of his men befriend Emiliano Zapata, then betray and eventually assassinate him. However, the *Zapatistas* still continued to fight. In 1920, President Carranza was assassinated and Alvaro Obregón became president. By this time, people were exhausted with the turmoil. The fighting slowly diminished and people returned to their work. Peasants began to sing songs such as this, called *corridos*:

> *Pancho Villa has surrendered*
> *In the city of Torreón,*
> *He is tired now of fighting*
> *And now cotton will be grown.*
>
> *Now we are all one party,*
> *There is no one left to fight;*
> *The war is ended, compañeros,*
> *Let us work, it is our right.*
>
> *I would like to be a great man*
> *With much wisdom in my head,*
> *But I would much rather have*
> *Every day my daily bread.*
>
> *Now the cornfields are in tassel*
> *The kernels are tight on the ear;*
> *It's the sustenance of man—*
> *The holiest thing that there is.*

## Phase 4

In 1934, Lázaro Cárdenas was elected president and finally began to enforce the 1917 Constitution. He enacted land reform, and by the end of his term, his administration had distributed more land to peasants than all of his predecessors combined—almost fifty million acres. Nearly one-third of all Mexicans received land, much of it to be used communally under the *ejido* system. This move was extremely controversial, since many wealthy people lost their title to the land.

Cárdenas also brought the profitable oil industry, which was made up of US and British-owned companies, under Mexican ownership. This eliminated foreign control of an important resource and export product. When he nationalized companies such as Standard Oil, the owners urged the US Congress to declare war on Mexico. Ultimately, the Mexican government paid $24 million to the foreign companies, and it began to channel profits from oil sales to build or improve Mexican schools, hospitals, roads and water systems. By the end of his term in 1940, the climax of the Mexican Revolution was reached.

---

## References

1. Meyers, William, *Forge of Progress, Crucible of Revolt*. Albuquerque, NM: University of New Mexico Press, 1994, p. 184.

2. Ibid., p. 117.

3. Hanrahan, Gene. *Documents on the Mexican Revolution*. Vol. III. Salisburg, NC: Docu-mentary Publications, 1978.

*Going to The Sources*

# Conservatives

In completing the research for your project, you will no doubt find a lot of information about the Mexican Revolution in books and encyclopedias. But did you even wonder what people involved in the Revolution itself had to say about events at that time?

The documents below are primary source documents—words actually spoken or written by people involved in the conflict. These documents should give you insights into the conflict that the encyclopedia never would! As you read these, reflect on the emotions the author is conveying and the intent of the author's words. Some of the language may seem difficult. If you are not sure about the meaning of something, ask your group members or your instructor.

T he speech at the bottom of this page was given by President Díaz on July 3, 1910. The US Embassy translated the speech and sent it to the US Secretary of State in Washington, DC. Henry Lane Wilson, the US Ambassador, wrote this accompanying message on July 5, 1910:

*"I have the honor to transmit herewith a translation of the remarks of President Díaz, made upon the occasion of the banquet given to him by some 1,700 political adherents, representing the wealthy, the most cultured and most progressive elements in Mexico. The occasion was peculiarly significant, as it was designed for the purpose of placing the seal of official approval upon Mr. Corral, the Vice President of the Republic, as the ultimate successor to President Díaz."*

## *President Díaz's Speech, July 3, 1910*

Gentlemen:

I owe to the kindness of all of you, and to your love of peace and your enthusiasm for progress, this beautiful feast with which you have honored me so much, and which brings to my soul most agreeable impressions on account of its democratic form and political significance. Here are found represented all the classes of the great Mexican family, and principally those who, by their labor, high spirit of honor and patriotism, have contributed much to national progress.

After my already long experience as a public man, in which I have had the fortune to pick out the good Mexicans and estimate their energy, their valor and their zeal for the welfare of their country, both in war and in peace, I can now say that it is they, with the help and unceasing labor of the noble populace of Mexico, who have brought about our present progress—that progress to which our ancestors aspired and to which they contributed with such patriotism and heroism. At my age, and having ended this Presidential term, it pleases me very much to receive from my countrymen the approval of my conduct, because they have a perfect right to judge it....

The Programme of my Government will be the same; but will be fitted as far as possible to the evolution of social and political progress, to the end that the free exercise of the rights and the citizens and the respect for the law by the governed and governing, may maintain that balance and harmony which makes for a great people and a powerful nation.

The principal basis of this programme will be the preservation of peace, and I shall be always on the alert to guarantee it to society.

Fortunately, peace is now the normal condition in which we live. It is the conviction of the populace, it is the aspiration of all, and it is sustained by the schools, railroads, factories, banks and all industrial activity, as well as by the prosperity of all classes. But if, on the other hand, any public disturbance should occur, as it might occur in any civilized country, the Government has the necessary means for quelling it at once...

The high credit of Mexico in foreign countries, to which you have referred, is truly a sympathetic note, since it reflects the judgment of the outside world concerning our present and future conditions; and this judgment is the more valuable when it is expressed without emotion, frankly and without partiality and rests on a sound economical basis, a constant observation and scientific studies....

Gentlemen: I am deeply obliged by all your favors and by your high expressions of confidence, and I invite you to drink in the progress of Mexico, under a sky of prosperity and prestige. [1]

---

Only a few days later, on July 8, 1910, Porfirio Díaz was re-elected President, a post he had held almost continuously since 1876. His main political rival, Francisco Madero, was in jail along with 60,000 supporters. Madero was released from jail eleven days after the election. He fled to Texas, where he began planning a rebellion against Díaz. Madero, Pascual Orozco and Pancho Villa led a successful attack on Ciudad Juárez, a city on the northern border, on May 10-11, 1911. This victory was a turning point, because it gave the rebels control of the northern part of the country and prompted many federal troops to desert the army. On May 26, 1911, President Díaz gave the following resignation letter to the Speaker of the Chamber of Deputies.

Sir:

The Mexican people, who have so generously lavished honors upon me; who [supported] me patriotically in all my endeavors to encourage the industry and commerce of the Republic, to strengthen her credit abroad and to give her a respected place in the concert of nations—that people, sir, has risen in armed bands declaring that my presence at the head of the executive is the cause of the insurrection.

.... I come before you now... to resign unreservedly, the high office of President of the Republic to which I was elevated by the vote of the nation, and I do it the more readily in that by retaining the office in question I should be exposing the country to further bloodshed, to the loss of its credit, to the destruction of its wealth, to the extinction of its activities and the risk of international intervention.

I hope, Honorable Deputies, that when the passions excited by this as by all revolutions shall have subsided, [that later reflections] will lend to a truer estimate of my actions, allowing me, when I die, to carry with me the consoling sense that I have in the end been understood by my countrymen, to whose welfare I have devoted and will continue to devote my entire energies.

With the highest respect, I remain,

Porfirio Díaz [2]

---

### References

1. Hanrahan, Gene, ed. *Documents on the Mexican Revolution*, Vol. II, Part 1. Salisbury, NC: Documentary Publications, 1976.

2. Hanrahan, Gene, ed. *Documents on the Mexican Revolution*, Vol. II, Part 2. Salisbury, NC: Documentary Publications, 1976.

Siquieros

## *Going to The Sources*
# Reformers

In completing the research for your project, you will no doubt find a lot of information about the Mexican Revolution in books and encyclopedias. But did you even wonder what people involved in the Revolution itself had to say about events at that time? The documents below are primary source documents—words actually spoken or written by people involved in the conflict. These documents should give you insights into the conflict that the encyclopedia never would! As you read these, reflect on the emotions the author is conveying and the intent of the author's words. Some of the language may seem difficult. If you are not sure about the meaning of something, ask your group members or your instructor.

---

Francisco Madero and other moderates called for the end of Porfirio Díaz's regime. In one of his many writings, Madero voiced the frustration and anger that many Mexican people felt about Díaz's hold on power. Madero wrote a book in 1908, calling for more honest elections and the formation of an opposition political party. He believed that Díaz's dictatorship and the lack of democracy were Mexico's worst problems, and suggested that if only people could vote in free and fair elections, the country's other problems would be solved. In the following writing, Madero opposes Díaz's re-election in the 1910 elections.

> In a word, General Díaz has gathered into his hands absolute power in order to be powerful enough to keep himself in power. Only in this way would he be able to govern the country according to his own will and without respecting the freedom of the press which could arouse the people and guide public opinion, or by ignoring the right of assembly which could have united public opinion against him...
>
> The Nation has taken account of this situation when it passed beyond the impact of the initial enthusiasm which caused it to enter into a new era of material progress; but it has understood that in order to gain its rights it would have to undertake a bloody revolution in order to overthrow General Díaz who would scarcely be expected to permit that he should be removed from power by legal means... The Nation has preferred to make the sacrifice of its freedom for a few years more on the alter of peace....
>
> It appears that the country is now willing to throw off its lethargy. But the awakening of the people can normally be a stormy process, and for us, those who pretend to guide public opinion with our writings, belongs the task of [channeling] popular energies along the wide road of democracy so as to avoid pitfalls which lead through the tortuous path of revolt and civil strife.[1]

On July 8, 1910, Porfirio Díaz was re-elected President of Mexico, a post he had held almost continuously since 1876. On the day the elections took place, Madero was in jail along with 60,000 supporters. He was released form jail 11 days later and fled to Texas, where he began planning a rebellion against Díaz.

In April, 1911, a journalist named Somerfeld interviewed Francisco Madero. Portions of the interview follow. In this interview, Madero mentions the primary goal of his followers—free elections. Although many people credit him with upholding democratic ideals, others criticize him for not taking a strong enough stand on issues. As you read this interview, keep in mind what Madero said about Díaz in the previous reading.

**MADERO:** [In a letter to an official in the Díaz government], I told him that the revolution would come if the Government did not grant the free ballot and respect the constitutional rights of the people.... Only the Government did not see it, or did not care to see the danger that menaced it and the nation if it continued the old policy of suppression. Now that we have taken up arms to obtain our constitutional rights, we will not lay them down until the general elections of... last year are declared void and the new elections will be entirely free....

**INTERVIEWER:** Don't you know that if existing conditions are not changed in a short time that intervention, armed intervention of the United States must follow?

**MADERO:** Nobody in Mexico wants American intervention.... The actual questions must be solved by ourselves. I do not believe that the American Government will intervene... Intervention would be an unfriendly act which would mean war against Mexico. The American and all the foreign [business] interests are respected by revolutionary and federal forces alike, and any question arising in that respect will be settled easily by diplomatic means.

**INTERVIEWER:** Don't you know that no matter how this revolution ends it would be a great mistake to force President Díaz out of office, even though you should have the physical power to do it?

**MADERO:** No, I do not know why it should be a mistake, and I do not see what reason you could have for making that statement.

**INTERVIEWER:** The reasons for my statement are these: If President Díaz should be forced out of office by this revolution the credit of your country would be hurt for years. Foreign governments would say: "What guarantee do we have that the next president will last longer than six weeks, since the revolutionists have been able to force out General Díaz, who has ruled the country for thirty-four years and was thought to have an absolutely secure hold upon the situation in Mexico?" Would you not regard it as good policy that Díaz should be permitted to remain in office, at least for a time, in order to save the credit of your country? In six or eight months, or, say, by the first of January, 1912, he could resign on account of old age or ill health, and in that manner dropping out gracefully without hurting the standing of Mexico.

**MADERO:** Your argument is very good and I will consider it. [2]

Madero's last comment gives us insights into his thinking about change in Mexico. His main concern was with bringing about political change—however it could be achieved. He seemed less concerned with major social changes in Mexico. When Madero began campaigning against Díaz, someone asked him why he did not give his family's hacienda lands back to the poor. He answered, "The Mexican people do not want land, they want liberty."

---

### Further Reading
To learn more about Madero's ideas for reform, ask a librarian to help you locate the *Plan of San Luis Potosí.*

### References
Madero Francisco. *The Presidential Succession of 1810.* Translated by Thomas Davis. New York: Peter Lang Publishing, 1990, pp. 102-103.

Hanrahan, Gene, ed. *Documents on the Mexican Revolution*, Vol 1, Part 2. Salisburg, NC: Documentary Publications, 1976.

Siquieros

## *Going to The Sources*
# Revolutionaries

In completing the research for your project, you will no doubt find a lot of information about the Mexican Revolution in books and encyclopedias. But did you even wonder what people involved in the Revolution itself had to say about events at that time? The documents below are primary source documents—words actually spoken or written by people involved in the conflict. These documents should give you insights into the conflict that the encyclopedia never would! As you read these, reflect on the emotions the author is conveying and the intent of the author's words. Some of the language may seem difficult. If you are not sure about the meaning of something, ask your group members or your instructor.

---

Many people who wanted to bring about change in Mexico became exiles in the United States to escape the repression of the Díaz government. One such person, Paulino Martinez, wrote the following article in a newspaper that was published in San Antonio, Texas.

## *Why I Write in a Foreign Country*

Public liberty has disappeared in my Country, particularly the right to write and publish articles on politics in the independent press.

To have honor and courage as a newspaperman in Mexico, to write truthfully and expose wrongdoing wherever it appears under the Despotic Government of General Díaz, requires that one resign himself to residence in a prison cell, and there to slowly die....

Newspapermen of courage are condemned to death in Mexico. Sometimes that sentence is executed by common assassins... or by torture in prison....

For the third time I have been forced to seek refuge in this Country [the US], searching for the liberties denied me by the Despotic Government of General Díaz at home.... The only crime I had committed against the Tyrannical Executioners of the Press was "telling the truth; fighting evil." I could not stand impassionately by and see the wrongs of ABSOLUTISM destroying my native country. I am firmly convinced that a Despotic Government can never produce real progress and happiness in a Nation. That is why I fight the system of Government established by Brute Force by General Díaz some 33 years ago. We all know that it was a coup that elevated him to power, and that this power has been maintained by deceit and violence....

All of this is inhumane. I have fought since my youth against the absolute power of General Díaz because of this. And I will go on fighting against it for as long as I live.... It is my wish that the absolute power of General Díaz end because it is leading us to ruin. It disgraces us and will bury us. This time the people will be fully resolved to embark upon a full democratic form of government, no longer suffering the "tutors" who deny them their rights. The people have demonstrated that they know how to exercise those rights in moderation. It is a crime against their legitimate aspirations, and an incentive to Revolution. They must take by force that which they are denied through peaceful means.

An honorable press should aid the people in this fight. The Government of General Díaz has stopped me from doing my duty as a citizen in my own Country. It has denied me access to my own press office.... It is for this reason that I now write on foreign soil, and because JUSTICE should be everywhere served, and the truth everyplace told.

Paulino Martinez
*Monitor Democratico*
San Antonio, Texas
February 5, 1910 [1]

---

Another writer in exile had this to say:

## The Kiss of Judas

The lack of respect and insolence shown the Mexican people, the easy violation of our own laws, the persecution of the newspapermen who raise their voices in defense of our languishing people.... Under the continuing "policy of Díaz," we face the loss of our autonomy if not our entire land, and our expulsion from our own nation as an inferior race.

If Díaz rules our destinies for another year more, hear me clearly:—We will see flying over our country "the Flag of the Stars and Stripes," and from the border to the hearth of our country, we will be occupied by our Masters and Señores, "The Yankees." We will be foreigners on our own land, as are now the downtrodden Texans. We will be dominated anew, if not by the Spaniards, then a bit worse.

Thinking of this disaster drives me out of my mind! The cunning with which the Yankees go on absorbing the Americas, first taking in all the land around our borders, then using their power of money to finish us off. All this is plain. It is not necessary to be a pundit to foretell the menace.

Mexican people: now is the time for us to help ourselves. All this peril comes from one man who is without patriotic feeling, without shame, without love of his country or brothers. That man is now in power; he is Judas; he is called Porfirio Díaz. Out with you, Dirty Traitor!

Miguel Albores
*Monitor Democratico*, San Antonio, Texas, September 25, 1910 [2]

Emiliano Zapata became an important leader to thousands of people in southern Mexico. He fought hard for land reform, which would give landless peasants some land of their own. In a conversation with then-President Madero, he said,

"What interests us is that, right away, lands be returned to the pueblos, and the promises which the revolution made be carried out."

Madero responded by saying that the land problem was a delicate and complicated issue which must follow the proper procedures. He reminded Zapata that they were in a new era, and urged Zapata to disband his army.

Zapata stood up and walked over to where Madero sat. He pointed at the gold watch chain Madero had on his vest. "Look, Señor Madero," he said, "if I take advantage of the fact that I'm armed and take away your watch and keep it, and after a while we meet, both of us armed the same, would you have a right to demand that I give it back?"

"Certainly," Madero told him.

"Well," Zapata concluded, "that's exactly what has happened to us in Morelos, where a few planters have taken over by force the villages' lands. My soldiers—the armed farmers and all the people in the villages—demand that I tell you, with full respect, that they want the restitution of their lands to be got underway right now." [3]

Zapata kept on saying, "I'll disband my boys as soon as the land is divided. What are you going to do?"

---

### References

1. Hanrahan, Gene, ed. *Documents on the Mexican Revolution*, Vol. 1, Part 1. Salisburg, NC: Documentary Publications, 1981.

2. Ibid.

3. Womack, John. *Zapata and the Mexican Revolution*. New York: Vintage Books, 1968, p. 96.

Siqueiros

## Going to The Sources
# Outside Interests

In completing the research for your project, you will no doubt find a lot of information about the Mexican Revolution in books and encyclopedias. But did you even wonder what people involved in the Revolution itself had to say about events at that time? The documents below are primary source documents—words actually spoken or written by people involved in the conflict. These documents should give you insights into the conflict that the encyclopedia never would! As you read these, reflect on the emotions the author is conveying and the intent of the author's words. Some of the language may seem difficult. If you are not sure about the meaning of something, ask your group members or your instructor.

---

**M**any people in the United States and countries watched what was happening in Mexico with great interest. The documents below reflect a variety of perspectives about events in Mexico.

The following communication was sent to the US Secretary of State by US Ambassador to Mexico, Henry Lane Wilson on June 27, 1910. Wilson was reporting the outcome of the June 26 primary elections in which Porfirio Díaz was re-nominated for the Presidency, a post he had held almost continuously since 1876. Francisco Madero began challenging Díaz in 1908 as a way to open up Mexico's political system. As elections approached on July 5, 1910, Díaz ordered Madero's arrest, and on the day of the elections, Madero was imprisoned along with 60,000 supporters throughout the country.

I have the honor to advise the Department of the national primary election of Mexico, which was held last Sunday, the 26th. According to reports received from our Consuls throughout the Republic, there was not a single sign of disturbance nor any transgressions of the law.... It is evident that the administration will continue to hold its own and that all the important interests of the country will as heretofore cooperate with the government to maintain its peaceful, prudent and progressive policy.

The Mexican electorate have been given a fair chance to express their opinion on political matters, and while it is true that several of the leaders of the opposition party have been under arrest for several weeks, this is largely due to the reprehensible methods employed in their campaign. They have not adhered to strict democratic methods in opposing the administration, their campaign having been one of personal defamation and revolutionary appeals to the masses.

Another one of the causes which has naturally kept all sober-minded and patriotic Mexicans from joining the opposition party is the absolute lack of personal prestige of the men they have put forward as the opponents of President Díaz and

Vice-President Corral. Mr. Madero, the anti-reelectionist candidate for the Presidency, is a wealthy farmer... wholly ignorant of government affairs, never has held a public office of any consequence, and for more than two years has been haranguing the Government by a series of abusive pamphlets and making seditious speeches throughout the Republic.

The Government has patiently permitted Madero to stump the country unmolested and without in any way interfering with his peculiar campaign methods. This prudent and moderate course undoubtedly encouraged the anti-reelectionist candidate and his followers to go beyond the limits of propriety and to abuse the freedom of discussion, and having lately assumed an attitude which might have brought about a lamentable agitation, from which the country would at least derive no benefits, the Government was finally forced to resort to drastic measures by placing Mr. Madero where, as a matter of fact, he ought to have been some time ago [in prison]....

This brief outline of the events of the election and the arrest of Madero may be of use to the Department in modifying the attacks of the sensational press which has recently been filled with highly colored accounts of the imprisonment of Madero and the impending revolution. [1]

---

Reformers and revolutionaries began organizing to unseat Díaz from power. Díaz responded with repression. He arranged to have his opponents thrown in jail. When dissidents such as Madero were released, they often went into exile in the US. The area along the border with Mexico became a hotbed of anti-Díaz organizing. Imagine if this happened today. How do you think the US government would respond? A telegram sent by the US Consul to the US Department of State gives us insights into the US government's response at that time.

There is evidence on both sides of border line of serious unrest and intrigue. Have situation on American side of border well in hand and with assistance of federal officers of Customs, Immigration, etc., United States Marshals, Bureau of Investigation Agents, United States Secret Service men, and United States Cavalry will keep it so. Will not ask for cavalry until absolutely necessary but have arranged with the Commander to have them ready to answer my call.

**Luther Ellsworth, US Consul**
**November 19, 1910**

---

Many anti-Díaz activists became frustrated with what they considered to be the heavy presence of US agents along the border, especially since the official US government policy was one of neutrality. Luther Ellsworth sent another letter to the Secretary of State on March 14, 1911 stating the following.

Sir:

I have the honor to advise that the "Press" in the American Border already has commenced to comment on the action of our Government regarding the rebellion in Mexico and the *Eagle Pass News and Guide* says in part:

"By what right the US officers spy upon and search out rebels against the Mexican government, and report their findings to the Mexican government is not clear. To attend meetings of persons opposed to the Mexican government, to keep a string of Secret Service men all along the border, to spy into everything that is going on and reporting the same to Mexican officials is not maintaining neutrality. In Uncle Sam's anxiety to help the Mexican government it appears he is setting a bad precedent. If the Mexican government denies the existence of a revolution, what in the name of General Hidalgo do they want the American troops for? Honestly, does it not appear that the Mexican government has given the American government to understand that it is unable to cope with the situation, and that the American government best hold itself in readiness to step in and protect American interests? The American side of the border is a solid, living mass of troops, marshals and officers of every description. The Mexican side of that same border is one vast blank spot—nary a darned officer in sight. What is the Mexican government doing to put down these disturbances by bandits? If Uncle Sam is to fight the battles of Mexico, let's have a square deal, and all those who want to fight on one side and those who want to fight on the other side — get in the game. Give us all a chance." [3]

---

As tensions mounted in Mexico, the future of US business interests became more uncertain. The Chief of the Bureau of Investigation (predecessor to the FBI) in the Department of Justice sent a memorandum to the Attorney General on April 26, 1911 with the following information.

My attention has just been called to the following extract of a report of one of our special agents operating at El Paso, Texas dated April 19, 1911. My informant gave me the following:

This party asked me if it were a fact that the [revolutionaries] were very short of money. I told him that I understood that they were very much in need of money. He then stated that he was representing a company who would furnish the [revolutionaries] with from $500,000 to $1,000,000 on the condition that the [revolutionaries] would issue to his company 6% gold bonds and a certain commercial concession which his company would ask of the [revolutionaries].... He then told us that if a meeting was brought about by us between him and a party representing the [revolutionaries], and if they could agree mutually on this concession he would make it pay us well for our time and services. We then took the matter up with a representative of the [revolutionaries] and then told him what this party wanted.... We then went... and got the Standard Oil party and... introduced him to the party representing the [revolutionaries].

... He showed him his credentials as to who he was and also showed him a letter from John Archbold of the Standard Oil Company, authorizing him to make contracts. He said that this Standard Oil party's desire was to get oil concessions in Mexico and they would be willing to lend the [revolutionaries] money under these conditions....

[He] felt sure that they would be able to close the trade in the next few days and that Madero would send a representative to El Paso who had authority to make the agreement.... Smith stated that the Standard Oil Co. has concession of the same nature in Mexico, but that these concessions had been canceled by the federal government and they were now operating through the Waters Pierce Oil Co. and that the federal government was imposing on the Waters Pierce Oil Co. by assessing them with unreasonable taxes. Consequently the Standard Oil Co. thought they would have better sailing under the [revolutionary] form of government. [4]

---

Many people in the US supported the goals of the reformers and revolutionaries. The San Francisco Labor Council sent a letter of solidarity and resolution on February 21, 1911 to President Taft. The resolution reads as follows:

WHEREAS, Governments derive their just powers from the consent of the governed and from no other source, and

WHEREAS, The intolerable tyranny of Díaz, Dictator of Mexico, is being successfully assailed by the Mexican people, and

WHEREAS, Díaz and his [supporters] have invariably shown themselves the blood thirsty enemies of Organized Labor, having on many occasions murdered numbers of Union men and organizers in cold blood, and

WHEREAS, By their continued suppression of the rights of free speech, free press and the right of the workers to organize, (it is a crime to organize a Union in Mexico), they have forfeited all right to be regarded as a civilized representative Government, and

WHEREAS, We recognize the necessity for the international solidarity of Labor,

BE IT RESOLVED, By the San Francisco Labor Council that we endorse the Mexican Revolution, and call upon the workers of America individually and collectively to render such aid and encouragement to the revolutionists as they may be able and to protest against any scheme seeking to use the forces of the United States to bulwark the tottering despotism of Díaz... [5]

### References

1. Hanrahan, Gene. *Documents on the Mexican Revolution*, Vol 11, Part 1. Salisburg, NC: Documentary Publications, 1976.

2. Hanrahan, Gene. *Documents on the Mexican Revolution*, Vol 1, Part 1. Salisburg, NC: Documentary Publications, 1976.

3. Ibid.

4. Hanrahan, Gene. *Documents on the Mexican Revolution*, Vol 1, Part 2. Salisburg, NC: Documentary Publications, 1976.

5. Hanrahan, Gene. *Documents on the Mexican Revolution*, Vol 1, Part 1. Salisburg, NC: Documentary Publications, 1976.

Siquieros

*An Exploring the Connections Lesson*

# Identity & Stereotypes
## A Guide to Understanding Cultures

This lesson explores questions of identity—how people understand and view themselves, and how others see them. We look at the practices and characteristics that contribute to creating identity and forming stereotypes. *Many Faces of Mexico* asks students to consider how identity affects the relationship between the people of the United States, Canada and Mexico.

The lesson begins with a session on cultures, defined as the way of life of a group of people. Contemporary Mexico is composed of many cultures, as are the US and Canada. Students look at some cultural traits associated with Mexican people and do a parallel look at those same traits in their own culture. The goal is to guide students through an objective, non-judgmental process to look at similarities and differences across cultures.

The second and third sessions focus on identity and stereotypes. Session Two addresses how many people in the US perceive Mexicans and how those perceptions have developed historically. We begin by analyzing images of Mexicans, some created more than 100 years ago. Through cartoons, a painting, a poster and a song, we see how people with particular interests in Mexico have tried to influence perceptions about Mexico and Mexicans in the US. We also have included illustrations from children's books, published between 1943-1967, which indicate particular attitudes toward Mexican people. By taking a historical view of biases and negative stereotypes, one can understand the deep and lingering impact such images and stereotypes have on the people of Mexico and the United States.

Session Three looks at how Mexican people are portrayed in the popular culture today, especially in advertising. Extension lessons are included for evaluating children's books about Mexico and/or Mexican people and for role-playing situations to practice confronting prejudice.

**Learner Objective**

- To compare and contrast cultural traits of North Americans.
- To develop an operational definition of stereotype and apply this to analysis of media images of the Mexican people.
- To demonstrate respect for human differences, particularly differences of culture and ethnicity.

**Concepts**

- Culture
- Nation
- Identity
- National Identity
- Stereotypes

**Major Questions to be Addressed**

- What are some cultural traits of North Americans?
- How have images of Mexican people been used to create stereotypes and manipulate US public opinion?
- How do children's books help form attitudes about other people?

**Exploring the Connections**

The main objective of this lesson is to recognize that positive perceptions and attitudes are fundamental to forming respectful relationships between peoples across cultures.

**Teaching Strategies**

- Reading and inquiry
- Image analysis, writing

**Materials Provided**

- Mexican Culture (Handout 1)
- Mexican National Identity (Handout 2)
- Key to the Images (Educator's Background Information)
- Images for Transparencies (Images 1-14)
- Image Analysis (Handout 3)
- Evaluation of a Children's Storybook (Handout 4)
- Confronting Prejudice (Handout 5)
- Guidelines for Challenging Bias (Handout 6)

**Additional Materials Needed**

- Overhead or projector—Session 2
- Poster board, markers, paste or tape, scissors—Session 3
- Magazines, newspapers, travel brochures, comic books, souvenirs, etc. for session 3. Also children's storybooks about Mexico from the library, especially those with illustrations—Session 3

**Time Required**

3 class sessions

*Note: This lesson can be used at any time during the curriculum. It is placed here because of its historical relevance.*

# Session 1
# Sequence of Lesson

| | |
|---|---|
| *Preparation* | Make one copy of Handouts 1 & 2 for each student |

*Anticipatory Set*
*5 minutes*

1. Ask students to think about who they identify with or feel a part of, such as a family, a cultural group, a team or school. Write their responses on the board and explain that it is human nature for people to identify with a group larger than themselves.

*Body of Lesson*
*40 minutes*

2. Write the word "culture" on the board and ask what this word means to your students. Explain that in this lesson we are using the sociological definition which suggests that culture is the way of life of a group of people.

3. Distribute Handout 1 and read aloud the first two paragraphs on culture. Instruct students to read this handout and answer the questions.

4. Have students form pairs and describe what they wrote about their own culture to the other student.

5. Explain that you are now going to go from studying *cultural practices* to studying *national identity*. National identity is a composite of cultural practices; however, some may be exaggerated while others are ignored. National identity is the face that outsiders commonly see of a nation or people. This symbolic faced cannot portray the diversity and complexity that actually make up a nation. National identity in Mexico began to be created in the 19th century, at a time when people felt more aligned with their family or cultural group, than with the nation as a whole. In order to accomplish certain objectives, there was a movement to develop a Mexican national identity, also called *Mexicanidad*. Distribute Handout 2 to the pairs and instruct students to read and answer the questions together.

*Closure*

6. Ask students to sum up what they learned about culture and national identity. Remind students that neither cultural practices, not national identity are static. Both change and are affected by things such as the times, new ideas, and the mobility of people as individuals and groups.

*Evaluation*

Collect Handouts 1 & 2 and assess the students' work.

*Assignment*

Ask students to find souvenirs, photos, cartoons, advertisements or drawings that refer to Mexico.
Bring to class for Session 3.

# Session 2
# Sequence of Lesson

*This session uses cartoons, posters and children's books published in the US to explore how pictures create our images and attitudes of Mexican people. We look at some images to see attempts to manipulate popular opinion, especially during war or conflict.*

*Preparation*

- Make transparencies of the images or copy a set of the images, mount on heavy paper and post around the room.
- Make one copy of Handout 3 for each student.

*Anticipatory Set*
*10 minutes*

1. Instruct students to write or draw on a piece of scratch paper what comes to mind when they hear the word "stereotype." Ask them to give examples of a stereotype. What do they think is the opposite of stereotype? Ask for volunteers to read or show their ideas.

*Body of Lesson*
*30 minutes*

2. Try to come to a consensus on a working definition of "stereotype." You may want to add that stereotyping is a way of organizing information. Stereotypes may accurately describe some people, but become problematic when they are applied generally or used for simplistic explanations. The following definition was written by participants at a National Conference of Christians and Jews in 1991, in an article "The American Indian and the Media." (News Media in Minnesota, 1993, p.79.:

   *Stereotypes are trite, uninformed, often banal images or mocking characterizations implying that all members of a group or race are alike. Stereotypes replace observation and thought with bias and patterned response. The beliefs and lifestyles of millions of individuals...cannot responsibly be reduced to a few simple equations.*

   Stereotypes can be divided into two categories: intentional and unintentional. Intentional stereotypes are created for a specific purpose, like gaining support for a particular point of view on an issue, or to support or undermine a specific group. Unintentional stereotypes may be a result of ignorance. However, both kinds adversely affect both the group doing the stereotyping and the group that is being stereotyped. According to the report issued by the Minnesota Advisory Committee to the US Commission on Civil Rights, when groups are stereotyped, "it not only impedes different racial and ethnic communities from understanding each other, but it also serves to reinforce racist and discriminatory attitudes."

3. Show the first set of cartoons and drawings (Images 1-10) on an overhead projector. As you show them, ask students to describe what they see and what message they think the image is trying to convey. Then read or talk from the *Key to the Images* on the *Educator's Bacground Information* sheet. This key explains

how the image has been used historically. Continue the process through image 10.

4. Show the second set of images (11 - 14) that are illustrations from children's storybooks. As you show the images, ask students to rank the illustrations between one and ten, with 10 signifying an accurate portrayal and 1 signifying a stereotypic generalization.

*Closure*

5. Ask students what they think teachers, librarians, parents, guardians and students can do about derogatory or biased materials. For example, if there are objectionable illustrations or references in a book, should it be removed or banned? Are there ways to creatively use objectionable materials for educational purposes? For example, students in Portland, Oregon put warning labels in books they found objectionable, and in a school library, a blank page was inserted for readers to "talk back" to the book with their comments.

*Assignment*

• Distribute the *Image Analysis* (Handout 3) for an assignment to collect the following day.
• Remind students to bring at least one picture, souvenir, etc. that refers to Mexico for the next session.

*Extension Lesson*

• Have students do a review of a children's story about Mexico or Mexican people. Distribute Handout 4 to use as a guide to evaluate a story and write a recommendation for its use.
• Encourage students to send the evaluation/recommendation to the library, author, publisher or local newspaper.

# Session 3
# Sequence of Lesson

*This session poses the question of whether the portrayal of Mexican people today has changed, and if so, how is it different. We use images from popular culture, especially from advertisements and souvenirs.*

**Preparation**
- Lay out the magazines, travel brochures, etc. that you have collected on a table so that they are accessible for students.
- Have poster board, markers, paste or tape, and scissors available.
- Write the following quotation on the board:

  *Wars come and go, yet the images we use to dehumanize our enemies remain strangely the same.*

**Anticipatory Set**
**10 minutes**

1. Have students show the image(s) they brought to class and very briefly tell where they found it.

**Body of Lesson**
**30 minutes**

2. Divide into groups of 4-5 students around tables or a desk. Distribute a sheet of poster board and a few markers to each group. Instruct students to write the word "Mexican People Today" at the top. Students should find and paste together images of Mexico and Mexican people, making a collage. They can also draw pictures or write words that reflect contemporary descriptions or attitudes of Mexican people.

3. After about 15 minutes, draw students' attention to the quotation you wrote on the board. Ask them to discuss this in light of their artwork. Ask them to put a large X through the images that they think dehumanize people, and a circle around those that are respectful. Then ask each student to write a sentence that begins, "Respectful relations across cultures are possible if....."

**Closure**

4. Have the groups post their artwork and read their sentence to the class.

**Evaluation**

Collect and assess the Image Analysis, Handout 3 and Handout 4 (if that Extension Lesson was done). Pay special attention to the remaking of the collage by the student.

**Extension Lesson**

Cut apart the scenarios from Handout 7, *Confronting Prejudice*, and discuss ways of handling each situation. You may wish to have students role play these scenarios to make them more real. Refer to the suggestions on the sheet, *Confronting Discriminatory Behavior*.

# MEXICAN CULTURE

Who are "The Mexicans"? What ties the people of Mexico together? Is it simply that they are people who occupy the same geographical territory or have the same federal government? Are there traditions and practices which unite the Mexican people and help to form a sense of common identity? To gain insight into these issues, we can ask the same questions about the United States and Canada. Who are "the Americans" or "the Canadians?" What do people in the respective countries have in common?

Mexico, the US and Canada are composed of various cultures, that is, groups of people who share common beliefs, practices and ways of life. The cultural heritage of a nation includes the different histories of all of its many people. Therefore, we can say that all the countries of North America have a diverse cultural heritage. The following passages contain generalized descriptions of these aspects of the Mexican people, with space to reflect on the cultural practices of your own country.

## MEXICAN FOOD

The Mexican diet is a blend of the basic foods of the Indians and the Spanish, along with contributions from other people. The foods the Mexican Indians cultivated included beans, corn, cocoa, potatoes, pumpkins, peanuts, pineapple, peppers, papaya, squash, sweet potatoes, tomatoes, vanilla, yams and zucchini. The Spanish brought with them bananas, citrus fruits and sugarcane, which originally were domesticated in Asia; onions, originally from Mongolia; and wheat, which originally came from Mesopotamia. Today it seems impossible to imagine a cup of cocoa without sugar, or a burrito without onions and tomatoes. This is an example of how cultural products and practices are blended together.

Within Mexico, food preparation varies according to the cultural heritage and availability of foods. Along the coast of the Gulf of Mexico, the food has an African flavor due to the population of people of African descent in that area, while in the northern mountains of Mexico, similar foods taste different as a result of that area's traditional methods of preparation.

**Using what you know about Mexican food, compare it to the foods you commonly eat:**

<u>Similarities</u>                                    <u>Differences</u>

# MEXICAN FAMILIES

Traditionally, the Mexican family is very close and united, with two or three generations living together. It is not uncommon to find grandparents, aunts and uncles living together in Mexican homes. Mexican families not only live together, but often work and play as a unit. If the family has a shop or a small business, employees are likely to be members of the family. Farming is usually a family affair, as well. Elderly people rarely live alone or are cared for in institutions such as nursing homes. Rather, they remain with their families and often have the important role of helping to raise and educate the children.

### What are some similarities and differences in families between your culture and that of Mexico?

Similarities                                                              Differences

# MEXICAN NAMES

The names of Mexican people often reflect a blend of Indian, African and Spanish cultures.  Examples include Paco IgnacioTaibo, Cuauhtémoc Cardenas, or Chango Rodriquez. In Roman Catholic families, it is traditional to name a child in honor of a saint, often including a religious term for a second name.  Examples of this would be María Rosario (Mary Rosary) or Jésus Domingo (Jesus Sunday). The child is  taught about the life of the saint for whom he/she is named and often observes the Saint's Day with a grand celebration.

As in much of the Spanish speaking world, the last name of Mexican people may be a combination of both parents' surnames. For example, the name of the early 20th century Mexican author Gregorio López y Fuentes indicates his father's last name was López and his mother's name was Fuentes. As names undergo change today, Gregorio might be tempted to modify his last name to López Fuentes or drop one of the names altogether.

### What are some similarities and differences in people's names or how people are named between the your culture and that of Mexico?

Similarities                                                              Differences

# MEXICAN CELEBRATIONS

The most popular of Mexico's many national holidays celebrate the country's independence from or victory over various foreign powers. On September 16, 1810 Mexico gained independence from Spain and each year the anniversary is commemorated with festivities called *Diez y Seis de Septiembre.* *Cinco de Mayo*, celebrated each May 5 with dancing and fireworks, commemorates Mexico's resistance to the French invasion in 1862. Fifty years after gaining independence from Spain, Napoleon III of France sent 7,000 soldiers to Veracruz to collect loans left over from the war of independence. Mexican soldiers held the French troops for almost a year before they were able to gain control of Mexico City.

Because the vast majority of Mexicans are Roman Catholic, many religious holidays are celebrated in Mexico, including Holy Week at Easter, Christmas and the Day of the Virgin of Guadalupe on December 12. Another prominent religious holiday is *la posada*, which in English means "the inn". This celebration reenacts Mary and Joseph's search for a place to stay in preparation for the birth of Jesus. The people go from house to house, singing and asking for a place to stay, until a large procession has come together. Finally, someone lets them into their home for a party.

Most parties, or *fiestas,* feature the breaking of a *piñata* for children. This originally was a clay water jug that was decorated with crepe paper and filled with candy. Children are blindfolded and take turns trying to break the *piñata* with a long stick. When it breaks, the children scramble to get the candy. Today, *piñatas* may be made of *papier maché* that is molded and decorated like an animal or a person. No matter what style, candy is always inside.

### How are the holidays you celebrate different or similar to those celebrated in Mexico?

<u>Similar</u>                                                          <u>Different</u>

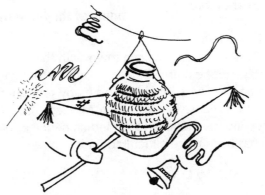

# MEXICAN NATIONAL IDENTITY

Before the Spanish invasion, diverse groups of people such as the Aztecs, Tarahumara, Otomí, Zapotecs, Mayan Lacandón and many others lived in the territory now known as Mexico. However, they did not view themselves as Mexican or as citizens of any nation beyond their group. Each group had its own distinct culture, despite many similarities and interaction among the groups.

When the Spanish settled in the hemisphere, they brought different cultural ways. During the colonial period, the Spanish and *Criollos* in New Spain imitated European art and architecture. They wore the same fashionable clothing they would have worn had they lived in Spain. Artists expressed themselves through music and literature in the Spanish style. The cities they built during the colonial era, like Guadalajara (wah-da-la-HAR-ah), were replicas of Spanish cities, often with the same name. Using Indian labor, the Spanish and *Criollos* also built cathedrals, government buildings and houses with Spanish-style architecture, which were furnished with materials imported from Europe.

The Spanish invasion and settlement brought momentous changes to the Mexican Indian people living in that area. The interactions between various Mexican Indian and Spanish cultures over time has resulted in an acculturation process. Acculturation is the altering of one another's culture. Modern Mexico reflects the acculturation process of the Spanish and Indian heritages. An example of acculturation can be found in language. Although more than 50 Indian languages are spoken in Mexico, the language the Spanish brought is used in business and government, and spoken by the majority of people. However, the Spanish language of Mexico has been altered to include many Indian words.

**Origins of the "new race"**

Some regions in Mexico are more predominantly Spanish or Indian in culture, and this is often reflected in the names of the communities. The southern Mexican town with the Indian name, Oaxaca (wah-HA-kah), has a traditional indigenous culture while the northern town of San Miguel de Allende was settled by the Spanish and today is inhabited by many foreigners. The regions that are more densely populated with Indians, like southern Mexico, reflect stronger resistance to Spanish culture and subsequently have retained their Indian heritage. Where fewer Indians live, such as northern Mexico, it has been more difficult to maintain Mexican Indian cultural ways.

Before the War of Independence in 1810, there probably was little discussion between different groups of people about a common identity or culture. But when the *Criollos* became more determined to gain independence from Spain, they needed allies. Thinking that people would join the army if they believed in a cause such as becoming an independent nation, they began to cultivate the image of *Mexicanidad* (meh-hee-KAHN-ee-dahd) or Mexican national identity. *Mexicanidad* was rooted in pre-Hispanic history and mythology, in part to appeal to Mexican Indians. For example, the symbol of Tenochtitlán was an eagle with a snake in its beak, sitting on a cactus. The Aztecs had an omen that where they saw this happen, they should build a grand city. The present day flag of the United States of Mexico has the same symbol in the center of its red, white and green stripes.

To promote this budding national identity, *Criollo*-owned newspapers began to print news about Mexico, rather than Europe. In literature, writers increasingly located their stories in Mexico and developed Mexican characters and events. *Criollo* and *Mestizo* artists created pictures in a "nativist" or "primitive" style that used Mexican Indian forms and bright primary colors.

*Mariachi* is a popular style of music in Mexico and is an example *Mexicanidad*. The violins, guitars and trumpets are modifications of Spanish instruments. The flashy clothing is Spanish while the huge hat worn by the musicians resembles an Indian sombrero, decorated with pompoms. Many people outside of Mexico associate *mariachi* music with Mexico, and believe that all Mexicans either play or like *mariachi*. However, this common perception of Mexican national identity does not reflect the diversity and complexity of the real Mexico.

Other examples of *Mexicanidad* can be found in the early 20th century art of Mexico, especially by artists Frida Kahlo and Diego Rivera. Although her father was from eastern Europe, her mother was Mexican Indian and Frida Kahlo wore braids and long skirts to look like an Indian peasant woman. However, her elaborate silver jewelry and fashionable clothing reflect the alteration of the traditional Indian culture. Artist Diego Rivera made the Mexican Indian the centerpiece of his murals and insisted that everything of value in Mexico was inspired by the Mexican Indians.

Another factor of Mexican identity is *la Raza*, or the new "race" of people who were conceived as a result of the Spanish invasion. There were very few women who came with the Spanish soldiers and migrants in the early years. Many Mexican Indian women were taken by or voluntarily went with Spanish men and bore their children who were called *Mestizos*. These children grew up with both Spanish and Mexican Indian cultural ways. The concept of *la Raza* originally was cultivated by the *Criollos*; today, Mexican-Americans often use the term *la Raza* to define their heritage.

# Respond to these questions regarding Mexico and your country:

<u>My Country</u>                    <u>Mexico</u>

What holidays,
symbols, colors,
monuments and
slogans promote
national identity?

_____

Who or what do you
think has created
national identity?

(To get you started,
think about your
answer to the question
above. Who created
these symbols of
national identity?
When? Why?)

_____

Imagine you are on a committee in your school or community to develop "spirit"
or loyalty. How would you go about this? What symbols, slogans, colors or events
might you use? What could you do to respect the diversity of all the people you
represent?

# Session 2
# Key to Images of Mexico & the Mexican People

*Note to Educator: This is a guide to the images included with this lesson. First, show the image and ask students to describe what they see and what they think is the message in the picture. Then read the following background information aloud to the class.*

## THE MEXICAN-AMERICAN WAR, 1846-1850

**Image 1**    Depending upon which side you were on, it was called either "The American Intervention in Mexico" or "The Mexican-American War." In the US, the Mexican-American War was an important time for the creation of national identity. It was one of the first wars fought on foreign territory, and thereby helped form how US citizens regarded their own country in relation to the world around them. The US public was extremely interested in the Mexican-American War, but at the onset, had little knowledge about Mexico. Image I is the cover of a book published in 1847 that helped inform people about Mexico. What do you think the readers of this book learned about Mexico? *("The Great Western Heroine of Fort Brown" from Incidents and Sufferings in the Mexican War. 1847)*

**Image 2**    The Mexican-American War was the first major event in US history to be reported by the "penny press," as newspapers were called. During the 1840s, newspapers began to compete with each other for sales. Publishers found the more dramatic or sensational the news, the more copies would be sold. Many major newspapers advocated territorial expansion of the US and pictures like this helped create the belief that some people were more worthy, and therefore deserved the land. This image shows a person scalping an Indian, with a statement by Sam Houston, commander of the rebel Texas army: "The Anglo-Saxon race must pervade the whole southern extremity of this vast continent. The Mexicans are no better than the Indians and I see no reason why we should not take their land..." *(500 Years of Chicano History)*

**Image 3**    There is an old saying, "In war, truth is the first casualty." The Mexican-American War was no exception. The US public was divided on whether or not to take Texas and, eventually, to expand to the Pacific Coast. However, politicians, businesspeople and others who supported its acquisition eventually persuaded the US government to declare war. Immediately, supplies, weapons and ammunition needed to be manufactured, ships purchased or built, materials transported, and more soldiers recruited. Wartime posters like Image 3 were published in newspapers and printed in large numbers to be posted in public places. *(Wartime poster, 1847)*

**Image 4**    In 1846, a mass meeting was organized in New York to celebrate Congress's passage of the war resolution. Writers, poets, dramatists and songwriters were called upon to appeal to "the patriotism of the people, call for the defense of America's freedom, and remind the nation of their duty to God." This song was written and sung to the tune of *Old Dan Tucker* for the war effort.

# THE MEXICAN REVOLUTION, 1907-1930

*Stereotypes do not vanish from peoples' minds once their original objective has been met. Stereotypes persist, change and are altered to fit the trend of the day. The portrayal of Mexico around the beginning of the 20th century changed. During this time, many US businesses were expanding into Mexico, partially due to President Porfirio Díaz's encouragement of foreign investment. Seventy-five percent of Mexico's trade was with the US, so there was a great deal of interest in Mexico among certain sectors in the US.*

**Image 5**    There was growing unrest and rebellion among Mexican people, directed toward the policies of their government and its foreign interests. By 1907, people had begun to organize their struggle for equality and respect. As a result, the US government was concerned about Mexico's order and stability, and about conflict between Mexico and Guatemala. *("More Trouble in the Nursery", Milwaukee Sentinel, 1907)*

**Image 6**    Note how all South American countries, including Mexico, are lumped together in this image. What do you think this cartoon implies? *("The South American Way", Minneapolis Journal.)*

**Image 7**    The fighting of the Mexican Revolution had been going on for five years when this cartoon was published. What do you think this cartoon is saying about Mexico's relationship with the governments of the rest the Americas? What do you think the impact of the struggle for land and liberty had on the landless peoples in the other countries in the Americas? *("United We Stand", St. Paul Daily News, 1915)*

# CONTEMPORARY MEXICO

*A variety of images of Mexicans are found in many places today.*

**Image 8**    This is the popular image of "The Mexican" that continually reappears. It has been found as a design for salt and pepper shakers, on calendars and tee shirts.

**Image 9**    These Mexicans appear on advertisements: Frito Bandito from the Frito-Lay Company; Emiliano Zapata with Elgin Watches; Pancho Villa promotes Old Crow Bourbon; and the generic lazy Mexican advertises a motel.

**Image 10**    This cartoon is adapted from one that was published by a major city newspaper in 1989. After it appeared, a reader wrote the following *Letter to the Editor* about the insensitivity of the cartoon. The following day the newspaper apologized for publishing the cartoon.

# IMAGES OF MEXICAN PEOPLE IN CHILDREN'S BOOKS

*There were not many books about Mexico for children published until recently. Here are illustrations taken from a few books published between 1942-1957. Ask students to describe the pictures and identify stereotypes they find. Include cultural, gender and age stereotypes.*

**Image 11**    *Pito's House* by Bryan and Madden; New York: Macmillan & Co. 1943.

**Image 12**    *Rosita and Panchito* by Edna Babcock: San Francisco: Harr Wagner Publishing Co. 1957.

**Image 13**    *Picture Tales from Mexico* by Dan Storm; Philadelphia: J.B.Lippincott Co. 1941.

**Image 14**    *In Mexico They Say* by Patricia Fent Ross; New York: Alfred Knopf. 1942; reprinted 1961.

*Note: To enrich this lesson show videos of Speedy Gonzalez, The Three Caballeros, or other cartoons that stereotype Mexicans.*

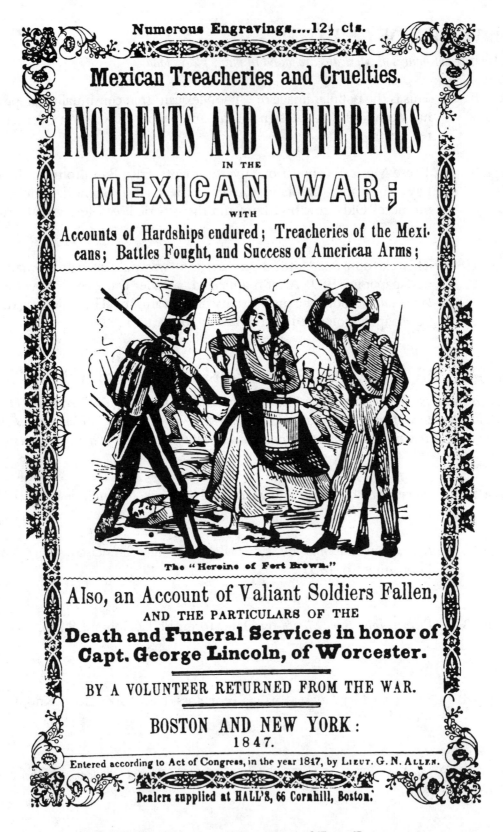

The Great Western Heroine of Fort Brown.
From *Incidents and Sufferings in the Mexican War* (1847).

"The Anglo-Saxon race must pervade the whole southern extremity of this vast continent.... The Mexicans are no better than the Indians and I see no reason why we should not take their land...."
— Sam Houston

*500 Years of Chicano History in Pictures*, Edited by Elizabeth Martinez. Albuquerque: South West Organizing Project. 1991

This song was written to celebrate the declaration of war against Mexico by the United States Congress in 1846, and is sung to the tune of Old Dan Tucker.

*The Mexicans are on our soil,*
*In war they wish us to embroil;*
*They've tried their best and worst to vex us*
*By murdering our brave men in Texas.*

*We're on our way to the Rio Grande,*
*On our way to Rio Grande,*
*On our way to Rio Grande,*
*And with arms they'll find us handy.*

*The God of War, the mighty Mars,*
*Has smiled upon our stripes and stars;*
*And spite of any ugly rumors*
*We'll vanquish all the Montezumas.*

*We're on our way to Matamoras,*
*On our way to Matamoras,*
*On our way to Matamoras,*
*And we'll conquer all before us!*

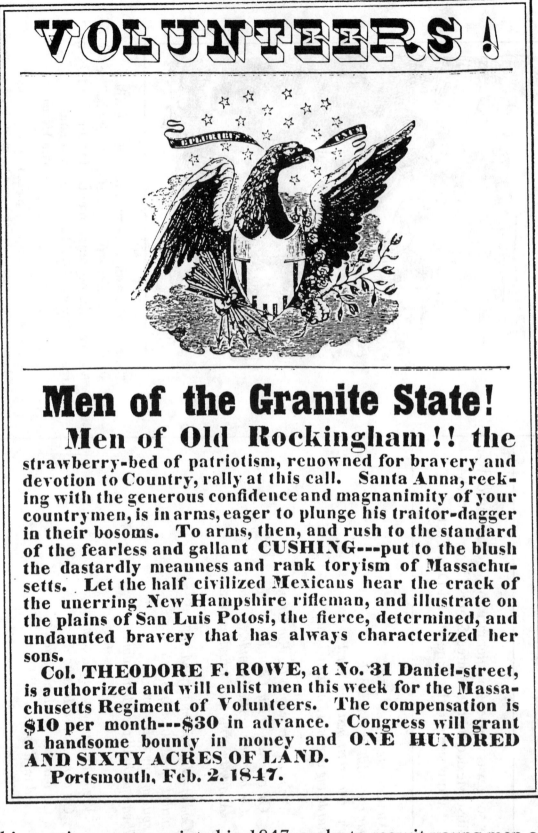

# VOLUNTEERS!

# Men of the Granite State!
## Men of Old Rockingham!! the

strawberry-bed of patriotism, renowned for bravery and devotion to Country, rally at this call. Santa Anna, reeking with the generous confidence and magnanimity of your countrymen, is in arms, eager to plunge his traitor-dagger in their bosoms. To arms, then, and rush to the standard of the fearless and gallant **CUSHING---**put to the blush the dastardly meanness and rank toryism of Massachusetts. Let the half civilized Mexicans hear the crack of the unerring New Hampshire rifleman, and illustrate on the plains of San Luis Potosi, the fierce, determined, and undaunted bravery that has always characterized her sons.

Col. **THEODORE F. ROWE,** at No. 31 Daniel-street, is authorized and will enlist men this week for the Massachusetts Regiment of Volunteers. The compensation is **$10** per month---**$30** in advance. Congress will grant a handsome bounty in money and **ONE HUNDRED AND SIXTY ACRES OF LAND.**

Portsmouth, Feb. 2. 1847.

This wartime poster, printed in 1847, seeks to recruit young men of the northeastern states to join the battles in Mexico.

## More Trouble in the Nursery
*Osborn, Milwaukee Sentinel*, 1907.
Reprinted by permission of the *Milwaukee Sentinel*.

**The South American Way**

Uncle Sam — What's the Row?

S.A. Republic — Just a revolution-it beats an election all hollow-why don't you try it?

*From the Minneapolis Journal.*

**United We Stand**

North and South America getting together on the Mexican situation.

Charles L. "Bart" Bartholomew, *St. Paul Daily News*, 1915.

Reprinted with the permission of the *St. Paul Dispatch*

**Frito Bandito
Advertises Frito Chips
for Frito-Lay, Inc.**

## THE NEW BREED

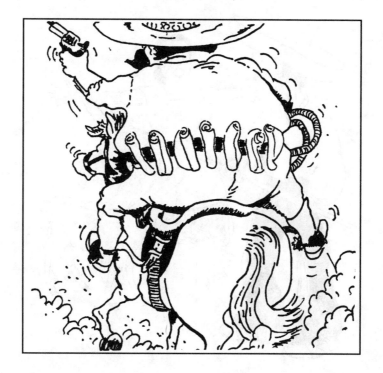

**Hernandez rides into town with ten tortillas on his belt.**

Letter to the Editor:

It was my distinct displeasure to have seen and read the "New Breed" cartoon. I was appalled at the lack of sensitivity to a minority culture and the racist concept directed, not only to Hispanics in general, but to those of us who happen to be named "Hernandez." I have always appreciated this paper for its creativity, understanding and, yes, even sensitivity to issues. However, this blatant racial depiction has possibly shown that the *Dispatch* needs to redress to its managers and editors what is appropriate in these days of intelligent journalism.

Joe Hernandez

The paper replies:

The newspaper apologizes for publishing the cartoon.

*All adapted from a cartoon, a letter to the editor regarding the cartoon, and the paper's reply which appeared in a major Midwestern newspaper in 1989.*

Los amigos de Rosita y Panchito vienen a la casa. Vienen a romper la piñata.

# IMAGE ANALYSIS

Creating stereotypes is not unique to specific historical periods or to particular countries such as Mexico, the US or Canada. There have been standard images used repeatedly to dehumanize people, images such as: a troublesome or simple-minded child; a lazy or unproductive person; an outlaw; a seductive or domineering woman; an anarchist; a monster or a beast; a snake or death itself.

**1. Study this cartoon and describe what you see.**

**TROUBLE ENOUGH FOR THE PRESENT**
The Little Fellows - What we need is the water cure.
Uncle Sam - The tub is full just now.
*From the Minneapolis Journal*

**2. What do you think the characters and objects represent? What is the issue?**

**3. Whose perspective is presented? What evidence do you have to support this?**

**4. Describe what you think may be stereotypes, inaccuracies or racial slurs.**

**5. What is your attitude toward this cartoon?**

*6. Redo the cartoon so it represents your perspective. You may mark up the cartoon or use the reverse side of this paper.*

# Evaluation of a Children's Storybook

**Title of Book** _____

**Author** _____

**Publisher** _____

**Date of Publication** _____

1.  Describe the story you read.  What ideas are presented?  Whose perspective is presented? What is the overall message?

2.  Describe the illustrations, particularly of the people and the setting. Are they realistic, cute, artistic, symbolic, or stereotypic? Give examples.

3.  What mood or feelings does the story evoke for you?

4.  Explain if and how the author uses or avoids stereotypes, including gender of characters, ethnic groups, economic classes, and ages of characters.

5.  Does the author promote respect and understanding? If yes, how? If no, what would you change?

6.  Do you like the story? Would you recommend it? To whom?

# Confronting Prejudice

## SCENARIO 1

Angie Velasquez is a new student at your school. She has recently moved here from southern California, where her family has lived since 1820. When you asked her if she was excited about living in a new place, she confided that is would be difficult living so far from her extended family. Besides, she is the only Chicana student in your school. Angie is introduced to the class and students greet her shyly. The following day, Angie and your teacher are talking in the hallway before the bell. As they walk into class you notice someone has written in big letters on the board, **GO HOME, BEANO!**

*There is a hushed silence in the room. What do you think will happen next? What do you think <u>should</u> happen next?*

## SCENARIO 2

You are attending a basketball game at the high school, and walk out to get some refreshments during half-time. You notice that the school's International Club is holding a fund-raiser for a trip to Mexico. At a concession stand, students are selling burritos, tacos and soft drinks. As you are standing in line to buy something, you hear a group of students nearby imitating Spanish accents. One starts singing, "Ay, ay, ay, ay..." Another says, "I bet this won't be as good as Taco Bell!" A third student shouts out, "No way, José!"

*Do you respond? If so, how?*

## SCENARIO 3

On one of your favorite TV shows, a Mexican-American guy named Carlos has begun dating one of the main characters, a blond Anglo named Brenda. As you are standing around your locker the next day talking about the show, one of your friends says, "I can't believe Brenda would date a *spic*. She could do much better."

*Do you respond? If so, how?*

## SCENARIO 4

One day you are standing in the lunch line. Ahead of you is a student from one of your classes with a tray full of food. His name is Pedro and he is Mexican-American. He looks like he's having some trouble with the person at the cash register. You overhear the cashier ask Pedro if he qualifies for the reduced lunch price. Pedro looks uncomfortable and glances over at you.

*Do you respond? If so, how?*

# Guidelines for Challenging Bias

1. **Don't Ignore It!** Silence can send the message that you are in agreement with such attitudes and behaviors. Make it clear you will not tolerate racial, ethnic, religious or sexual jokes or slurs, or any actions that demean any person or group.

2. **Acknowledge that people are different from one another but avoid stereotypical thinking.** Recognizing obvious differences is not the problem, but placing negative value judgements on those differences <u>is</u>! Stereotypes about those differences are hurtful because they generalize, limit and deny people's full humanity.

3. **Be honest with yourself about your own attitudes, stereotypes and biases.** We all have been socialized to believe many myths and misconceptions and none of us remain untouched by the discriminatory messages. Practice not getting defensive when discriminatory attitudes or behaviors are pointed out.

4. **Be aware of your own hesitancy to intervene.** Confront your own fears about interrupting discrimination and remember tension or conflict may be unavoidable in certain situations. Practice response-ability!!

5. **Actively listen to and learn from others' experiences.** Educate yourself about your own and other's cultures. Do not expect people from different backgrounds to always educate you about their culture and history, or to explain racism or sexism to you. Make an effort to see situation through their eyes.

6. **Use language and behavior that are non-biased and inclusive** of all people regardless of race, ethnicity, gender, disabilities, sexual orientation, class, age or religion.

7. **Project a feeling of understanding, love and support** when confronting bias. Without preaching, state how you feel and firmly address the hurtful behavior or attitude while supporting the dignity of the person or persons who are involved.

8. **Be a role model** and be willing to take the risks this demands. Practice positive values. Remember issues of human dignity, justice and safety are non-negotiable.

9. **Work collectively with others.** Organize and support efforts that combat bias and oppression in all its forms. Social change is a long term struggle and it's easy to get discouraged, but together we have strength and vision to make a difference.

Adapted from *Guidelines for Challenging Racism and Other Forms of Oppression* by Patti DeRosa, Cross-Cultural Consultation, 28 S. Main #177, Randolph, MA 02368. 617-986-6150.

# Frida Kahlo & Diego Rivera

*Mexico Through the Artist's Eye*

The art of Mexico is as old as its oldest civilizations, communicating through time and across cultures. Art offers an avenue for understanding mutual experiences, such as happiness and sorrow, life and death, and the importance of family. Art is the expression of our common humanity.

When one looks at Mexican visual art in the first half of the 20th century, one finds a unique blend of personal and political metaphors, reflecting the changing conditions in Mexico. This lesson looks at two of the most renowned artists of the era, Frida Kahlo and Diego Rivera. Rivera painted huge historical panoramas on the walls of public buildings so everyone would have access to his works. Kahlo's works of art were usually small in size and almost always included a self-portrait. If you choose to extend the lesson, you may want to consider additional prominent artists, such as José Clemente Orozco, David Alfaro Siqueiros and Rufino Tamayo.

This lesson considers questions commonly posed in the world of art such as: What is the artist trying to communicate?" How does the artist communicate? The exercise leads students through a process developed by art critics to become familiar with a work of art and then talk about it in a knowledgeable way.

We are not able to include quality reproductions of art in this book. Therefore, we suggest you locate art prints for this lesson in public libraries or collaborate with a colleague in the art department. You also may wish to develop an additional interdisciplinary lesson or unit on Mexican art. One suggestion is to have students work together to create a mural.

**Learner Objectives**
- To examine Mexican works of art and explain how they portray social movements and personal perspectives.
- To explain the role that art has played in 20th century Mexico.
- To develop skills used in art criticism to describe, analyze and interpret works of Mexican artists in the 20th century.

**Concepts**
- Windows of Access
- Political art
- Self-reflective art

**Major Questions to be Addressed**
- Why do people make art?
- What to people communicate through art?
- How do people communicate through art?

**Teaching Strategies**

Inquiry, Discussion

**Materials Provided**
- Biographical Information on Frida Kahloand Diego Rivera (Handout 1)
- Windows of Access (Handout 2)
- Art Criticism Worksheet (Handout 3)

**Materials Needed**
- At least two color pictures, one each by Frida Kahlo and Diego Rivera, to be used for the art criticism project. Recommended works by Kahlo are *Necklace of Thorns, The Two Fridas* or *Self-portrait on the Borderline*. Recommended works by Rivera are murals from the National Palace that portray the history of the Mexican people. Have the prints or pictures from books available for classroom use. Consult your art department or library for prints. There are also calendars with excellent reproductions of the artists' paintings.
- Reproductions of early indigenous and 20th century Mexican art, by artists such as José Clemente Orozco, David Alfaro Siqueiros, Rufino Tamayo and Maria Izquierdo. Use these to supplement or extend the lesson.

**Time Required**

1 class session

**Preparation for this Lesson**
- Make six copies of Handout 2 (adapted from a worksheet by Barbara Rogers Bridges), one for each small group.
- Make one copy of Handouts 1 & 3 for each student.
- Make overheads of at least two pictures you have chosen to use for this lesson. Display other pictures.

# Sequence of Lesson

| | |
|---|---|
| *Anticipatory Set*<br>*5 minutes* | 1. Display several pictures of Mexican art to illustrate the diversity of styles and themes among Mexican artists. Pose and discuss the question, Why do you think people make art? |
| *Body of Lesson*<br>*40 minutes* | 2. Refer to a variety of pictures and ask students if they have different feelings about or reactions to the different pieces. These reactions are the first step in art criticism. Explain that art criticism is a way of judging and talking about art. It is based on description of what one sees, interpretation of the meaning of the work of art, and evaluation of how individuals feel about the work of art. |
| | 3. On the overhead or slide projector, show the two works of art you have selected by Kahlo and Rivera and ask students to describe in detail what they see. Distribute Handout 1 for students to read in class. |
| | 4. Divide the class into six groups. Distribute Handout 2 and assign one of the questions, or *Windows of Access,* to each group to complete in class, referring to the works of art by Kahlo and Rivera. Each *Window of Access* is one component that art critics use to analyze art. |
| | 5. After 10-15 minutes, ask each group to give a 2-3 minute presentation to the class on its *Window of Access.* Students should take notes on Handout 1 to use for an assignment. |
| | 6. Distribute copies of Handout 3, *Art Criticism Worksheet.* Have the two works of art available for students to study throughout the assignment. Ask students to complete as much of the worksheet as they can in the remaining class time and to complete the rest as a homework assignment. |
| *Evaluation* | Collect and evaluate the *Windows of Access* and *Art Criticism* worksheets. |

# Frida Kahlo & Diego Rivera

## Biographical Sketches

**Frida Kahlo's** paintings expressed her ambivalence toward life, illness and death. She is famous for her self portraits, expressing the anguish of her life of physical pain. Her fame as an artist has grown over the years since her death in 1954. Born in Mexico City, Frida lived there most of her early life. Her father, Guillermo, was a well educated Eastern European who emigrated to Mexico. He was a jeweler and a photographer. Her mother, Matilde, was part Indian from Oaxaca.

Frida suffered a series of medical problems, beginning with polio, when she was six years old. This illness required that she spend nine months in isolation, and it left her with one leg shorter than the other. During this period she began to paint, using an easel her father built to go over her bed. At age eighteen, Frida was seriously injured in a street car accident. Damage to her spine and internal organs, and many surgical operations influenced her outlook on life. Her self portraits where she appeared as a wounded deer or with the thorns around her neck reflected this view.

During her early years, Frida attended private schools. She observed artists such as Diego Rivera painting murals in Mexico City, and in 1922, she asked him to critique one of her pieces. In 1929, she and Diego were married, and they traveled together to the US where he was commissioned to paint murals. By 1938, Frida's art was attracting notice and she was asked to exhibit in the US as well. In addition to her painting, she and Diego led an active social and political life during the post-revolutionary period in Mexico. Their life together was both dramatic and stormy. Frida's health declined, and in 1953, she became bed-ridden after her injured leg was amputated. She continued to paint, finding the artistic expression to be a relief from intense physical pain. At age 47 Frida Kahlo died, ending a remarkable life reflected in artistic images and expression.

**Diego Rivera** was born in 1866 in the city of Guanajuato, a mountainous area in central Mexico, where his father was a teacher. His family moved to Mexico City when he was six. At age thirteen, he entered San Carlos School of Fine Arts. Diego preferred to paint scenes and events of Mexican life, even though he was taught classical painting. As a student activist, he made political posters for groups opposing the re-election of President Porfirio Díaz.

Diego traveled to Europe where he spent most of the next twenty years studying and painting in Spain, France and Italy. He returned to Mexico in 1910, the same year the Mexican Revolution began. He was part of a group of artists who used art as a means to create awareness about the country's social conditions and history. Diego painted huge murals in public places in Mexico and the US and began the enormous mural on the walls of the Mexican Palace in 1922. The painting chronicles major events in Mexico's history and portrays the lives of Indians, Mestizos and the Spanish. This mural was completed in 1955, two years before his death at age 71.

# FRIDA KAHLO & DIEGO RIVERA
## "Windows of Access"

Art criticism involves more than just opinions and feelings about the beauty of a piece of art. Critics also use other criteria to describe, interpret and evaluate art. One method, called "Windows of Access," helps viewers to understand and appreciate the complexity of a piece of art and how people interact with it. These "windows" include such things as the artist's intention, placement of the art, formal aesthetic properties, historical and cultural factors and audience expectations.

    **DIRECTIONS**: Your group is assigned to respond to ONE of the following six windows of access. As you complete the questions raised in the window of access, begin your sentences with either the phrase "We know..." or "We think.." to differentiate facts from opinions.

1. **ARTIST'S INTENTION:** What do you think the artist was trying to convey? What were her/his beliefs or values? What techniques did s/he use to convey them?

2. **PLACEMENT:** Can you tell where the work of art is placed? What is its size in relation to the space around it? Who has access to it? How does the placement help convey the metaphor or message?

3. **FORMAL AESTHETIC PROPERTIES:** Describe the elements of design — lines, colors, shapes, textures. How are the designs put together - symmetry, asymmetry, repetition, variation? What is the first thing you see?

4. **HISTORICAL CONTEXT:** How does the artist incorporate the past into the work of art?

5. **CULTURAL CONTEXT:** What are the key events or issues at the time the work of art was created? How does the artist reflect her/his era?

6. **AUDIENCE EXPECTATIONS:** Look at the works of art from the perspectives of a Mexican worker and a director of the Mexican Arts Commission. Considering each perspective, does your reaction to these works of art differ? How?

# Art Criticism Worksheet

***DIRECTIONS:*** *Study these works of art by Frida Kahlo and Diego Rivera and select one to write about in the following paragraphs.*

**Name of artist** _____

**Symbolism**     The symbolism included in this work of art is:

**Mood**     The personal feelings this work of art produces are:

**Meaning**     The meaning and purpose of this work of art is:

**Judging**     I like or do not like this work of art because:

# Bringing History to Life

## *Stories from the Revolutionary Era*

The stories in Lesson 15 continue the portrayal of six people from families in six regions of Mexico begun in Lesson 9. It is now early in the Twentieth Century. We visit descendants of the families described in Lesson 9, and learn how they relate to the dynamic situation in their country during the tumultuous years of the Mexican Revolution. In some regions, the people are intimately involved in the war; in others, they hear only rumors of fighting and don't know what to believe. No one is oblivious, however, and all are concerned about how the fighting will affect their immediate needs and future lives.

Students should work in the same small group as in Lesson 9 for the first part of the lesson while they read and discuss their story. Then students "jigsaw" and form new groups with one representative of each region. That person tells the story of his or her family. Students use the note taking grid to record information about the lives of the people.

| Learner Objectives | • | To describe important events that occurred in people's lives during the Revolutionary era. |
|---|---|---|
| | • | To assess the impact these events by identifying ways in which people's lives changed during the Mexican Revolution. |
| | • | To develop an understanding of different perspectives about changes in Mexico during the Revolutionary era. |

**Concepts**
- Customs
- Social change
- Continuity

**Major Question to be Addressed**

How did economic, social and political changes affect people's lives in Revolutionary Mexico?

**Teaching Strategies**
- Reading and discussion in small groups
- Jigsawing and teaching others

**Materials Provided**
- Six stories from the Revolutionary Era (Handouts 1a-1f)
- Note-taking Grid (Handout 2)
- Family Time-line (from Lesson 9)
- Chart of Descendants (Image)

**Additional Materials Needed**
- Student journals
- Overhead projector and transparency of Chart of Descendants

**Time Required**

1 class session

**Preparation for this Lesson**
- Make copies of the six stories from Handout 1 — one story per small group with enough copies for each student in the small group.
- Make one copy of Handout 2 (*Note-taking Grid*)for each student.
- Ask students to bring to class the *Family Time-line* from Lesson 9
- Make an overhead of the *Chart of Descendants* to help students understand the continuity between stories. Save for the next story lesson, Lesson 22.

# Sequence of Lesson

*Anticipatory Set*
*10 minutes*

1. Divide students into the same small groups as Lesson 9. Instruct students to jot down on plain paper all they can recall about the story of the person from their region during the Colonial time. Show overhead of the Chart of Descendants so they can track the person.

*Body of Lesson*
*40 minutes*

2. Use same instructions as Lesson 9 for the remainder of this lesson.

## Story from Region 1 — North
# Revolutionary Era

Ochaván, also known as Diego Rodriguez, was one of the many Tarahumara Indians who sought refuge in the mountains to escape the Spanish. As in all the regions where the Spanish invaded, the Tarahumaras rebelled. The first organized rebellion in the north took place in 1648, and was repressed bloodily by the Spanish. Other major rebellions took place in 1652 and 1697 and the fight continued until the second half of the eighteenth century.

The life of the Tarahumara people continued with few changes during the Mexican Revolution. Most people remained in the mountains and avoided contact with outsiders. There were a few exceptions in which Tarahumaras migrated to Spanish villages. That was the case of one of Ochaván's descendants, Manuela Rodriguez. Her family had left the mountains, and in 1916 she was living in Durango. During this time, Pancho Villa was leading the revolution in the north. In 1916 Villa launched an attack on the city of Columbus, New Mexico, which was then a US territory. This became the pretext for the US cavalry to march onto Mexican soil.

My name is Manuela Rodriguez, and I am 23 years old. I am a Tarahumara Indian, originally from the mountains of Chihuahua. Now I live on a *hacienda* (ha-see-EN-dah) in Durango, where the owners raise cattle and harvest corn. I was married two years ago, but my husband left with Pancho Villa's troops after they raided the *hacienda*. I think Villa was looking for supplies for his troops.

These are hard times because my husband is gone and I don't know where he is. I wonder if he is alive or if he is dead. I wish he had taken me with him. Many wives go with their husbands to the war front and move wherever the troops go. Women cook for their husbands and the other soldiers. Some of the women even give birth on the journey.

I think these women have a hard life because most of them also have to fight. Each woman is given a rifle, but usually not a horse. The women have to carry their cooking utensils and their rations in one hand, a rifle in the other hand, and a baby on their back. They have to endure long walks behind the horses that the men ride.

It has been six long years since the war started. A lot of people have died on both sides, along with many bystanders. Two days ago Mexican troops entered one of the nearby towns and hanged fourteen men and five women suspected of being part of Villas' people.

Now the *gringos*, those green-clad US soldiers, have sent their cavalry down to capture Pancho Villa. Maybe Villa made a big mistake by attacking the town of Columbus, New Mexico, because the *gringos* have come armed to the teeth with cannons, machine guns and even airplanes. I don't think they are going to catch him because the people here help him. Everyone I know likes Villa and thinks very highly of him.

Meanwhile, things have changed since Mexican government troops have taken this territory. The troops do whatever they want, and have no respect for anybody. I think that instead of staying here abusing people, they should be fighting the *gringos* that have invaded Mexico from the north. The *gringos* say they want to get Pancho Villa. I think they want another piece of my people's territory. Would you agree with me?

## Story from Region 2 — North Central
# Revolutionary Era

---

Don Francisco Alvarado de Ojeda died a rich man in northern Mexico. His wife died shortly thereafter. He left most of his wealth to his daughters, who married into very wealthy families in the area. The Alvarados' blood line continued, although the last name Alvarado was lost when one of the daughters married into the Gutierrez family. This is the story of Delores Gutierrez Mujica, a direct descendant who inherited most of the Alvarados' wealth. By the time of the Mexican Revolution, she had several *haciendas* (ha-see EN-dahs). As a landowner, she owned and controlled huge areas of land.

---

My name is Delores Gutierrez. I have one daughter and two sons. I own six *haciendas* and my husband owns two. On each of our *haciendas* we have a large house which is surrounded by a thick wall. On the far side of the wall are shacks where the workers live.

We raise cattle, sheep and horses, and we also grow grain. We hire some people to administer the *haciendas* and others to take care of the animals. Those who administer the *hacienda* have proven to be very loyal and are rewarded well.

There also are many Indians who come to the area to work on our land. These people mainly work in the fields from dawn to dusk,

taking care of the corn. They are very resilient, and because they are Indians, we can make them work as much as we want. At times some of them protest and refuse to work. But the Indians who are loyal to me always take care of them. Last night they hanged one of the Indians because he refused to work. He only wanted to get drunk.

On the *hacienda* we have armed guards who control the land and the people who work for us, because there is talk of revolution. There is a lot of unrest in the country right now. Those rebels Pancho Villa and Emiliano Zapata are planting ideas in the heads of the Indians to revolt against the *hacienda* owners. I am confident, however, that everything is going to be all right, because the federal army reinforcements arrived yesterday from Mexico City. They are on their way to crush the forces loyal to Villa, the "bandit" who is in this territory.

The laws of the Mexican government protect our right to own and control our land. We also have the support of the Catholic Church, which we visit every Sunday. The priest has told us that the eyes of God are watching us closely and will protect our lives and our property. The priest also said those who are foolish enough to follow the ideas of the revolution will go directly to hell.

In two days I will be 55 years old, and our family and friends from other *haciendas* are coming for the birthday festivities. We will kill seven cows for the feast, and it will be a grand party! All kinds of food will be served in the main house, and many good friends will honor me with their visits.

After the Indians prepare the food and decorate the house for the party, I will give them some time off. They will probably sing and get drunk, just as they usually do.

## Story from Region 3 — South Central

# Revolutionary Era

---

By the time of the Mexican Revolution, the descendants of Martín de Muñoz had many children and grandchildren. They lived mainly in Mexico City, but some moved throughout the central part of the republic. Martín had received land and Indians as payment for his work as a soldier, and over the centuries, the value of the land increased. The family's wealth also grew; they owned businesses and many held high positions in the government of Porfirio Díaz, the dictator of the Mexican Republic. A descendant of Martín de Muñoz, Luis Muñoz, was a captain for the federal army during the revolution.

---

My name is Luís Muñoz. I am 35 years old and I am a prominent captain in the Mexican army. I live in Mexico City with my wife and five children. My children attend private school, and we also have a tutor come to our house to give the children music lessons. I am proud of my children, especially my sons.

The war began in 1910 because the Indians invaded *hacienda* (ha-see-EN-dah) lands. It is now 1911, and there seems to be no end in sight to the war. Maybe it will never end. There are several rebels in the republic who have brought my country into this bloody war, rebels such as Emiliano Zapata in the state of Morelos. These rebels claim that the Indians own the land. Zapata uses the motto, "Land and Liberty," and yet they take land away from the people who now own the land. We have legal titles to the land that we got from the government, and we deserve the freedom to harvest its resources.

Those Indians used to be lazy, but now they have gotten too ambitious. They have invaded land where my friends grow sugar cane, and they also have killed several landowners. Their actions affect not only this area, but also the economy of the entire country.

I am really worried about the future of Mexico. We had been doing so well with Don Porfirio Díaz heading the government. He started to build the railroad system in the countryside, and was constructing majestic buildings in Mexico City. Furthermore, he invited many foreign investors to put their money to work in Mexico. Several US mining companies invested their capital in the north, which provided jobs for many people. Investors from Europe also were beginning to arrive, because they believed Mexico had become more civilized. Now this Indian revolt has scared many investors away.

Fighting the Indians is not an easy task. They know the terrain well and fight to the last drop of blood. Luckily we have machine guns and cannons while they rely on old guns and horses.

There is much confusion because so many factions are fighting each other. In the south, the situation is more clearly defined. The fight is against Emiliano Zapata's army, and we know where he is. In the north, things are different. In the state of Chihuahua, it is hard to know who is fighting whom. Obregón is fighting Villa; Villa is fighting Madero, and Carranza is chasing Villa. We have to put an end to this mess and start working together again, just as we did before.

## Story from Region 4 — Gulf Coast
# Revolutionary Era

Josefina Silva and her husband died on the cane plantation where they worked all their lives. Her children and grandchildren continued to work under many of the same conditions as their ancestors, even though slavery had been abolished in 1810. African people gained some freedom, although a caste system was created. In this system, people of Spanish origin regarded themselves as superior and treated African and Indian people as if they had little or no value. Most of the African people remained along the Gulf coast; others migrated to the interior of the Mexican Republic to find work. Many married Indians and Mestizos. This is an account of Sabino Silva Jimenez, a descendant of Josefina Silva. Sabino lived in the Veracruz area during the revolution, where he worked on a large *hacienda* (ah-see-EN-dah).

Sabino Silva Jimenez is my name. I am 33 years old and I work for Señor Mendoza, the owner of this *hacienda* where we grow sugar cane. My father and mother once worked in the sugar cane fields near here, as did their parents. There are many workers in the fields, but I don't know many because I spend most of my time working in the stables not far from the house. I feed and care for Señor Mendoza's horses.

The Mendozas own several sugar and coffee *haciendas*. Señor Mendoza is a very rich man. He is always visiting his other *haciendas* to make sure everything is in order. When Señor Mendoza is away, we have to deal with his son, Alberto Mendoza, who is the second boss of this *hacienda*.

Alberto is a young man who has no respect for anyone, and he often mistreats the workers. He

raped two of the girls who work in the kitchen and was never punished. Not long ago he killed one of the Indians who worked in the fields, just because the Indian could not pay what he owed to the *hacienda* store. Alberto tied the Indian to his horse and dragged him around until he was dead.

We buy what we need for our families at the *hacienda* store. We earn so little money that we are not able to pay cash, so we buy our food, clothing and alcohol on credit. The amount of money we owe to the store keeps piling up, along with interest. Some workers will never leave the *hacienda* because they owe so much money on

their debt. In fact, I know a worker who will not be able to pay back his father's debt in his lifetime, and neither will his children.

My job is not so bad as long as Alberto is not around. Besides, I don't know any other life than this one. But I wonder if things will change pretty soon around here. The other night I went out to a cane field where I heard some workers talking and singing around the bonfire. When I joined them, I was well received. They knew I worked in the big house. There were mostly Indians and others who looked like me. I never had seen so many workers from the *hacienda* together. Maybe that's because I rarely go out.

I truly enjoyed being part of the celebration, although I had to leave early to get up the next morning for work.

During the gathering I overheard some people talking about events that were happening outside of the *hacienda*. I heard that a war had started against the Mexican government and the *hacienda* owners. The little news which we receive from the outside is brought by men who transport sugar to the trains. Sometimes the news we get is only rumors, but whether rumor or truth, people here are restless. Everybody is tired from mistreatment and injustice.

Personally, I think that even if war is not good, we need a change around here. I don't know what kind of change it should be, but something has to happen.

## Story from Region 5 — Pacific South
# Revolutionary Era

During the Colonial Era, the Zapotec people were an integral part of the Spanish empire. They mined silver and wove cloth which was sent to the Spanish crown, and the owners and exporters of these products became very wealthy. After independence, Europeans planted coffee on land that they had taken from the Zapotecs and the Mixtecs, and thousands of Indian people became laborers for this export crop. During the revolution, several armed groups formed to fight for their rights. The legendary Emiliano Zapata, whose motto was "Land and Liberty," was a leader in the southern part of Mexico.

Xochitl's descendants stayed in this region of mountains and ocean, and continued the line of artists. One of them became a follower of Zapata. Although a jeweler by profession and not a soldier, Feliciano Mendieta saw the suffering of other landless people and decided to join the revolutionary.

My name is Feliciano Mendieta. I am 44 years old. I was born in the Oaxaca (wah-HA-kah) region to a family of jewelers. We are Zapotecs, but we also have some Spanish blood in us. Therefore, I am called a *Mestizo*. I don't look Indian or Spanish, but rather a mixture of both.

I spent my childhood in a small village near the ocean, and I often went to the beach with my brothers. These were some of the most memorable times of my childhood. When I was 11, I started helping my father in his workshop, learning the art of jewelry-making. When I was 15, my family moved to a *hacienda* (ah-see-EN-dah) that belonged to a very rich man. We were invited there because the owner wanted my father to make jewelry for his family. I, too, made jewelry using the silver that comes from the mines near here.

We were treated very well compared to other people on the *hacienda*. They were mostly Indians or Mestizos, and they had difficult lives, working from sunrise to sunset tending the coffee bushes. They lived in dismal little houses, and they were beaten by the owners. I made friends with some of the workers, and they told me about their resentment toward the owners. When the revolution started, the owners moved to their other *hacienda* because they believed the war would not reach them there. I think they must have known how their workers felt.

Along with others on our *hacienda*, I decided to join the revolution. We went to the state of Morelos, where Emiliano Zapata gathered fellow Indians and convinced them to help to take the land back from the rich. Seven of us from the same village in Oaxaca joined his army. Zapata was a very strong-willed man with a soft heart. Sometimes he was stubborn. Perhaps my most exciting memory is when we triumphantly entered Mexico City after we had defeated the army in a series of battles.

But the war was also tragic. After one encounter with the army, I came across my brother lying on the ground, killed by several bullets. While bullets whizzed by, I held him in my arms. He was the brother who took me by the hand to the beach. He was my oldest brother, and there he was lying on the ground in an army uniform. I couldn't understand what had happened. I knew he had left home to find work in the mines. I understood why he had left. But why was he with the government troops? Had he been forced to fight on their side?

In war, there is so much confusion. I knew some had been taken prisoner and forced to fight against their own people under threat of death. Some of these men were later retaken as prisoners by their own people. After a while, nobody knows who is fighting for whom. But it torments me to think about how my brother died. Did one of my bullets take his life?

## Story from Region 6 — Southeast
# Revolutionary Era

After several years passed, Ana Santiago gained her freedom from the Gonzalez family and returned to the little village where she had been born. There she married a Tzeltal Indian and lived with him and their four children for the rest of her life. During this time, the Spanish founded more cities. The Indian resistance continued and more Indians were converted forcibly to Christianity.

Many generations passed since the days of Ana Santiago. Descendants of the original Spanish people settled in the best lands of the region. Things did not change much for the local Mayans; they either lived in poverty in their villages or worked in Spanish homes. In 1991, rumors of the Mexican Revolution had reached this territory and there were a few revolutionary groups in the area. This is an account of one of the descendants of Ana Santiago.

My name is Manuel Santiago, and I am 27 years old. I live in a small village in the highlands not far from San Cristobal. In the season of corn my wife and I plant a small crop in the skirts of the mountain, and when the season is over I cut firewood for a Spanish family. Traveling from our small house to the fields early in the morning, I walk the same paths that my people have walked for generations. The land gives me strength.

My wife and I have two sons. She stays home to cook the meals, take care of the boys and raise a few hens and turkeys. It is sometimes a struggle for me to provide enough food for my family. We don't have much money. In exchange for the firewood that I cut we get some money or clothes that the Spanish family doesn't wear anymore. We used to have more land to grow corn, but the government charges us more and more for use of the land. If we do not pay, the government takes the land from us, even though the land always has been ours. And then we have nothing.

My boys can speak a little Spanish because they go to the Catholic Church two days a week. A priest comes from San Cristobal to teach religion to the children. Everything is taught in Spanish. My boys don't like to go to those sessions very much. They say they'd rather go out with me to learn how to work the fields. Sometimes I think they are right. They look happier when they go to the mountain with me to harvest corn or to hunt armadillo.

But I guess it is important to learn Spanish ways. I think my sons will be treated better if they learn the Spanish language and about Christianity. I speak both Spanish and our native Tzeltal, but my wife speaks only Tzeltal. She refuses to learn Spanish, because she thinks Spanish people don't mean with their hearts what they say.

I am concerned because people say there is war to the north of here. Somebody called Emiliano Zapata has recruited a group of Indian peasants. This leader, Zapata, is said to be fighting for the land that the Spanish took from the Indians. People also say somebody called "Pancho" is fighting in the north against the government of Porfirio Díaz up in Mexico City. I don't know what to think. These may only be rumors, so I don't know what is really happening because we are very isolated. But I am sure of one thing—the people here are very unhappy with the treatment that we receive from the government.

More Spanish people from San Cristobal are moving onto land near our village. They are nervous because they fear that Indians like me are going to join the revolution and take our land back. These settlers are so afraid that they have asked for help from the Mexican army several times. A few times I have seen federal soldiers come to San Cristobal. Then I was afraid.

# NOTE-TAKING GRID for the REVOLUTIONARY ERA

*Use this grid to fill in the information about the five other regions*

| | Who is the story about? Describe the person and their way of life. | How do events in Mexico affect her / him? |
|---|---|---|
| REGION _____ | | |
| REGION _____ | | |
| REGION _____ | | |
| REGION _____ | | |
| REGION _____ | | |

# CHART OF DESCENDANTS

|  | COLONIAL ERA | REVOLUTIONARY ERA | CONTEMPORARY ERA |
|---|---|---|---|
| **REGION 1**<br>North | **OCHAVÁN**<br>Tarahumara Medicine Man | *Descendant of Ochaván*<br>**MANUELA RODRIGUEZ**<br>Hacienda Worker | *Great granddaughter of Manuela Rodriguez*<br>**MAGDALENA HERNANDEZ**<br>Maquila Worker |
| **REGION 2**<br>North Central | **FRANCISCO ALVARADO**<br>Criollo Landholder | *Descendant of Francisco Alvarado*<br>**DELORES GUTIERREZ**<br>Hacienda Owner | *Great grandson of Delores Gutierrez*<br>**ALEJANDRO GUTIERREZ**<br>Store Owner |
| **REGION 3**<br>South Central | **MARTÍN DE MUÑOZ**<br>Spanish Immigrant / Soldier | *Descendent of Martín de Muñoz*<br>**LUIS MUÑOZ**<br>Mexican Army Captain | *Great granddaughter of Luis Muñoz*<br>**ELEONORA QUINTANILLA**<br>Tour Agency Owner |
| **REGION 4**<br>Gulf | **JOSEFINA SILVA**<br>African Slave | *Descendant of Josefina Silva*<br>**SABINO SILVA JIMENEZ**<br>Plantation Worker | *Great grandson of Sabino Silva Jimenez*<br>**JACINTO SILVA LAGOS**<br>Petroleum Worker |
| **REGION 5**<br>Pacific South | **XOCHITL**<br>*Zapotec Weaver* | *Descendant of Xochitl*<br>**FELICIANO MENDIETA**<br>Jeweler | *Great granddaughter of Feliciano Mendieta*<br>**MARÍA MENDIETA**<br>Jeweler, Migrant Worker |
| **REGION 6**<br>Southeast | **ANA SANTIAGO**<br>Tzeltal Servant | *Descendant of Ana Santiago*<br>**MANUEL SANTIAGO**<br>Corn Farmer | *Great granddaughter of Manuel Santiago*<br>**MARÍA SANTIS LÓPEZ**<br>Zapatista Guerrilla |

*An Exploring the Connections Lesson*

# Political Reform
## *Chronicling the 1968 Student Movement*

This lesson bridges the time span between the Mexican Revolution and contemporary Mexico, emphasizing Mexico's political system. In structure, the Mexican system is similar to the US; in practice, the government has been dominated by one party, the Institutional Revolutionary Party (Partido Revolucionario Institucional or PRI) for several decades and since 1929, every president of Mexico has been from the same party. The body of this lesson contains substantial information on the structure and functioning of the Mexican political system.

To learn about this complex topic, we have recounted a sequence of events in 1968 when university students challenged the lack of democracy in the Mexican political system. The Student Movement galvanized popular discontent, at least for a brief period of time. The students also gained worldwide attention, and like students in France, the US, and elsewhere at the time, they exposed vast contradictions in the government and other institutions. Beginning in July, the movement climaxed on October 2 ,1968, ten days before the Olympic Games were to begin in Mexico City. On this date, the police and army fired on thousands of demonstrators.

It is very important for students to understand some of the dynamics of Mexico's system before they can comprehend why there was dissent. Therefore, we suggest you use much of one class period for reading the background paper, *Governing Mexico*. This is a challenging reading, so we suggest you take time to discuss the concepts and main points thoroughly.

The second part of the lesson follows the same format as Lesson Six, *The Spanish Invasion*, to demonstrate the similarities of the events. Ironically, the tragic incident of October 1968 took place in the same location as the Spanish massacre of the Aztecs at Tlatelolco, almost 500 years before. This part of the lesson contains narrative readings, pauses for discussion and a writing assignment. Primary source material, printed in italics, are used almost exclusively. Most of the documents, eye-witness accounts and testimonies, are from the book *Massacre in Mexico* by Elena Poniatowska. She is a journalist and writer of testimonial literature. Her brother was killed during the riots in 1968.

Part II opens with a news flash about the student massacre on October 2. Students then read a chronological account of events, including a description of a silent march held on September 13, 1968, and a poem written to honor those who died on October 2. Also included are the students' demands, the government's responses, and comments from a variety of people who either were involved in, or observed, the events.

**Learner Objectives**

- To analyze the policies and practices of Mexico's ruling party.
- To analyze conflict situations and brainstorm when and how to alleviate tensions.
- To compare testimonies and documents of students, government officials and observers to recognize their divergent views of political change and democracy.

**Concepts**

- Democracy
- Conflict
- Resistance
- Co-optation

**Major Questions to be Addressed**

- What is the purpose of government?
- What can citizens do to change government?
- What are some strategies to resolve conflict?
- Could there have been another outcome to the events of 1968?

**Exploring the Connections**

This lesson examines Mexico's political system. Although there are many similarities in the structure between the US and Mexican governments, there are important differences in the ways in which governmental institutions, political parties, and citizens interact. In the first part of this lesson, we encourage students to think about these similarities and differences.

**Teaching Strategies**

- Interviews

- Reading
- Discussion
- Writing

**Materials Provided**
- Governing Mexico (Handout 1)
- Students Confront the Mexican Government (Handout 2)

**Time Required**
2-3 class sessions

**Vocabulary**
- Chapultepec
- La Noche Triste
- Tlatelolco

**Preparation
for this Lesson**
- Make one copy of Handout 1 for each student.
- Make at least one copy of Handout 2, and cut into sections for students to read aloud, or make copies for each student.
- A few days prior to the lesson, ask students to talk to someone who has been involved in a group protest or a movement to bring about change. This could be through a neighborhood group, labor union, civil rights work, etc. Students are encouraged to find out how and why the person became involved, what tactics were used, and what the outcome was. If they don't know anyone, they could read articles or other accounts of a movement.

# Sequence of Lesson

*Anticipatory Set
10 minutes*

1. Ask students to write what they think is the purpose of government. What should be its function? Ask volunteers to express their opinions and then follow up with a discussion.

*Body of Lesson
60 minutes*

2. Distribute Handout 1 and instruct students to read it and write responses to the questions during class.

3. Ask students to recall their interviews with people involved in a movement or protest. List on the board the kinds of protest students found. Listen to their stories. Indicate that the next part of the lesson will focus on an important protest movement in Mexico.

4. Introduce the next section by explaining that in democratic societies, citizens are expected to monitor their governments. In 1968 in many places in the world, students and others were doing just that — trying to influence their governments. In Mexico students also exercised their rights and responsibilities as citizens, and this is the story about what happened. Distribute sections from Handout 2. Take turns reading the sections aloud in the sequence indicated. Pause for discussions as indicated within the text. You may wish to copy the

students' *Six-point Petition* on a transparency or blackboard, as it is referred to frequently in the narrative readings.

*Closure*        4.   Do a 3-5 minute free writing exercise that begins, *If I was an athlete preparing for the 1968 Olympic Games, I would ...*

*Assignment*          Imagine you are either a student, a parent of a student, or a government official in Mexico in 1968. Write a 2-3 page letter to explain your beliefs and your role regarding the student movement and government's response. Include a paragraph that begins *I feel so strongly about ... that I am willing to...*

## Footnotes for Narrative Readings in <u>Students Confront the Government</u>

1.   Poniatowska, Elena. *Massacre in Mexico*. New York: Viking Penguin Press, 1975, p. 29.
2.   Ibid, p. 45.
3.   Interview with Mexican human rights advocate, Mariclaire Acosta, December 3, 1993.
4.   Poniatowska, pp. 8-9.
5.   Ibid., p. 14.
6.   Ibid., p. 79.
7.   Ibid., p. 57.
8.   Ibid., p. 78.
9.   Interview with Gilberto Vasquez, March 15, 1995.
10.  Ibid., p. 47.
11.  Ibid., p. 52.
12.  Ibid., pp. 53-54.
13.  Ibid., pp. 54-55.
14.  Ibid., pp. 55.
15.  Ibid.
16.  *New York Times*, Sept. 14, 1968
17.  Ibid., p. 80.
18.  Ibid., p. 7.
19.  Ibid., pp. 171-172.
20.  Wigg, Richard. "Mexico's Image Crumbles as the Riots Continue," *The Times*, London: October 4, 1968, p. A11.
21.  Delmas, Gladys. "Troops' Show of Force Stuns Mexicans," *The Washington Post*, October 4, 1968, p. A3.
22.  Nix, Robert. Address to the Mexico-United States Interparliamentary Group, Report of the Ninth Conference on the Mexico-United States Interparliamentary Group. Aguascalientes, Mexico, April 1969. Washington, DC: US Government Printing Office, 1969, pp. 3-4.
23.  Alvarado, José. *Siempre!*, October 6, 1968, p. 302.
24.  Interview with Mexican human rights advocate, Mariclaire Acosta, December 3, 1993.
25.  Ibid.

# Governing Mexico

## The Mexican Government

In structure, the United States of Mexico is a republic that was modeled after the United States of America. Each of its thirty-one states elects its own governor, legislature and four senators. Like the US, the Mexican federal government consists of a president, congress and supreme court.

The president is elected to a six-year term by a simple majority and is prohibited from seeking re-election. The president appoints members of the cabinet, ambassadors, generals and admirals, subject to ratification by the senate. As in the US, the president is commander-in-chief of the armed forces. There is no vice-president, which makes unforeseen successions complicated.

Congress consists of two chambers: a 128-seat Senate and a 500-seat Chamber of Deputies. The Mexican congress has virtually the same powers as the US congress. However, the congress has never seriously challenged any proposals or budgets presented by the president. That is mainly because the majority of members are from the same political party as the president.

Like the US, Mexico has a constitution. Adopted in 1917, the Mexican Constitution reflects the goals of the Mexican revolution to provide a better life for all Mexican people. It outlines the authority of the government by defining the role of the president and congress; it also limits the powers of the church and religious organizations. The Constitution of 1917 declares that primary education should be free and compulsory. Article 27 called for land reform, including a decree to re-establish an ejido system of communal land holdings. It also states that land must serve a "useful social function" and "only Mexicans by birth or naturalization have the right to acquire ownership of lands." Article 123 provides for an eight-hour workday, a six-day workweek, a minimum wage, and equal pay for equal work regardless of sex or nationality. This article also gives labor the right to organize, bargain collectively and go on strike.

The Mexican congress is able to make amendments to the constitution. In 1983, in one day, the congress amended Article 27 to read that responsibility for land reform lay with state governors. Within a few years, hundreds of thousands of parcels of ejido land had changed hands for foreigners to grow food for export.

---

**What are some of the similarities and differences in the political structure between your country and Mexico?**

**SIMILARITIES**                          **DIFFERENCES**

# Mexico's Political Party, the PRI

Although there are many similarities in the political structure of the United States and Mexico, in practice there are profound differences. In Mexico, one political party, the Institutional Revolutionary Party (Partido Revolutionario Institucional or PRI) controls the government and has controlled it since 1929. Every president since 1929 has been from the PRI (or its parent party the PRM), and has won with as much as 90 percent of the vote.

The PRI identifies itself with the Mexican Revolution, largely because it was originally organized to unite various revolutionary groups after the Mexican Revolution. The party is made up of different sectors, or interest groups, such as labor, agriculture and a popular sector that includes teachers, small business people, professionals, bureaucrats, youth and women. However, in the PRI's attempt to bring unity to Mexico, it has turned Mexico into a one party "democracy". In fact, many believe the Mexican presidency is more like a dictatorship.

The Mexican congress is essentially an arm of the PRI and is composed almost exclusively of PRI members. There are opposition parties, such as the conservative National Action Party (PAN) or parties who also claim the revolutionary tradition, such as the Democratic Revolutionary Party (PRD). However, these parties have few representatives in congress and have been considered to be little more than pressure groups until recently.

---

**1. What are the major political parties in your country? In Mexico?**
**2. Which party is the most powerful right now? Why?**

**YOUR COUNTRY**                                        **MEXICO**

The PRI is not just the majority party led by the president. The PRI holds legal authority to govern Mexico. Although states are supposed to have separate powers from the federal government, no one becomes a state governor without the approval of the president. The president is able to have governors removed from office, too. The president also appoints judges and the heads of the police, labor unions and farmers' groups. Although the military and political sectors are separate entities, top military officers always have had interests in line with the ruling PRI elite. The president has mechanisms to control the military and keep the army subordinate to the civil government.

One strategy used by the PRI to maintain political stability is called co-optation. When there has been dissent and people have pressured for reform, the PRI has incorporated these groups into their party. The largest workers' union in Mexico, the CTM, was brought into a formal relationship with the party in the late 1940s. When an opposition newspaper was published in the 1970s, the PRI allowed it to remain a voice of opposition, but put it under PRI control. As a result, the PRI includes—and controls—a wide range of political ideologies from left to right.

---

**1. What are some of the ways individuals and groups express their opposition to government policies and practices in your country? In Mexico?**

**2. What are some of the ways the government responds to political opposition in your country? In Mexico?**

**YOUR COUNTRY**                    **MEXICO**

# The PRI from 1934-1968

During the first years of the PRI and through the presidency of Lázaro Cárdenas (1934-1940) the government finally began to fulfill some of the promises of the Mexican Revolution. Efforts were made to bring about significant social changes that would benefit the majority of the people. Cárdenas worked to implement land reform and strengthen the labor movement. He doubled the budget for rural education and appointed a secretary of education to design new curricula for primary and secondary schools. To pay for these reforms, Cárdenas nationalized the holdings of oil companies operating in Mexico. The new oil monopoly, controlled by the Mexican government, was called PEMEX. Needless to say, companies like Standard Oil were outraged and some politicians in the US called for intervention in Mexico.

After Cárdenas' term, the pace of social reform slowed. The PRI leadership was more interested in expanding Mexico's economic base through industrialization. Mexico's economy grew steadily, as did the number of new millionaires. However, the increased wealth was not distributed equitably. Although there was the appearance of overall prosperity, large sectors of Mexican society were being left behind by "progress." Quality of life for the growing lower class was decreasing.

# Mexican Students Challenge their Government

By the mid 1960s many Mexicans, especially students, believed that this economic "progress" was at the expense of their freedom as guaranteed in the 1917 Constitution. When many university students studied economics and political science and then observed the reality around them, they recognized contradictions between the ideals of the Mexican Revolution and the reality of Mexico of 1968.

Octavio Paz, Mexican Ambassador to India in 1968 and renowned author, described Mexico in the 1960s:

> *In reality, our poor Revolution had long since been the victim of a two-fold takeover: it had been co-opted politically by the official government Party, a bureaucracy that is similar in more than one respect to the Communist bureaucracies of Eastern Europe, and it had been co-opted economically and socially by a financial oligarchy that had intimate ties to huge American corporations.*

(Elena Poniatowska, *Massacre in Mexico*, (NY: Viking Penguin Press, 1975) pp xiv-xv.)

---

## Reference

Information about Mexico's political system was drawn from *Democracy and Human Rights in Mexico* (New York: World Policy Institute, New School for Social Research, 1995).

# Students Confront the Government

### 1. Narrator's Announcement

Attention! Attention! Serious fighting has been reported in Mexico City. Last night, October 2, 1968, police and federal troops fired on university students when they were having a demonstration in the plaza at Tlatelolco (tlot-e-LOL-co). The government reports that twenty-nine people are dead and eighty are wounded. A spokesperson for the students says at least 500 were killed on the spot and 1000 are seriously wounded. How did this happen? Who is responsible? *Why* did this happen?  Let's go back to the beginning.

### 2. Reader

In Mexico in the mid-sixties, students complained that they had no voice in the government nor in the universities they attended. When they did try to speak out, the police brutally attacked them. When students had a strike at the National University in 1966, federal troops were sent in to restore order. What began as a grievance in 1968 quickly became a movement that attracted tens of thousands of Mexicans who were discontent with the government. The students focused their attention on the police, the corruption in the government and the unwillingness of the government tomeet with them. Basically the student movement was an attempt to confront the lack of true democracy in Mexico.

### 3. Reader

The following petition was issued by a committee of students in the summer of 1968. It addressed their concerns regarding police brutality and the issue of impunity, which means to not be punished for human rights' violations. Students sent the petition to Mexican President Gustavo Díaz Ordaz and distributed it widely throughout Mexico City.  This is what the petition requested:

### Six-point Petition:
1. *Disband the riot police force*
2. *Dismiss top police officials*
3. *Restore autonomy, or self-rule, to the National University of Mexico*
4. *Free all "political prisoners"*
5. *Repeal the anti-subversive article in the criminal code which punishes Mexicans for challenging the status quo*
6. *Compensate the wounded and the families of all those killed in clashes with the police*

### 4. Reader

In other parts of the world in 1968, students were challenging government policies and practices. Students organized demonstrations in Egypt, Italy, Yugoslavia, and Uruguay. In France, the university was closed down by student protesters. In the US, students —and others — were protesting the war in Vietnam and were involved in the civil rights movement. Most of these demonstrations were focused against the respective governments' policies and practices.

### 5. Reader

The Olympic Games were scheduled to begin in Mexico City on October 12, 1968. Millions of pesos went into the construction of stadiums, hotels, housing for athletes, and a new subway system to move the tourists around. The Olympics were an opportunity to show the world that Mexico was a modern, progressive country. Many Mexicans applauded this and wanted to increase tourism in Mexico. The Olympic Games were an opportunity to bring in millions of tourist dollars. Other Mexicans questioned the millions of pesos that were taken away from programs to alleviate widespread poverty among Mexicans.

### 6. Reader

In mid-August, as city workers were putting the finishing touches on the various construction projects before the Olympics, university students held a huge demonstration on their campus. The rally lasted well into the night, until the government moved tanks and armored cars into the area.

## Pause for Discussion

Why do you think the students chose this particular time for a demonstration?
What do you think happened next?

### 7. Narrator

At least one student was killed that night. In response to the confrontation with the students and the students' petition, the government issued this statement:

> The Government of the Republic is most willing to meet with the representatives of teachers and students at educational institutions connected with the present problem, in order to exchange views with them and acquaint itself directly with their demands and suggestions, with the aim of definitely resolving the conflict that our capital has experienced in recent weeks, a conflict which in fact has affected the lives of all its inhabitants to some degree. —Luis Echeverría, August 22, 1968. Secretary of Internal Affairs and future President of Mexico, 1970-76.[1]

### 8. Reader

The meeting the government proposed never took place. When students protested the brutal response of the government, the President of Mexico, Gustavo Díaz Ordaz, made the following remarks in his State of the Union address, September 1, 1968:

> We have been so tolerant that we have been criticized for our excessive leniency, but there is a limit to everything, and the irremediable (unacceptable) violations of law and order that have occurred recently before the very eyes of the entire nation cannot be allowed to continue.[2]

## Pause for Discussion

Imagine you were a government official in charge of student affairs.
How would you describe the student movement to the president?
What would you recommend that the government do?
Do you think this conflict could be settled without more violence at this point?

## 9. Narrator

Who are the people involved in the protests? Where do they come from? Why did they get involved in the student movement?

## 10. Reader

The people who were involved in the 1968 movement were mainly university students and intellectuals, although workers and artists in and around Mexico City joined the protests. Most of the students were from the middle class, including approximately a quarter from lower middle class families. These students generally were the first generation in their family to be able to get "higher education." Although many of the students benefited from the government's emphasis on education, they lacked an effective voice in their education or in the affairs of their nation.

## 11. Reader

University students in Mexico are accustomed to being involved in political discussions; challenging the system is expected of students. The universities are training grounds for politicians and the National University was designed to be autonomous, or free from outside control. In 1968, the student movement was a loosely-knit organization of students that did not have a specific ideology. They did have a goal, however, which was to open up the political process so their voices would be heard.

## 12. Reader

When asked how she got involved in the student movement, a University student replied, "I was totally and absolutely fed up with authoritarianism. I just couldn't take it any more. It was affecting every important thing in my life."
    — Human Rights Advocate[3]

## 13. Reader

*Young peasants, workers and students are facing a very dim future, since job opportunities are being created for the benefit of special interests rather than society as a whole. We are constantly told, "You are the future of the country." But we are constantly denied any opportunity to participate in the political decisions that are being made today...We want to and ARE ABLE to participate today, not when we are 70 years old.*
    — Gustavo Gordillo, student [4]

## 14. Reader

*Everybody shuts himself up in his own little world. Adults look to anything young people do as an attack on their principles and their moral code. That's the reason behind their illogical hostility toward long hair. What does long hair have to do with decency or whether a kid's good or bad? I like having long hair.*
    — Gustavo Gordillo, student [5]

### 15. Reader

Students made banners to carry at demonstrations and put handbills on every post they could find. They also made up chants that they repeated during marches. This is what they said:

**Mexico-Freedom-Mexico-Freedom-Mexico-Freedom**
-Chant at demonstrations

**THE AGITATORS ARE IGNORANCE, HUNGER, AND POVERTY**
-Banner at a demonstration

**PEOPLE, OPEN YOUR EYES!**
-Handbill

**DON'T SHOOT, SOLDIER: YOU'RE ONE OF THE PEOPLE TOO**
-Banner at a demonstration

---

## Pause for Discussion
How would you describe the students?
What do the students want?

---

### 16. Narrator

The student demonstrations attracted attention throughout Mexico. People responded with comments like these:

---

### 17. Reader

*I didn't get any kind of a formal education because my folks couldn't afford to send me to school. But if education nowadays is the sort that produces students like that, I'm glad I didn't go to school. I've never in my life seen such disrespectful, vulgar, foul-tongued people.*
— José Alvarez Castaneda, cab driver[6]

---

### 18. Reader

*The student movement is not the work of delinquents, nor does it intend to subvert Mexican institutions. The student leaders are ready and willing to initiate a dialogue with the highest authorities in the country.*
—Heberto Castillo, engineer [7]

---

### 19. Reader

*Students aren't worth a damn. When the government represses them, they retaliate by yelling and throwing stones. They do lots of shouting every time, but that's all. What's needed are firearms.*
— Cleofas Magdaleno Pantojo Segura, peasant [8]

---

### 20. Reader

*They're just a bunch of long-haired hippies.*
— Tlatelolco resident

## 21. Reader

*It took all our family savings to send our son to the University, and first thing we knew, he was involved in some protests. As soon as I learned what he was doing, I got on a bus, went to Mexico City, and brought him home.*
— Parent of a University student [9]

## 22. Reader

*The government is convinced there's only one public opinion in Mexico: the one that applauds it, that toadies to it. But there's another public opinion: one that criticizes, that doesn't believe a word the government says, and yet another one, one that doesn't give a damn, that turns a deaf ear to any more promises, that hasn't been taken in, that's indifferent, that no one has been able to take advantage of, a public opinion that despite its suspicious attitude and its ignorance is a free opinion.*
— José Fuente Herrera, engineer [10]

## 23. Reader

*What do you punks think you're doing? Do you really think you're such hot stuff you can overthrow the government? That'll be the day!*
— Police officer to student [11]

## Pause for Discussion
The above statements were taken from interviews by a journalist.
What are some of the different perceptions you find in these statements?
Why do you think there was such diverse reaction?
If you were interviewed about the student activists, what would you say?

## 24. Narrator

After the students sent their petition to the government, they continued to press for dialogue. Some of their protests were spontaneous actions, while others were in the form of strikes and rallies. Actions were coordinated by the student National Strike Committee. The police responded by occupying school campuses in the city. Following the government's orders, police arrested students they considered disorderly, and they injured hundreds of others.

## 25. Reader

In response to police occupation of the campus, students organized a demonstration that was called "the silent march." They distributed the following flyer that also included the six points from the petition:

**TO THE PEOPLE:**
*The National Strike Committee invites all workers, peasants, teachers, students and the general public to the*
**GREAT SILENT MARCH** *in support of our six-point petition:*

*We have called this march to press for the immediate and complete satisfaction of our demands by the Executive Power.*
*The day has come when our silence will be more eloquent than our words, which yesterday were stilled by bayonets.*[12]

**26. Reader**
One of the student organizers, Luis González de Alba, wrote this description of the Silent March which took place on Friday, September 13, 1968:

*The helicopter hovered overhead just above the treetops. Finally, at the appointed hour, 4:00 pm, the march began in absolute silence. This time the authorities could not even claim that we had provoked them by shouting insults. A number of delegates maintained that if the demonstration was a silent one, it would fail to show people how angry we were. Others said that none of the demonstrators would keep their mouths shut. What chance was there of controlling and shutting up several hundred thousand boisterous young people who were in the habit of singing and shouting and chanting at demonstrations? It was an impossible task, and if we failed it would betray the weakness of our organization. That's why the youngest kids wore adhesive tape over their mouths. They themselves chose to do that: they put tape over each other's lips to make sure they wouldn't make a sound. We told them, "If a single one of you fails, we all fail."* [13]

**27. Narrator**
*This is what happened next. As soon as we left Chapultepec (sha-PUL-tay-pec) Park, just a few blocks farther on, hundreds of people began to join our ranks. All along the Paseo de la Reforma, the sidewalks, the median strips, the monuments, and even the trees were full of people, and every hundred yards our ranks doubled. And the only sound from those tens of thousands and then hundreds of thousands of people were their footfalls. Footfalls on the pavement, the sound of thousands of marching feet, the sound of thousands of feet walking on, step by step. The silence was more impressive than the huge crowd. It seemed as though we were trampling all the politicians' torrents or words underfoot, all their speeches that are always the same....*

*Since we had resolved not to shout or talk as we had during the other demonstrations, we were able to hear—for the first time—the applause and the shouts of approval from the dense crowds supporting us along the line of march, and thousands of hands were raised in the symbol that soon covered the entire city and was even seen at public functions, on television, at official ceremonies: the V of Venceremos ("We shall win")...This symbol of unswerving, incorruptible, indomitable will appeared in the most unexpected places, from that time on till the massacre later. Even after Tlatelolco, the V kept appearing, even at the Olympic ceremonies, in the form of the people's two uplifted fingers.* [14]

**28. Reader**
After the Silent March a handbill was distributed throughout Mexico City that said, *You can see that we're not vandals or rebels without a cause—the label that's constantly been pinned on us. Our silence proves it.* [15]

**29. Reader**
The next day *The New York Times* gave this description of the September demonstration:

*...the students have plastered the walls and bulletin boards with revolutionary mottoes. In the School of Economics, quotations from Mao Tse-tung are seen...The auditorium of the School of Philosophy and Letters has been renamed 'Auditorium Ernesto Che Guevara,' and classroom doors have been painted with such names as 'Lenin Room' or 'Ho Chi Minh Room.' ...From almost all the students come expressions denoting great lack of respect for governing officials, the PRI, which has ruled under various names for almost 40 years...* [16]

## Pause for Discussion
What are the references used by The *New York Times* meant to imply?
What do you think its perspective is on the student movement?

### 30. Reader
*A policeman climbed up on the platform to speak at a meeting; he said he was a decent person, took his uniform off and stamped on it, and then asked us for money to go back to the part of the country he came from. He was so angry that tears were streaming down his face.*
— Julián Acevedo Maldonado, student [17]

### 31. Reader
*Mexico had never seen such huge and enormously enthusiastic spontaneous demonstrations as the ones organized by the students. There was one demonstration, in support of the Cuban Revolution, some years ago, but it was not nearly as wide in scope. The 1968 student movement really shook Mexican society to its foundations, and that's why the government began to be so afraid of it.*
— Félix Lucio Hernández Gamundi[18]

## Pause for Discussion
What do you think will happen next?
What do you think could be done now to prevent further violence?

### 32. Narrator
The place was Tlatelolco, a large plaza in Mexico City. The date was October 2, 1968. An estimated 4,000-10,000 people gathered in Mexico City at Tlatelolco to listen to student speakers demand that the government listen to their grievances. On that same night, Mexico's Interior and Defense Ministesr gave orders to the army to move in on the student protest at Tlatelolco.

### 33. Reader
At approximately 7:00 pm riot police moved into the crowd, swinging clubs and chains against protesters and spectators. People in the crowd tried to defend themselves, using rocks and bare fists. Snipers in a nearby building responded, supposedly to protect the crowd. Within minutes the army entered the area with armored vehicles and automatic weapons. Three hundred tanks, assault troops, jeeps and troop transports surrounded the entire area. Thousands of Mexicans were caught in crossfire. Anyone who moved was fired upon.

### 34. Reader
The terror lasted until 4:00 am, when the army crushed the demonstration and gained control. By then, at least 500 students and spectators were killed and at least a 1,000 were seriously wounded. Two thousand people were jailed. The incident took place on the same spot on which the Aztecs made their last stand of major resistance against the Spaniards under Cortés in 1521, which was the original *Noche Triste*. It is also the site of ancient Aztec human sacrifice rituals.

**35. Narrator**
A week later, the 1968 Olympic Games began in Mexico City as though nothing had happened.

**Read aloud**

## IN MEMORY OF TLATELOLCO

Darkness breeds violence
and violence seeks darkness
to carry out its bloody deeds.
That is why on October 2 they waited for nightfall
so that no one would see the hand
that held the gun, only its sudden lightening flash.

And who is there in the last pale light of day?
Who is the killer?
Who are those who writhe in agony, those who are dying?
Those who flee in panic, leaving their shoes behind?
Those who fall into the dark pit of prison?
Those rotting in a hospital?
Those who become forever mute, from sheer terror?

Who are they? How many are there? Not a one.
Not a trace of any of them the next day.
By dawn the following morning the Plaza had been swept clean.
The lead stories in the papers
were about the weather.
And on TV, on the radio, at the movie theaters
the programs went on as scheduled,
no interruptions for an announcement,
not a moment of reverent silence at the festivities.
(Because the celebration went right on, according to plan.)

Don't search for something there are no signs of now:
traces of blood, dead bodies,
because it was all an offering to a goddess,
the Eater of Excrement.
Don't search in the files, because no records have been kept.

But I feel pain when I probe right here: here in my memory
it hurts, so the wound is real. Blood mingling with blood
and if I call it my own blood, I betray one and all.

I remember, we remember.
This is our way of hastening the dawn,
of shedding a ray of light on so many consciences that bear a heavy burden,
on angry pronouncements, yawning prison gates,
faces hidden behind masks.
I remember, let us all remember
until justice comes to sit among us.

— *Rosario Castellanos* [19]

### 36. Narrator

News of the massacre at Tlatelolco spread throughout the world. In Paris, 2,000-3,000 students demonstrated in support of Mexican students and workers. Police took 400 persons into custody for identity checks after police clashed with students proclaiming their solidarity with students of Mexico.

---

### 37. Reader

International Olympic Committee President Avery Brundage announced that the Olympic Games would open in Mexico City as scheduled on October 12, 1968, despite the clash between students and the police.

---

### 38. Reader

Octavio Paz resigned his prestigious position as Mexico's Ambassador to India, because he felt he could no longer represent a country that murders its youth.

---

### 39. Reader

An editorial/letter to *The Times*, a London newspaper, states that *Mexico's prestige is being seriously affected by the disturbances and "bloodletting." Mexican President Gustavo Díaz Ordaz has decided that everything must be subordinated to restoring foreign confidence in 'Latin America's most stable country, and that everything is being done to reassure foreign investors and tourists that the country is stable.*
　　　　　*——The Times*, October 4, 1968 [20]

---

### 40. Reader

Mexico's Secretary of Finance returned from Europe on October 3, 1968 after meetings with European Foreign Ministers and representatives from the International Monetary Fund. The Secretary came with a large loan in his pocket, proof that confidence in Mexico was as strong as ever.

　　*The growth rate for 1968,* he said, *would certainly reach 7 percent and there had been no flight from the peso during the recent disturbances.*
　　　　　—*The Washington Post*, October 5, 1968[21]

---

### 41. Reader

Until recently, Mexican history textbooks have omitted the story of the 1968 Student Movement.

---

### 42. Reader

There was no mention of the Mexico City riots at a high-level conference on Mexico-United States affairs, held in Mexico in April 1969. A US representative stated, *Mexicans and Americans have common values and shared attitudes. Our two countries are committed to decency and justice; they are opposed to tyranny and oppression...*
　　　　　—Report of the Ninth Conference on the Mexico-United States Interparliamentary Group, 1969[22]

## 43. Reader

Two weeks later in a Mexican newspaper, the following editorial was printed:

*There was beauty and a bright glow in the souls of these dead youngsters. They wanted to make Mexico a land of truth and justice. They dreamed of a marvelous republic free of poverty and deceit. They were demanding freedom, bread, and schooling for those who were oppressed and forgotten, and were fighting to do away with the sad expression in the eyes of children, the frustration of teenagers, the cynicism of older people. In some of them there were perhaps the seeds of a philosopher, a teacher, an artist, an engineer, a doctor. But now they are merely physiological processes come to a sudden end inside skins cruelly ripped apart. Their death has wounded each and every one of us and left a horrible scar on the nation's life.*

— Editorial by José Alvarado, *Siempre!*, October 16, 1968 [23]

## 44. Narrator

Every year on October 2, memorial services are held to remember the victims of the student massacre. In 1993, on the 25th anniversary, a commemoration was held in the Plaza Tlatelolco, to which about 100,000 people came. Private citizens built a monument inscribed with the names of the known victims, and decorated it with flowers and candles.

As a result of this gathering, survivors met and formed a Truth Commission. They called upon lawyers, prominent Mexican leaders, and people concerned with human rights to investigate the actions of 1968. One of the first tasks was to find out how many people were killed and who they were. A member of the commission said,

*One of the first things that the members of the Commission did was to write to all of the responsible government officials and to get the files of 1968...And none of them has responded favorably. But people are coming in with their testimonies, and they are sending their testimonies. The trouble is that there was a lot of intimidation on these people not to talk."*

She goes on to say,

*This is a Truth Commission that emerges 25 years after an event in a regime that has basically remained unchanged, although there has been a tremendous move towards democracy in Mexico on the part of society. And it is a completely spontaneous civilian kind of effort with no government support whatsoever.*

— Human Rights Advocate [24]

## 45. Reader

*I think it has taken me about 25 years to realize and to understand what actually happened to us as a generation. Thanks to the 25-year commemoration, I think a lot of us now have, for the first time, been able to really sit down and talk about this.*

— Human Rights Advocate [25]

*An Exploring the Connections Lesson*

# Uprising in Chiapas
## *Analyzing the Media*

Everyone interested in contemporary Mexico faces the challenge of finding current, accurate information that represents a wide range of perspectives. Generally, the media presents the opinions of privileged people in positions of power, such as the president, governmental officials and business executives. Rarely does the mainstream media carry comments or analysis from the perspective of ordinary people.

This lesson focuses on one event—the uprising in Chiapas that began on January 1, 1994. The uprising began when thousands of people in the state of Chiapas in southern Mexico took up arms. Although their grandparents fought in the Mexican Revolution for economic, political and social reforms, the people still had not experienced significant improvement in their standard of living after almost 75 years. People in Chiapas were prepared to fight so their children and grandchildren could realize the promises of the past.

In this lesson, students are encouraged to find different accounts of the Chiapas uprising, including newspapers, journals, computer networks, films, etc. In addition, we have provided an interview with a person from Chiapas. Students are asked to compare and contrast the various sources to discern the perspectives and accuracy of the information.

| **Learner Objectives** | • | To gather and evaluate information from a variety of sources about the uprising in Chiapas, Mexico in January 1994. |
| | • | To develop skills for analyzing media coverage of Mexico. |

| **Concepts** | • | Media |
| | • | Perspective |
| | • | Bias |

| **Major Questions to be Addressed** | • | How does one find and evaluate information on current events? |
| | • | What are alternative sources of information? |
| | • | Why did some Mexican citizens resort to rebellion again in 1994? |

| **Exploring the Connections** | • | Information and news is basic to developing an understanding of the connections between peoples of North America. This lesson explores some of the ways we know about and understand one another as we learn about events and people across borders. |

| **Teaching Strategies** | • | Reading, Analysis, Discussion |

| **Materials Provided** | • | Analyzing the Media Worksheet (Handout 1) |
| | • | The Uprising in Chiapas (Handout 2) |

| **Additional Materials Needed** | | Student Journals |

| **Time Required** | | 1 class session, plus time to search for articles and information |

| **Preparation for Lesson** | • | Have students collect articles about the Chiapas uprising that began January 1, 1994. Use the computer and library to search for a variety of sources, including radio, TV, daily newspapers, and weekly periodicals. Try to include various sources, such as the *Christian Science Monitor, Wall Street Journal, New York Times, Miami Herald, World Press Review, Los Angeles Times, Report on the Americas* by NACLA, and Internet (try usi@infi.net). Tack articles on a bulletin board. |
| | • | Make two copies of Handout 1 for each student (one for the assignment prior to class and the other for use in class). |
| | • | Make one copy of Handout 2 for each student. |
| | • | On the day before the lesson, select 5-6 articles from the bulletin board that represent diverse viewpoints and styles of reporting. Include at least one article that is from Chiapas. Copy and divide the articles so each student has at least one to read prior to the lesson. Distribute Handout 1 to each student. Ask students to complete Handout 1 using the article they have read. |

# Sequence of Lesson

*Anticipatory Set*
*5 minutes*

1. Ask students where they go to find news about things that interest them. To whom do they talk or listen? What do they read? Follow up with a question about where they think people who are interested in Mexico, including Mexicans living in the US or Canada, would go to find news about the country.

*Body of Lesson*
*30-35 minutes*

2. Prior to class, list on the board the titles and sources of the articles the students read on Chiapas. Choose students to briefly summarize each article. Use Handout 1 to guide the reports and discussion. Using a show of hands, ask students which article they think is the most balanced and which they think is the most biased. Record the votes on the board next to the titles.

3. Distribute Handout 2, *The Uprising in Chiapas* written by Octavio Ruiz. As a native of Chiapas who now lives in the US, Octavio frequently responds to questions from secondary school students about his country. Ask students to read his interview silently or aloud in class and to answer the questions on Handout 1 based on the reading. Use Handout 1 as a guide to lead a discussion on *The Uprising in Chiapas*.

4. Expand the discussion. Ask students what the criteria for reporting the news should be. What kinds of sources are the best sources of information? Why?

*Closure*

5. In journals, write at least one page that begins "Things I still wonder about how the news is reported..."

*Evaluation*

Collect both copies of Handout 1 to assess students' work. During the next class, select 5-6 students to read their journal entries.

# Analyzing the Media

We get our news about current events from many places — TV, radio, lectures, personal experiences and print media, such as newspapers, magazines and newsletters. One of the most recent sources of news and information is computer networks, such as the World Wide Web of the Internet. Within hours of the January 1, 1994 uprising in Chiapas, computer screens around the world issued news written by the combatants themselves. Using a laptop computer, spokespersons for the Zapatistas, an army of Mayan Indians, sent communiqués throughout the globe "as a block against disinformation" of the Mexican government. As a result, many Mexicans and other citizens around the world have heard the words of the rebels themselves and have responded to their cause.

Most information goes through many filters before it is disseminated or circulated to the public. At one level, news producers and editors make decisions about which stories or events qualify as "news." They edit stories, shorten them, or ignore them all together. There are other, more subtle interpretations put on the news — the voice intonations of the radio commentator, the set used for TV coverage or the headlines of a newspaper article. All of this affects what news we see or hear and how it is interpreted by us. As consumers of news, we need to learn to decipher between facts, different interpretations, and the "spin" put on the events by commentators and others. Becoming a critical consumer of the news takes practice and commitment.

As you read, watch or listen to news accounts of the Chiapas uprising — or any news for that matter — think about and try to answer the following questions:

**Who is the author?**

**Who is the publisher?**

**Where is it published?**

**Is the coverage on-the-scene?**

**Who is quoted?**

**Is there enough information to understand the situation?**

Are there pictures? What do they show?

Describe what you think the author's point of view is. How do you think this point of view was formed?

Is this report designed to appeal to a certain audience?

What does the article claim was the cause of the problem?

What does the article claim has been the response to the problem?

What questions does the article raise or leave unanswered?

# The Uprising in Chiapas

*A Perspective from Chiapas by Octavio Ruiz*

Octavio Ruiz was born and raised in the state of Chiapas, Mexico. Before coming to the United States in 1988, he studied anthropology at the University of Chiapas. Since then he graduated from the University of Minnesota. Octavio frequently speaks to student groups in the US about the situation in Chiapas, where war broke out on January 1, 1994. The following article responds to questions students most commonly ask.

***Octavio, how do students find out about the situation in Chiapas?***

If I had been born in the US, perhaps I would not have heard about the Chiapas uprising. Maybe I wouldn't even know where Chiapas is located. If I did know, perhaps I would have heard about it in a two-second segment on the evening news or read about it in a two-inch article on the last page of a newspaper, in the lower right corner, beside the food coupons. If I was curious and had the sophistication and resources, I could get sufficient information through the Internet. Either way, the distance from the snowy north to the rainforest and mountains of southern Mexico might seem to be enough to justify ignorance about the subject. Personally, I cannot ignore it.

***Where are you from?***

I was born in the state of Chiapas, Mexico, in the Mayan area, which comprises southern Mexico, Guatemala, Belize, Honduras and El Salvador. I am Mayan Indian and I belong to the Mayan Tzotzil group. I came to live to the state of Minnesota in 1988. That was quite a change!

***What happened in Chiapas in 1994?***

On January 1, 1994, a war started in Chiapas. An army of 3,000 Mayan Indians stormed into four important cities in the state and several other small villages in the area. This army is the *Ejercito Zapatista de Liberación Nacional*, or EZLN, also called the Zapatistas. The following days the Mexican army of 25,000 soldiers arrived, equipped with US-made weapons, tanks, helicopters and airplanes. The Mexican army bombed villages and the battles were intense. The media reported there were 145 war casualties, many of whom were civilians. These civilians had nothing to do with the conflict, except they were Indian, and therefore, were suspected of collaborating with the EZLN.

There were massive arrests and torture of prisoners, who were both soldiers and civilians. National and international press reporting was hindered by the Mexican army, so news coverage was incomplete. Then, on January 12, the two armies agreed to a cease-fire and they began to negotiate for peace.

*Why did this war start? I thought Mexico was a stable country! Travel agencies show Mexico as a place where everybody smiles and enjoys the sunny beaches. The media portrays Mexico as a country ready to join the "First World." Didn't the US and Canadian governments just sign a trade agreement with Mexico?*

Yes, the North American countries did sign a trade agreement, NAFTA. But is Mexico a stable country where everyone is happy? No!

On January 1, 1994, Mexico's mask was taken off and Mexico's ugly face was revealed to the world. For years, the Mexican elite had tried to hide the problems in southern Mexico from foreign eyes.

There are three main reasons why the EZLN went to war: democracy, the North American Free Trade Agreement, and the 500 years of oppression which people in this continent have endured. Let me explain.

Democracy. It is a beautiful word that is pronounced with pride by most people in the US and Canada. Democracy is what my people are fighting for too! Isn't it ironic that the US government and US citizens are willing to sacrifice their young people in order to defend democracy abroad, but they do not support a small group of Mayan Indians who are willing to die for democracy? Instead the US government has chosen to support a 65-year dictatorship of one party rule in Mexico. This is the dictatorship of the Institutional Revolutionary Party, or what we call the PRI. Sixty five years!

You, my friends, you who know more about democracy than I do, please tell me if 65 years of one party in power is a real democracy?

The North American Free Trade Agreement. What does the fighting in Chiapas have to do with the NAFTA deal? In the first place, NAFTA was signed by the Mexican government with almost no participation of the Mexican Indian

population. The Mexican government says NAFTA will improve economic relations between the US and Canada by reducing tariffs and taxes. The EZLN believes NAFTA has a negative effect on the Indian people, not just in Chiapas, but throughout the country. NAFTA gives license to international business to exploit Indian labor for their profits. It legalizes the theft of my people's land. NAFTA also has a detrimental impact on the environment.

Furthermore, Mexico is not equipped to compete in the international markets, either technologically or financially. Going into NAFTA is like Mexico being invited to play a game of cards, but the other countries have all the aces. US farmers produce large quantities of corn in a few months with their modern machinery, while the Mexican Indian campesino can hardly produce one harvest a year. In Chiapas, we say "a good harvest happens only if the bank robbers are having a good day, the campesinos have voted for the PRI, and the ancient Aztec gods are in a good mood to send the rain!"

The third reason for the war in Chiapas is the 500 years of oppression which has been experienced by the Indian people of this continent.

*Discussion of the 500 years is heard repeatedly in this country. American Indian people talk about it all the time. But that was so long ago. What difference does it make today?*

For us, the first inhabitants of this continent, 500 years is not a long time ago. A long time ago is 65,000,000 years when the dinosaurs disappeared. But Indian people are still here. We are everywhere on this continent, trying to cope with the loss of culture / soul. We are trying "the new ways" to survive so that finally somebody will call us "civilized."

I remember the days of my childhood in Jovel. That's the Indian name for San Cristobal de las Casas, the second largest city in the state of Chiapas. Jovel is where those of us who understood our Mayan language were taught to be ashamed of it. We had to learn Spanish. Jovel is where, not long ago, an Indian had to get off the sidewalk so that the *ladino,* or Spanish descendant, could pass by. Jovel, the proud city of Spanish architecture where the *ladinos,* and those who deny any connection with their Indian past, will not mix with those who have committed the sin of being born brown and looking Indian, speaking an Indian language or dressing in Indian clothes. Racism and its unspoken rules still exist in that city and all over the state of Chiapas. Actually, it exists all over Mexico, and it doesn't stop at the borders.

***Let's go back to the Chiapas war. What happened after the fighting in January 1994?***

Peace talks took place between the two armies involved in the confrontation. On the one hand, the government tried very hard, they say, to agree to the demands of the EZLN. Meanwhile, the politicians in power assassinated each other. For their part, the EZLN made a major effort to hold their fire. The high command of the EZLN called several times for "national democratic conventions," or meetings of different sectors to discuss solutions. I think these national democratic conventions have demonstrated the willingness of the Zapatistas to resolve the conflict in a peaceful way. Furthermore, the national democratic conventions have demonstrated the capabilities of the civilians in Mexican society to achieve democracy.

In August, 1994, presidential and state elections were held in Mexico. The results were another slap in the face of the Mexican Indian and in particular to the efforts of the Zapatistas to achieve democracy in the country. Why? Because once again, candidates from the PRI party won the elections. Although an effort was made to monitor the elections, there is proof of a great deal of fraud in Chiapas.

***What happened to the Mexican Revolution? I thought the goals of the revolution were to redistribute the land and improve the standard of living for all Mexicans, including Indian people. What went wrong in Chiapas?***

It is paradoxical that the state of Chiapas, which is one of the richest states in natural resources, is also one of the poorest. People in my state still die of diarrhea and other curable diseases, such as pneumonia and chicken pox. There are hardly any medical services for the Indian population and let's not forget education; education is a luxury in the Indian villages.

***What do you think needs to happen to bring about peace in Mexico?***

My feeling about the state of Chiapas and in general about Mexico is that there needs to be change, a radical change in the way Mexican "democracy" is being handled. Otherwise other groups will rise just as the Mayans in Chiapas have done.

# At What Price?

## *A Simulation on Mexican Economic Culture*

Students often have a difficult time understanding the ways in which economic structures, social class, and culture influence people's economic realities. When discussing the fairness of a competitive market economy in the United States, some students may argue that the poor are unwilling to work hard and learn skills to improve their economic situation. Others may argue that the poor face significant challenges and constraints in their climb out of poverty. Students form these ideas, in part, from frequent debates about issues such as wealth distribution among citizens, politicians, business leaders, and the media. Given the context of an increasingly global economy, students undoubtedly form ideas and impressions about the ways other economies function as well.

Students are exposed to numerous images of peoples' lives in Mexico and Central and South America, yet it may be difficult for them to identify with the circumstances in which many people live. In order to help students experience how Mexicans might function within a given social and economic context, this simulation gives students an opportunity to experience the daily social and economic struggles that occur in Mexico.

This lesson may seem complicated when you first read the instructions. Don't despair! When students follow their assigned role they quickly catch on. Any simulation contains significant generalizations and simplifications. Educators and participants should understand that while exercises such as this have limitations, they also can help students to experience, at least superficially, complex issues and events.

| | |
|---|---|
| **Learner Objectives** | • To practice critical thinking, problem-solving and negotiating skills as students simulate a real-life conflict concerning economic conditions in Mexico. |
| | • To describe differences in economic and social power between people of different social classes. |
| **Concepts** | • Social Class |
| | • Market economy |
| **Major Questions to be Addressed by Lesson** | • How does economic reality differ for people of different social classes in Mexico? |
| | • How does the structure of the Mexican economy influence these economic realities? |
| **Teaching Strategies** | Simulation, Discussion |
| **Materials Provided** | • Rules Sheet (Handout 1) |
| | • Group Description Sheets (Handouts 2a - 2c) |
| | • Educator Worksheet |
| | • Goal Sheet (Image 1) |
| | • Social Class Designator Cards (Image 2) |
| | • Goods and Services Cards (Image 3) |
| | • Play money (Image 4) |
| **Materials Needed** | • Box for the "bank" and visor or hat for the banker |
| | • Stopwatch for timing the "days" (optional) |
| | • Overhead projector and transparency (optional) |
| **Time Required** | 1-2 class sessions |
| **Preparation for this Lesson** | • Make 1 copy of Handout 1 for each student. |
| | • Make enough copies of Handout 2 for students to share in small groups. |
| | • Determine the number of students per social class. Photocopy Image 2 to make small cards that designate the social class and cut into individual pieces. |
| | • Determine the money you will need for the simulation using the Educator Worksheet. After calculating the total amount needed, add 75 $1 bills for the bank. Copy, using Image 4, and cut up the needed amount of play money. |
| | • Determine the number of goods and services cards using the Educator Worksheet. Photocopy Image 3 as noted. |

**Basic Necessity Cards     GREEN**
Worth $1—represent the basics such as food and clothing. Everyone needs a minimum of one green card every day.

**Middle Class Items Cards     BLUE**
Worth $5—represent middle-class housing, educational opportunities, appliances, etc.

**Luxury Cards      GOLD**
Worth $20—represent items available generally to the elite, such as expensive homes, fancy cars, travel abroad and private education.
**Labor Cards    RED**
Value varies—represent work units worth one day's labor. The workers give them to their employers when they are hired and should receive some payment in return at the end of the day.

- Prepackage the money and cards, clipping them together, for each student in advance of the simulation.
- Give students the Rules Sheet (Handout 1) prior to class to read; ask them to bring the Rules Sheet to class. Have extra copies on hand for students who forget their copies.
- Make a transparency of the Goal Sheet (Image 1) to display during the simulation. (Optional)

# Sequence of Lesson

*Introduction*
*15 minutes*

1. Explain that peoples' lives are intimately linked to their country's economic structure. This is a simulation of Mexico's economy; however the same dynamics apply to most other countries, including the US and Canada.

   Ask for a volunteer to be the banker. Give him/her the bank box. Have the rest of the students draw a social class designation (Image 2) from a bowl and divide students into three social groups in separate areas of the room. Distribute the prepackaged money and cards. The income disparity gives students a feeling for the initial inequality in society.

2. Make sure students have a copy of the *Rules Sheet*. Explain the roles the various social classes play in society so students can identify with the class in which they find themselves. For instance, tell the Upper Class that they are wealthy entrepreneurs and large landowners. The Middle Class students most likely represent store owners, health care providers and government workers. The Lower Class students should identify with teachers, factory employees and other workers, subsistence farmers, street vendors, etc. Distribute copies of the *Group Description sheets* (Handout 2) to members in each group and ask them to read this either individually or in the group. Instruct students to think about their group's goals and strategies, as listed on the *Rules Sheet*.

3. Review the goals and responsibilities of the individuals in the various social classes (have students follow along on the *Rules Sheet*). For instance, since the Middle Class represents the mercantile aspect of the culture, it is given Blue Cards and Gold Cards to sell.

*Body of Lesson*
*30 minutes*
*for simulation*

4.  Begin the simulation. The actual simulation time is divided into four "days," each of which is 5 to 7 minutes long. Teachers can vary the length of the "days" according to how the interaction is progressing. At the end of each "day," allow some extra time so students can assess what they have acquired and what they still need to purchase or sell. Encourage students to strategize among their sectors to figure out ways to "survive."

    During each of the "days" the Middle Class sells Blue and Gold Cards to the Upper Class, while members the Lower Class try to sell their labor (Red Cards) and basic necessities (Green Cards) to the Middle Class and Upper Class. Labor can be bought and sold on a daily basis or contracted for all the "days." Encourage members of both the Upper and Middle Classes to hire the workers to buy and sell goods and services for them. Members of the Lower Class may use this as an opportunity to make additional money.

    All students must pay a one-time $2 tax at some time during the simulation, no matter what their income, although some may creatively avoid payment. The purpose of this is to help them appreciate the inequities of a non-differentiated tax structure. The instructor is encouraged to take on this task as a way of interacting with students. Students' hands may be stamped to indicate they have paid the tax.

    Students should begin to interact quickly, and negotiating, bargaining, buying and selling will fill the classroom. You may wish to put on the overhead a copy of the *Goals Sheet* to avoid having to answer questions during the simulation.

    The instructor should keep the time for each day. The instructor may need to intervene if students decide, for example, to "quit" the simulation and migrate to the United States. In this instance, you may need to act as an INS agent and not allow students to enter the US. The instructor also may wish to suggest quietly that workers unionize or form some other form of collective arrangement. The instructor should try to avoid intervening if events like theft of money and cards occur.

    Before the last day begins, announce there is a crisis. The lack of rain throughout Mexico has resulted in widespread shortages of food. Therefore, everyone must obtain one additional green basic necessity card in order to survive.

6.  After the last day of the simulation, tally the cards. Students should first make sure they possess the required cards necessary for their survival. If they do not have the necessary cards, they must subtract the face value of the missing cards from their cash holdings. For instance, if one from the Lower Class has only 3 Green cards instead of the required 4, s/he would subtract $1 from the total cash holdings.

    The second step in the tally process is for students to tally their total assets (cards and money) for their grade. This demonstrates the serious nature of economic realities—that for many people their very survival is at stake. You may wish to put the following grading scale on the board for the students' reference. If the student fails to meet the minimum requirement, they in effect fail to "survive."

A= over $76;  B = $61 - 75;  C = $41 - 60;
D = $20 - 40;  F = below $20.

*Discussion*
*20 –30 minutes*

6. After you have ended the simulation, facilitate a discussion by asking students to relate what happened to them during the simulation and how they responded. Other discussion questions could include:

To all students:
• How did you feel about the way the other social classes treated you?
• What strategies did you use in the simulation?

To members of the Lower Class:
• How did you react when you saw that there would not be enough work for all the workers and peasants and that you might starve?
• Was there competition between people of the Lower Class or did people pretty much stick together?  Why?

To the Middle Class and Upper Class:
• When you hired people to work, how did you decide how much to pay? Was it enough for them to survive?
• Were you worried that the poor might unite and demand higher wages or overthrow the system of ownership? Did you do anything to prevent this from happening?
• What would determine whether you would help the Lower Class try to make conditions in your country more fair?

Final Question:
• What do you think the future of this economic system will be?

*Closure*

Ask students to write about their reactions to the simulation in their journals and how they might respond to their situation. Explain that the economic realities many Mexicans face forces them to make difficult decisions in order to survive. One of these decisions is whether to leave family and friends to search for better opportunities.

This simulation is adapted from Bruce and Sharon Reichenbach's article "Simulating Latin American Economic Culture," *Social Education* 55(3), 1991 and from "Life and Land in El Salvador," in *El Salvador: Conflict and Change*, Resource Center of the Americas, 1992.

# RULES SHEET

**Goal**  Your goal is to survive and support your family. For some, your goal may be to increase your power and status, which is represented by your money. With the money given out at the beginning of the game you will buy and sell goods (basic necessities, other items, or luxury goods) and pay for work performed. Your money and cards will be totaled at the end and used to buy your grade for the day.

**Time**  The simulation time will be divided into four "days." Each day lasts about six minutes. At the end of each day you will return to your respective social class to evaluate what you have bought and sold.

**Roles**  10 percent—Upper Class (Large landowners, wealthy entrepreneurs)
20 percent—Middle Class (store owners, government workers)
70 percent—Lower Class (peasant farmers, teachers, workers)
1 Banker

**Cards**  Labor (Red) = Work units are worth one day's work.  Give to your employer when you are hired.
Basic Necessities (Green) = $1 - Basics such as food and clothing
Middle-class Items (Blue) = $5 - Items such as appliances, education, housing
Luxury Items (Gold) = $20 - Items such as mansions, cars, travel, private education

## UPPER CLASS
You will begin with $200.
Responsibilities:
1.  You must buy 8 green cards, 4 blue cards and 4 gold cards. You will be docked  the value of any missing cards (Blue, Green, Gold or Red) at the end of the simulation.  Extra cards have no monetary value.
2.  You (or someone you hire to do so) must hire 3 workers for each of 4 days, so that at the end of the simulation you will have employed at least 12  worker-units and have 12 Red cards. You are responsible for ensuring that these workers are hired. Minimum wage is $2 a day, but you can pay what you want and the workers probably will accept.  You may send your workers out to purchase items you need.

## MIDDLE CLASS
You will begin with $20, 6 Blue cards, and 2 Gold Cards to sell or keep.  You will get additional money by selling goods in the form of cards.
Responsibilities:
1.  You must have 8 Green Cards and 5 Blue Cards at the end of play. You will be docked  the value of any missing cards (Blue, Green, Gold or Red) at the end of the simulation.  Extra cards have no monetary value.
2.  You must hire 1 worker for each day, so that at the end of 4 days you will have employed at least 4 worker-units and have 4 Red cards.  Minimum wage is $2 a day, but you can pay what you want and the workers probably will accept. You may send your workers out to purchase items you need.

## LOWER CLASS
You will begin with $10, 8 Green Cards and 4 Red cards. You will get additional money by selling Green cards (produce) and Red cards (labor) to members of other social classes. Begging and other forms of creative income arrangements are allowed.
Responsibilities:
1.  At the end of 4 days you must have 4 Green cards. You will be docked the value of any missing Green cards at the end of the simulation. Any extra cards have no monetary value.

## BANKER
You will begin with $75 in small bills.
Responsibilities:
1.  You will set up a desk in the room to serve as your bank. Your job will be to change money when people need smaller bills and to make loans to individuals, depending on their ability to repay or if they are friends. You should charge an interest rate of at least 50%. On the last day, you may want to close the bank to collect the loans due the bank. You may hire someone to help you with collections.

**Tax:**  Everyone pays a one-time flat fee of $2 to the tax collector.

**Grades:**  Total your money and subtract the face value of the cards you are missing.  DO NOT ADD THE VALUE OF THE REQUIRED CARDS TO YOUR MONETARY SUM.

## Group Description
# UPPER CLASS

**You represent about 10% of the population of Mexico.**
**You probably are a large landowner or a wealthy entrepreneur.**

### If you are a large landowner...

...you are part of an elite group that owns over 60% of Mexico's agricultural land. You are very, very wealthy—a millionaire. You grow cotton, wheat, sugar, coffee and other crops for export, because you can make more money on these export crops than you can growing corn, beans and vegetables for consumption within Mexico. Most of the exports from your plantation are shipped to the US, Canada or Europe and you make a large profit. You often travel to the US and you have a house in Miami. You have many friends in the US and Canada, some of whom are very influential.

You hire peasants to work on your plantation. You see your role as one of providing jobs and creating wealth. You strongly believe in the free enterprise system. You pay the workers very little, but they take the jobs because there are no other jobs available.

You know that many Mexicans are poor and do not own any land. You know that they want land to grow food to feed themselves and their children. You believe that if they did receive land, they would not know how to farm it. You also may feel threatened, because you are outnumbered by the massive numbers of poor people who want land. To enable you to feel more secure, you might consider hiring a couple of peasants, fairly cheaply, to guard your plantation and be your bodyguards.

### If you are a wealthy businessperson...

...you probably oversee several large manufacturing operations that have international connections. Your companies produce all kinds of products for export to the United States and Europe, including clothing, automobile parts and other manufactured goods. Sales to the US are booming, and you are very proud that the company is so successful financially.

You believe that it is important to keep unions from gaining strength in your Mexican factories. If unions are successful, you are concerned that this will open the door for other workers to organize throughout other local factories, thereby driving up wages and forcing your company to spend money things like benefits, such as health and child care. Your bottom line is your responsibility to company shareholders to continue to make a profit for them.

## Group Description
# MIDDLE CLASS

### You may be a store owner, a health care provider or a government worker...

...you live in a small house or apartment furnished with a TV and radio. You own a car, but it is expensive and you live on a fairly tight budget. You would like to be able to buy things to make life a little easier, such as a new refrigerator or even a microwave oven, but you just aren't able to get ahead.

You know there are people much poorer than you, and you know that things are unfair in Mexico. Sometimes, church workers and community organizers ask you to join them to work for change, but often you feel that to keep what you have safe, you'd better not say anything. You could join those who are working for and demanding a more fair distribution of the land and just wages, but to do so might be risky.

Besides, there isn't much that you can do to solve the big problems in Mexico. The country has some major problems, and sometimes all you want to do at the end of the day is just come home and watch TV. On TV, you see how the wealthy people live in Mexico and the rest of North America. You dream about owning a fancy house or car like they have. Even if that is a fantasy, you wish that you could take a vacation to a beautiful place, or afford to send your daughter or son to a good university in the United States. Sometimes, you think about getting another job so that you could afford some of those luxuries in life.

## Group Description
# LOWER CLASS

### You own little except for your ability to work...

...Mexico has very high unemployment, and it is extremely difficult to find a job. You and your children are undernourished. You live in a house with dirt floors, outdoor latrines and running water that is available only a few hours during the night. Your home's exterior walls are made of scrap wood, corrugated metal, or mud with whitewash covering. The roof is corrugated metal—on hot days the house is like an oven; on rainy days the noise inside is deafening.

You want a job that pays a living wage, or land on which you can grow corn and vegetables for yourselves and your children. You want access to health care and wish your children would be able to go to school. You are well aware of the inequalities in Mexico. You know things need to change. You also know that people who speak out are often beaten or "disappeared."

You can try to convince the wealthy plantation owner that you are a very good worker, and that s/he should hire you. You can go to the factory to apply for an assembly job because there a few openings. Someone has to be hired. Or you can sell candy that you make to people on the streets, but you need to save money in order to buy ingredients.

You may turn to crime and steal from people who own property.

You can join together together with other people to demand land distribution or jobs. You can ask others to help you. But there may be consequences to these actions.

You can try to find a better life in another country.

# EDUCATOR WORKSHEET

Compute the number of cards/money you will need to begin the simulation by multiplying the number of students in your class by the following formula. When you have finished calculating the total number of cards and total amount of money needed for each social class (Upper Class, Middle Class and Lower Class), add each of these subtotals to determine the total amount needed for the simulation.

---

**UPPER CLASS** - 10%
*Calculate the number of students in this category:*
10% multiplied by # of students= x students

**Cards**:  None

**Money**:
$200 multiplied by ____ students = $____
*(Give mostly in denominations of $20s, but include some $10s and $5s.)*

*EXAMPLE: For a class with 30 students, you would make the following calculations:*
10% multiplied by 30 students = 3 students

**Cards**:  None

**Money**
$200 multiplied by  3  students = $ 600

---

**MIDDLE CLASS** - 20%
*Calculate the number of students in this category:*
20% multiplied by # of students = x students

**Cards**
6 Blue cards multiplied by ___ =___Blue cards
2 Gold cards multiplied by ___ =___Gold cards

**Money**
$20 multiplied by ____ students =$_____
*(Give in $10, $5 and 5 $1 denominations.)*

*EXAMPLE:*
*For a class with 30 students:*
20% multiplied by 30 students = 6 students

**Cards**
6 Blue cards multiplied by 6 = 36 Blue cards
2 Gold cards multiplied by 6 = 12 Gold cards

**Money**
$20 multiplied by  6  students = $ 120

---

**LOWER CLASS** - 70%
*Calculate the number of students in this category:*
70% multiplied by # of students = x students

**Cards**
8 Green cards mult. by ___ =___Green cards
4 Red cards multiplied by ___ =___Red cards

**Money**
$10 multiplied by ___ students = $_____
*(Give in $1 denominations.)*

*EXAMPLE: For a class with 30 students:*

70% multiplied by 30 students =  21  students

**Cards**
8 Green Cards multiplied by 21 = 168
4 Red Cards multiplied by 21 = 84

**Money**
$10 multiplied by 21 students = $ 210

---

**BANKER**
1 student

**Money**
$75 in single dollar bills.

> **FOR 30 PARTICIPANTS**
> Total Gold cards needed: 12
> Total Blue cards needed: 36
> Total Green cards needed: 168
> Total Red cards needed: 84
> Total money needed: $1005

# GOALS: At the end of the simulation, you should have:

**UPPER CLASS**
8 Green cards
4 Blue cards
4 Gold cards
12 Red cards

**MIDDLE CLASS**
8 Green cards
5 Blue cards
4 Red cards

**LOWER CLASS**
4 Green Cards

## EVERYONE

You will be docked the value of any missing cards (Blue, Green, Gold, or Red) at the end of the simulation.

## How to Tally your Score:

1. The chart above lists the color & number of cards you should have. Check what you have against this chart.

2. For each card that you are missing, subtract the value of that card from your money. Cards are worth the following amounts: Gold: $20 each, Blue: $5 each, Green: $1 each.

3. Add up your cash and the value of your remaining cards to determine your grade.

# Social Class Designator Cards

By chance you were born
into the Upper Class

By chance you were born
into the Lower Class

By chance you were born
into the Upper Class

By chance you were born
into the Lower Class

By chance you were born
into the Upper Class

By chance you were born
into the Lower Class

By chance you were born
into the Lower Class

By chance you were born
into the Middle Class

By chance you were born
into the Lower Class

By chance you were born
into the Middle Class

By chance you were born
into the Lower Class

By chance you were born
into the Middle Class

By chance you were born
into the Lower Class

By chance you were born
into the Middle Class

By chance you were born
into the Lower Class

By chance you were born
into the Middle Class

By chance you were born
into the Lower Class

By chance you were born
into the Middle Class

# GOODS & SERVICES

| | |
|---|---|
| **Basic Necessities** food, clothing | **Basic Necessities** food, clothing |
| **Basic Necessities** food, clothing | **Basic Necessities** food, clothing |
| **Middle Class Items** appliances, better education | **Middle Class Items** appliances, better education |
| **Luxury Items** fancy cars/ houses, vacations | **Luxury Items** fancy cars/ houses, vacations |
| **Labor** | **Labor** |

# MONEY

| | |
|---|---|
| $1 | $1 |
| $1 | $1 |
| $5 | $5 |
| $10 | $10 |
| $20 | $20 |

*An Exploring the Connections Lesson*

# Who is Being Fed?

## *Food Pathways in North America*

The foods we eat every day usually have traveled a long way before they enter our mouths. Unless we raise our own food, we rarely are aware of where food comes from or the circumstances surrounding its production. Food is something everyone has in common; it links all people together through a universal necessity. Food is an excellent theme to help students cross borders and consider their connection with others.

Prior to the lesson, students should read a background piece on Mexico's agricultural system. It includes primary sources that present a variety of perspectives about the complex topic of food and the globalization of the agricultural system. This is difficult reading, but we think it is important for students to gain familiarity with the concepts.

The lesson activity is a tour of the stages of production for a tomato we call *Tomasito*. The tomato is grown in Mexico from a seed hybridized in the US and then eaten in Canada. After students read about this food pathway, they are given hypothetical problems that could interrupt the production and distribution. They are asked to help solve the problems. This hypothetical tour is based on information from an education kit, *Economic Integration of the Americas* (see bibliography).

For an extension to this lesson, we suggest showing the video, "Dirty Business: Food Exports to the US," produced by the Manitoba Labour Education Committee. The video focuses on the problems of those working for a transnational corporation which operates in Mexico. The video explores the problems of low wages, child labor, weak labor laws and the devastating pollution caused by corporate farming and food processing. The video presents a strong critique of food corporations, so you may want to balance the assessment of the food export industry with a different point of view such as a speaker from a transnational corporation or the Department of Labor or Commerce. If this is not possible, get information from the public library on a transnational food corporation to gain its perspective.

| Learner Objectives | • To explain Mexico's complex agricultural system. |
| --- | --- |
| | • To trace the production and distribution of foods that link Mexico, the US and Canada. |
| | • To articulate a personal perspective on one's choices regarding food and the food system. |

| Concepts | • Agricultural system |
| --- | --- |
| | • Traditional and non-traditional crops |
| | • Transnational corporations |
| | • Global economy |
| | • Food security |

| Major Questions to be Addressed | • How might one characterize Mexico's agricultural system? |
| --- | --- |
| | • What are the connections via food between consumers in the US and Canada, and producers in Mexico? |
| | • What are some of the consequences of the North American agricultural system, such as patterns of land ownership, diversity of food products, cost, effect on the environment, and the health and safety of the producer and consumer? |

| Exploring the Connections | Students investigate their connections to Mexico via its agricultural products. The pathway of the tomato demonstrates the complex linkages between Mexico, the US and Canada. |
| --- | --- |

| Teaching Strategies | Reading, writing, small group work |
| --- | --- |

| Materials Provided | • Mexico's Agricultural System: Who is being Fed? (Handout 1) preparatory reading |
| --- | --- |
| | • Tomasito's Tour (Handout 2) |
| | • Tomasito's Troubles (Handout 3) |

| Additional Materials | Newsprint and Markers |
| --- | --- |

| Time Required | 2 class sessions |
| --- | --- |

| Vocabulary | • *Ejido* |
| --- | --- |
| | • *Campesino* |

| Preparation for Lesson | • Make one copy of Handout 1 and distribute it prior to class as homework. Ask students to circle the key concept in each section of the reading and to jot down questions that arise. |
| --- | --- |
| | • Make one copy of Handout 2 for each student. |
| | • Make one copy of Handout 3 and cut into seven sections. |

## Sequence of Lesson

| *Anticipatory set* *10 minutes* | 1. In class, introduce the idea of exploring the origin of foods we eat, emphasizing imports from Mexico. Ask volunteers to tell you what they ate the day before. Write foods on the board. Ask students to hypothesize about which foods came from Mexico and why they were imported. |
| --- | --- |

*Body of Lesson*
*50-60 minutes*

2. Ask students to summarize the article, *Mexico's Agricultural System*, prior to class. List the key concepts and the questions generated from the article on the board. Encourage discussion.

3. The next activity is an exploration of the connections between Mexico, the US and Canada via *Tomasito the Tomato*. Remind students that the tomato has been grown in Mexico by Indian peoples for thousands of years. It is still grown in Mexico, but many tons of tomatoes are now shipped north to the US and Canada. Distribute Handout 2 and take turns reading it aloud.

4. Divide into seven groups. Give each group newsprint, a marker and one of the sections from Handout 3, *Tomasito's Troubles*. Instruct members of each group to read their problem and talk about it. Write the following questions on the board to guide students' discussion and preparation for a presentation:
   • What is the trouble?
   • What are the effects of the trouble at your stop?
   • What are the effects of the trouble at the other stops?
   • What do you recommend for solving the problem?

   Students need to decide how to present their problem to the class using the newsprint and markers.

5. Reconvene the class and starting with Stop 1, ask small groups to read their problem aloud and make a presentation based on their responses to the four questions. Explain that the troubles are hypothetical, but they are to conider them as though they could actually happen. Follow-up with a discussion about their observations and these suggested questions:

   • What surprises you about the agricultural system that links Mexico, the US and Canada?
   • What do you think are some of the positive and negative outcomes of this system? *(impact on land ownership, diversity of food products, cost, effect on the environment, and the health and safety of the producer and consumer, etc.)*
   • What would take for there to be changes in the food system? What kinds of changes would you like to see?

   Option: For group presentations, have students act out their stop, their problem and their recommendations.

*Closure*

6. Explain that the tomato is only one example of the many products that link Mexico, the US and Canada. The choices we make for much of the food we eat has a ripple effect throughout North America. Food sustains people, but often the system of food production does not. Ask students to discuss or write about how consumers can be involved in creating a more equitable and sustainable food system.

# Mexico's Agricultural System: Who is Being Fed?

*In 1990, Mexico was the third largest export market for US agricultural commodities, including wheat, corn and dairy products. US exports to Mexico were $28 billion.*

*In 1990, Mexico was the second largest supplier of US agricultural imports, including coffee, vegetables, fruits, nuts and cattle. Mexican exports to the US were $31 billion.*

*Mexico is one of the wealthiest nations in the world, judged by its place as one of the top 15 food-producing countries and one of the largest oil producers. Yet, an estimated 40 to 50% of the population have not been able to obtain minimum levels of calories for adequate health, growth and a productive life.*

—Statistics from *Poverty and Hunger: A World Bank Policy Study*
(Washington, DC, 1990)

## Who is Being Fed?

Global trade is bringing US and Canadian consumers a year-round supply of fresh flowers; fresh and processed fruits such as tomatoes, melons, pineapples, strawberries, and mangos; and fresh vegetables such as artichokes, cucumbers, cabbage, cauliflower, green beans, peppers, broccoli, snow peas and asparagus. All these are flown in daily from Mexico. In addition, there are the traditional exports that feed Mexico's northern neighbors, such as sugar, coffee, bananas and cattle. During the winter and spring, over half of the fresh vegetables that are consumed in the US come from Mexico.

The growth of these exports have bittersweet outcomes, depending on one's perspective. These products have proven very profitable for foreign investors, transnational food corporations and many large-scale Mexican farmers. These exports both satisfy the appetites of North American consumers and create jobs in Mexico. On the other hand, these exports have serious economic, personal and environmental effects, and cause grave problems for small-scale farmers, or *campesinos* (cahm-pay-SEE-nohs).

## Mexico's Dual Agricultural Structure

Mexico has essentially two agricultural systems, operating parallel to each other. Producing foods as cash crops for export is the primary goal of large-scale farmers. Although only about 15% of Mexico's land is arable, or suitable for cultivation, 88% of the arable land is used for cultivation of export crops and for grazing cattle. What large-scale farmers produce is determined by what brings the highest prices in international markets. Since the 1970s, most large-scale farmers have been producing the non-traditional crops listed above. They sell to transnational corporations that process or directly transport the products to warehouses and eventually to grocers.

Among the beneficiaries of the large-scale agricultural system are transnational corporations, such as Del Monte, Green Giant, Heinz, United Brands, Castle and Cooke, PepsiCo, Ralston Purina, Campbell's, General Foods, Beatrice Foods, Gerber, Kellogg, Kraft and Nestlé. Rarely do these corporations own land. Instead, they contract with large-scale farmers. The corporations have capital to invest in technology, seeds, fertilizers and pesticides, transport systems and marketing.

The other agricultural system involves about 60% of Mexico's farmers who have access to the remaining 12% of arable land. This includes individual small-scale farms that produce for local markets, and farms known as *ejidos*. Ejidos are a system of community-owned lands which, in some cases, have been owned "in trust" by communities for centuries. Ejido lands were protected from sale as a result of the Mexican Revolution. However, a significant amount of ejido land passed into private hands during the 1980s and 1990s due to extreme credit pressures and changes to Article 27 of the Mexican Constitution. These constitutional changes allow, for the first time since the Revolution, the sale of ejido land to private owners. The changes were a crucial concession by Mexico to ensure the passage of the North American Free Trade Agreement in 1993.

Ejido lands rarely have been more than

subsistence farms, where corn and beans are grown for the consumption of campesinos and their families. They have, however, provided a way for poor families to at least provide basic grains for themselves. With the on-going loss of ejidos to private producers and the general inability of campesinos to gain access to other arable land, there is a growing problem of malnutrition in Mexico. It is estimated that half of all rural Mexican children are malnourished.

Furthermore, small-scale farmers have considerable difficulties competing with large-scale farms because they lack access to money for seeds, water, transportation and information required for success in agribusiness. They tend to be unfamiliar with non-traditional crops and production

technology. Gaining entry into the export market is very difficult for small farmers, if that is what they choose to do.

## A Mexican Campesino

To give you a better idea of the challenges small farmers face, here is the story of one man named Emetario Pantaleón.

"The old man works the earth most days before the sun pulls itself over the eastern ridges. With his horse grazing on the grassy borders of his field, he stoops over the black dirt, tilling the soil, removing weeds, and harvesting fresh vegetables and herbs. Those, in addition to dried beans and corn that is made into tortillas, provide breakfast, lunch and supper for him and the other families who share this land, 365 days of the year.

He has spent most of his 97 years here, his world defined by the dry hills that ring this little valley, his soul anchored to this piece of ground. His name is E m e t a r i o Pantaleón, and he is one of the few remaining members of the guerrilla army led by Emiliano Zapata during the Mexican Revolution. It was a war for the land, fought by the many who had nothing against the few who held almost all of it. It was a peasant's struggle, as bloody as any in the world.

'The days I come here I am content,' Emetario says, his voice rising and his body shimmering with enthusiasm. 'I need to feel the earth in my hands.'

But now, just three generations after the revolt that won them their land, many of Mexico's *ejido* farmers face losing it once again. Emetario Pantaleón pulls off his sandals and lifts his face to the sun. 'It is sad that the people leave the farms. It is the earth that sustains us,' the old rebel says. 'It is the earth that sets the mind free and cures the body of life's indignities. It is the earth that endures. This land. This very dirt. This life. This is what matters. These lands are not for sale.'"

*—Interview with Emetario Pantaleón, "The Bitter Harvest" The Houston Chronicle, December 12, 1994.*

## Health and Safety

Raising cash crops for export has a great cost on the health of the Mexican people and environment of Mexico. The production of export foods is characterized by the heavy use of chemical fertilizers, herbicides and pesticides. Although pesticides can bring short-term benefits in controlling insects, heavy pesticide use has several adverse effects. When pesticides are applied too heavily or too close to harvest time, the residues accumulate in foods at levels that often exceed health standards for consumers. Pesticide residues also can pollute the environment, particularly water sources, soils and vegetation. There are few enforced laws concerning the dumping of wastes and emission of pesticides in Mexico.

Herbicides and pesticides also put farm workers' health at risk. Increasing numbers of people are being exposed and harmed. It is not uncommon for airplanes to spray fields while people are working below, or for farm workers to use toxic products without being provided protection for their skin or lungs. Acute poisonings and chronic illness have become common among farm workers and their families.

## Food Security

The growth of agricultural exports and the resultant change in land use has affected the food supply that is available for local consumption in Mexico. Land devoted to basic food crops—corn, wheat, beans and rice—fell 25% between 1960-1970 and has continued to decline since. While Mexico is the second largest supplier of cattle to the US, beef consumption in Mexico has decreased by 50%. Meanwhile, Mexico imports 25% of its corn and wheat.

"This shift can hinder food security," says Isabel Cruz who heads a national association of rural credit unions. "The government policy will drive out the small producers. Where will they go? The government doesn't concern itself with that."

The two different agricultural sectors have very different concepts of food security. One argument, expressed by small-scale farmer organizations, is to structure agricultural policy to make Mexico self-sufficient in basic food production: invest in infrastructure that helps small-scale farms; provide loans and reduce the interest rate which hovers between 50-90% in the mid-'90s; and raise, or at least enforce, the minimum wage of $3.90 per day for farm workers.

A very different approach to food security is advocated by decision makers who believe that crop production should be based on a country's comparative advantage. Comparative advantage means that a country can produce a good or service at a lower cost than another country. According to this way of thinking, countries should specialize and take advantage of the quantity and quality of resources they have.

In Mexico, the larger producers' approach to food security supports the policy of increasing agricultural exports. Proponents argue that the foreign exchange earned through sale of crops should be used to purchase food that is grown more cheaply in the US, Canada or elsewhere. The Mexican Agriculture Ministry suggests growing fruits and vegetables to export to the US, Canada and other countries. Since there is a limited amount of irrigated land in Mexico, these policy makers believe that priority should be given to crops that can only be produced with a constant supply of water, namely fruits and vegetables. The Ministry encourages using Mexico's comparative advantages such as cheap labor, irrigated land and mild climate. The Ministry agrees with the NAFTA guidelines to end price supports and eliminate tariffs and trade barriers such as import licenses.

## Impact on the Majority of Mexicans

The first to feel the impact of the export-oriented, neo-liberal policies have been the *campesino* families, the 25 million Mexicans who depend on corn, beans and other grains for their livelihood. In addition, millions of urban poor in Mexico are hungry because agricultural production is not designed to meet the nutritional needs of the majority of people.     Like people in both rich and poor nations, thousands of Mexicans have been leaving the countryside for years. Most of the peasants have moved to Mexico's cities, where they join the millions of others already living in the shanty towns on the fringe of urban areas. In 1995, 72% of Mexico's population lived in cities.  Many also head for the United States to work as migrant laborers.

### References

1.  Barry, Tom. *Mexico Country Guide.* Albuquerque, NM: Interhemispheric Resource Center, 1991.
2.  "The Bitter Harvest," *The Houston Chronicle*, 12, December, 1994.
3.  Thrupp, Lori Ann. "New Harvests, Old Problems." *Report on the Americas.* Vol.28, No. 3. November /December 1994.
4.  World Bank. *Poverty and Hunger: A World Bank Policy Study.* Washington, DC, 1990.

Analyze and write your impressions about the cartoon above.
Then re-draw the picture so it shows a more equitable food system.

# Tomasito's Tour

## *A Guide to America's Food*

Stop 1. Tomasito's tour begins on **land in the state of Jalisco, Mexico.** The land was acquired by the US-based Jolly Green Giant Company in partnership with a Mexican development corporation. Mexican farmers used to work this land together on communally owned cooperative farms called *ejidos* (aye-HE-does). Reforms in the 1980s opened up Mexican agriculture to large scale private investment and pushed small landholders off the land.

Stop 7. Our final stop is a **fine Canadian restaurant** where a customer orders a juicy tomato salad. The waitress, a Canadian woman, is serving up Tomasito. She was formerly employed in a food processing plant that closed down and moved production to Mexico. Workers in Canada and the US are losing their jobs because they cannot afford to compete with low Mexican wages which are kept far below their actual level of productivity. The waitress is now working part-time for a minimum wage with no benefits. Like her Mexican friends in Canada, she cannot afford to order her food in this restaurant. And it's no coincidence that she is a woman, since women usually get jobs with the lowest wages.

Stop 6. To take Tomasito and his friends to their final destiny, **truckers** drive across Mexico, through the US and to Canada. Tomasito begins the trip with a poorly paid, non-union Mexican driver who can only take the produce as far north as the border. There, the tomatoes are transferred to a warehouse while they wait for a new driver. Because the US driver is a member of the Teamsters union, this driver earns significantly more money for the same work as the Mexican.

Stop 2. The next stop on Tomasito's tour is **Davis, California,** headquarters of Calgene Inc. where the tomato seed that produced Tomasito was developed. The seed is a hybrid, patented and owned by this trans-national company. The seed was originally developed from a Mexican strain. With a research grant paid for by US taxpayers, trans-national companies are fighting for longer and stronger protection of their seed patents.

Stop 3. Now Tomasito stops in **St. Louis, Missouri,** headquarters of Monsanto Corporation, a large trans-national chemical manufacturer. To prepare the land for the mass cultivation and export of tomatoes, the land is first fumigated with chemicals. After the crops are planted, they are sprayed with more chemicals to kill insects and weeds. Monsanto produces these chemicals, and is one of the largest polluters in the Americas.

Stop 4. Our tour now takes us to **Emelle, Alabama,** a poor, predominantly African-American community. Production waste from the Monsanto manufacturing plant is shipped here to the world's largest hazardous waste landfill. Birth defects have increased in the community, as well as other unusual illnesses.

Stop 5. Tomasito takes us back to **Mexico**, where we meet local farm workers who make approximately US$2.50 per day cultivating the land and harvesting the food which is exported. These workers are given no protection from the pesticides. They have no gloves, masks or safety instructions, and no access to health care. The farm workers no longer have land on which to produce their own food, and cannot afford to buy the tomatoes they grow on the wages they earn.

# Tomasito's Troubles

*Cut apart the seven sections and give one to each small group.*

---

**Stop 1.** **Tomasito's potential growth has been interrupted.**
**Land in Jalisco, Mexico** that was owned by Green Giant Company and a Mexican development corporation has been returned to the Mexican farmers who were its owners. The *campesinos* plan to work it cooperatively and to grow food to feed their community. The new president of Mexico has reinstated the original 1917 Mexican Constitution which states that only Mexicans have the right to own Mexican land.

---

**Stop 2.** **Tomasito's offspring might not resemble their parent.**
Calgene Inc. in **Davis, California** received another research grant so they could work with grocery store chains to develop a new tomato. The result of the research is a hybrid seed which produces tomatoes that are square so they can be packaged and displayed more efficiently. The square tomatoes will not roll off the counter onto the floor, which saves clean up costs and loss of produce. However, the seed for the square tomatoes costs three times that of the old seed.

---

**Stop 3.** **Chemicals that feed and protect Tomasito are in question.**
Inspectors from the Health and Safety Office have given notice to Monsanto Corporation in **St. Louis, Missouri** that their plant will be closed down unless they comply with new environmental regulations. The chemicals that Monsanto exports to Mexico cost much less to produce, but they are so toxic to people and the environment that they are banned in the US and Canada. The "North American Health and Safety Commission" has a new law that requires the same standards for Mexico as the US and Canada. Until and unless Monsanto complies, the company will be required to stop production of all chemicals.

---

**Stop 4.** **By-products from Tomasito's food are trapped in a traffic jam.**
Residents from **Emelle, Alabama** have blockaded all roads that lead to the hazardous waste landfill. Trucks from across the US have been prevented from dumping their loads for two weeks. The trucks are caught in a huge traffic jam! Other landfill sites across the south of the US will not accept hazardous waste, so the inabilty to dispose of the chemical waste shipped to Emelle from Monsanto Corporation could potentially slow down production.

**Stop 5.** **Tomasito's care-givers may go on strike.**

Farm workers in **Jalisco, Mexico** have formed a union and are requesting higher wages, shorter hours and better working conditions. They have threatened to go on strike unless their demands are met. The Mexican government has appointed a mediator to try to negotiate a settlement between the farm workers and their employers.

---

**Stop 6.** **Truckers who transport Tomasito expand their territory.**

As a result of NAFTA, the **truckers** who are Mexican have been granted the right to carry produce anywhere in the United States and into Canada. Although they are still not unionized and still have low wages, they are able to get more work now. However, the members of the Teamster Union in the US are upset. They do not want non-union drivers working in their area and possibly taking work from them.

---

**Stop 7.** **Tomasito remains waiting on the plate while new troubles brew.**

Canadian Immigration officers have raided the **fine Canadian restaurant** and are holding Mexican dishwashers in a detention center. The workers do not have the necessary legal documents to allow them to work in Canada. The media has been covering the story and townspeople are concerned. Some folks have set up a picket line to try to convince potential customers to eat elsewhere. A group of church and community people have gone to the detention center and are trying to help the men get work permits so they can stay in Canada with their families. A group of loyal customers say they don't care who serves them as long as the food is good. Meanwhile, Tomasito ripens.

# Casting a Vote
## *Simulating Mexico's Electoral System*

What constitutes a democracy? Responses to this question vary. Common elements that might be agreed upon are universal adult suffrage, regular elections, secret ballots and partisan competition. If one applied even these minimum requirements to Mexico's political system, few would consider Mexico a democracy. Every president since 1929 has been from the Institutional Revolutionary Party (PRI). The main role of the PRI has been domination, not power sharing. The state controls the bureaucracies which direct most labor unions, student groups, peasant organizations and almost every other facet of organized society. The PRI has built an empire by weaving an intricate web of power. Even when challenged by massive demonstrations and protests, the party has maintained its dominant position in the Mexican government.

Students examining Mexico's political system may find it difficult to understand how the PRI has accumulated so much power. The structure of the Mexican government looks very much like that of the US, with a president, a congress and a supreme court. However, in practice it operates quite differently. It is nearly impossible to capture the complexity of Mexico's political system in one or two lessons; therefore, we focus on one characteristic of Mexican politics—electoral practices.

Many analysts of Mexican politics contend that the PRI has been able to build a political empire through irregular elections. Students are asked to analyze portions of a speech given by 1994 presidential candidate Ernesto Zedillo, outlining the PRI party platform. They are then are asked to brainstorm ideas for a hypothetical opposition candidate's position on these same issues. Next, students are asked to vote for one of the candidates, but the election is rigged according to a number of strategies allegedly used by the PRI. We consulted individuals who observed the 1994 presidential elections, and they related ways in which the PRI was able to maintain its 65-year winning streak at the polls.

| Learner Objectives | • To brainstorm and construct an opposition candidate's proposals or reforms on key issues in contemporary Mexico. |
|---|---|

**Learner Objectives**

- To brainstorm and construct an opposition candidate's proposals or reforms on key issues in contemporary Mexico.
- To observe and differentiate between various forms of voting practices, and to document observations and articulate them.
- To hypothesize about the impact voting irregularities have on political participation and democracy in Mexico.

**Concepts**

- Electoral Process
- Citizenship
- Democracy

**Major Questions to be Addressed**

- What are some methods used to influence the outcome of elections in Mexico?
- What are the implications for political participation and democracy?

**Teaching Strategy**

Voting Simulation

**Materials Provided**

- PRI Party Platform (Handout 1)
- Sample voting ballots (Handouts 2a–2c)
- Reflecting on the Meaning of Democracy (Handout 3)
- Voting Roster (Educator's Worksheet)

**Materials Needed**

- Make a ballot box (shoe box with rectangular slit cut in top).
- Ink pad and a stamp (for marking students' hands)

**Time Required**

1-2 class sessions

**Preparation for this Lesson**

1. Make one copy of Handout 1 for each student. Ask students to read it and respond to the questions as homework prior to class. For more information on Mexican politics, refer to previous lessons (16–18) to provide a context for this lesson.
2. Write the names of students on the Voting Roster (Educator's Worksheet) to simulate an actual voter registration list.
3. Make copies of the Ballots (Handouts 2a-2e) to give to each student in the class, as instructed below. You may wish to keep this list at hand as you conduct the simulation.

**Ballot A** *Need 2 ballots (1 each for 2 students)*
This ballot should be given to students *who will be among the first voters.* After voting they should approach someone in line and urge that person to vote for the PRI. (*Intended to simulate intervention/intimidation of a PRI official at voting place. Election observers we consulted indicated that PRI officials sometimes would enter the voting booth with an individual as s/he marked his or her ballot.*)

**Ballot B** *Need 4 ballots (2 each for 2 students)*
Two students are given **two** ballots each (should be assigned to students *who will be among the first voters*). After student votes the first time and sits down, student gets up and votes again. Other students should notice that student has voted previously

because hand is stamped. Allow student to vote twice. *(Intended to simulate what Mexicans call "Carousel Voting," or people who vote over and over again, often using false ID cards).*

**Ballot C**    *Need 6 ballots (2 each for 3 students)*

Students are given **two** ballots, should mark both ballots and roll them together and stuff both into the ballot box.*(Intended to simulate what Mexicans call "The Taco," in which some people are able to obtain extra ballots and stuff the ballot box.)*

**Ballot D**    *Need 2 ballots (1 each for 2 students)*

Ballot is in a language that students will not be able to understand; therefore, it is unclear what students will choose to do in this scenario. S/he may choose to cast the vote along with others, not participate, etc. *(Intended to simulate the problem that with over 50 indigenous languages in Mexico, many citizens may not understand instructions written in Spanish.)*

**Ballot E**    *Make enough copies of this ballot for the rest of the students in your classroom to cast a vote, plus 10 additional copies for you to mark for the PRI and stuff in the ballot box before the voting begins.*

Suggested Procedure

This election is "rigged" in a number of ways. First, the instructions on the ballots suggest a number of fraudulent methods. In addition, we encourage the instructor to incorporate at least some of the following methods to ensure that the PRI "win" the election.

A    (Strongly Suggested) As you prepare the ballot box, place the extra ballots marked PRI in the ballot box before class.

B    (Optional) On the Voting Roster, there are three symbols randomly placed on the page. They are there as a reminder that when a student comes forward to register, you should take the action specified in the key at the bottom of the page.

The circle represents an event which happened to many voters in Mexico. When they arrived at their designated polling place to vote, they were told that they were at the wrong polling place and directed to another one, which often was quite far away. These citizens effectively were denied the right to vote.

The X represents another common effort to invalidate votes for an opposition candidate. As a student comes forward to vote, simply take ballot out of his/her hand and check the vote. If the student voted for the opposition candidate, indicate to that student that s/he did not mark the X exactly in the right place (not exactly in the square or any other excuse). Rip up the ballot in front of him/her and indicate that the ballet is invalid.

The "#" symbol represents "shaving." When a Mexican voter with a valid ID came forward to register, that person was told that his or her name did not appear on the voter registration list (that name was "shaved" off of the list). The person was sent away from the polling place without having the opportunity to vote.

# Sequence of Lesson

*Anticipatory Set*
*10 minutes*

1. Ask students how many of them have participated in an election, such as in school or other organizations in which they might be involved. Next, ask students to describe the election process. How did they cast their vote? By raising their hands? Saying aye or nay? Using a secret ballot? Were there steps taken to ensure that the vote was fair? What were these steps?

2. Indicate that the class will be conducting a mock election for Mexico's President. Students need to identify an opposition candidate to the PRI candidate. Ask students to take out a copy of Handout 1, which they should have read as homework.

*Body of Lesson*
*40 minutes*

3. On the board or overhead, make two columns: "PRI" and "Opposition." Ask students to restate or summarize the main points of the PRI platform (Handout 1) and list responses under the PRI column. Possible questions for discussion are:
   - What seems to be the main point of the PRI regarding economic (or health/education) reforms? How much do you think these reforms would bring about change in the current situation in Mexico?
   - Who do you think will benefit the most from these reforms? The least?

4. Next, ask students to create a hypothetical opposition candidate in the presidential race. Design a party platform that responds to students' concerns regarding Mexico. Try to elicit at least one concrete proposal to give students a better idea of an alternative plan to that of the PRI. Ask students to brainstorm responses to the following questions:
   - What ideas or proposals do you think an opposition candidate might have to address these same issues (economy, health, education)? What creative ideas do you have to respond to the needs of the majority of the Mexican population?
   - What proposals would address urban or rural poverty, or another issue that affects a large number of people?
   - What should we call this "alternative" party?
   - What are the pros and cons of each party's platform?

5. Indicate to students that the time has come to vote for the platform and the party of their choice. Distribute the ballots. At the bottom of each ballot will be instructions as to what students are to do. *Emphasize that students should not read one another's ballots, discuss their ballot with one another, or ask for directions.* Discuss with students the procedure for voting. We suggest that students mark their ballots at their seats. As students come forward, check off their name on the Voting Roster and allow them to cast their ballot. When students have cast their ballot, stamp their hands to indicate they have voted.

Indicate to students that they will be wearing two different "hats" during this simulation. They should follow the instructions listed on their ballot, and they should watch carefully for cases of fraud. When they see something suspicious, they should jot it down to discuss only after everyone has had a chance to vote and the ballots are tallied.

6.  Let the voting begin! Place the Ballot Box and Voting Roster on a table in a conspicuous place. The instructor should sit next to the Ballot Box and check students' names off the Roster.

    When the voting is over, ask a class member to help you tally the votes on the board as you read off each ballot. If you have "rigged" the elections well, the PRI should win with a clear majority. Class members also should see that the number of votes tallied exceeds the class size, due to your prior ballot box stuffing, the "Carousel Voters," and the "Taco" voters.

    Encourage students to begin identifying suspicious activities they saw occurring. List responses on the board.

7.  Debrief the simulation with students. Refer to the information provided on the ballots as well as the actions you took (ballot stuffing, "shaving," etc.). Indicate to students what each of these was intended to simulate. Ask students how they felt watching the examples of voting fraud. Suggested questions:
    *   How do you think you might feel towards a government that you suspected was not elected fairly? Would you feel a sense of loyalty to it?
    *   What impact do you think voting fraud has on political participation in Mexico? If you knew voting fraud had occurred for the past 65 years, would you still vote?
    *   Do you think other governments should pressure Mexico to become more democratic? Why or why not? What steps could be taken to do this?

*Closure*

8.  Remind students that this was a mock vote—a simulation of voting fraud. It is highly unlikely all of the methods they saw would occur all at once. However, none of these reported activities is fictional—all methods were witnessed by, or reported to international election observers. These examples also are only some of the methods the PRI uses to maintain its dominance. Many potential opposition candidates do not run because of intimidation and there have been a number of assassinations in Mexico in recent years.

    Finally, remind students of the all-important outcome... in this simulation, the PRI extended its winning streak and power.

*Assessment*

Give students participation points for the day's lesson.

*Assignment*

Distribute copies of Handout 4. Ask students to reflect on the definition of democracy given and to write their responses to the questions on the handout.

# PRI Party Platform

Before the 1994 Presidential election took place in Mexico, the Institutional Revolutionary Party's (PRI) Secretary for International Affairs sent a letter to members of the international community. In it, he outlined PRI candidate Ernesto Zedillo's position on important issues and enclosed excerpts from a Zedillo speech.

Although Dr. Zedillo outlined a 10-point program in his speech, two key issues—his plan for the economy and education and health—are outlined here. Analyze the words and think about the persistent problems in Mexico.

## Economy

The government I propose to lead will place highest priority on encouraging investment. We will create an environment in which investments can grow, and with them, jobs. Foreign investment will continue to be a complement to national investment as it enables us to acquire the most advanced technologies and link with international flows of both trade and production....

Foreign trade is necessary for Mexico to produce more and better. Through trade we can specialize in the production of those things that we produce and thus our working hours will be more profitable and our people will live better. We need to do more to promote our exports.

## Education and Health

The central objective of my economic policy proposal is to increase the well-being of Mexican families. It is therefore essential that special attention be paid to investments in people. Better education, more training and better health services will be the social platform for more productive and better paid workers. We must undertake a national crusade to solve the backlogs that still persist in our education system and we must elevate the quality of that system....

We also must focus our attention on health. Health represents one of the essential factors that determines the productivity of men and women. At the same time, we must be careful that the financing of institutions which tend to the health of workers do not unnecessarily elevate companies' costs.

Analyze Dr. Zedillo's speech and write your responses to the following questions in your notebook/journal:

Q: Who do you think these reforms will help in Mexico? Who do you think will benefit the most? The least?

Q: Imagine an opposition candidate in the Presidential race. If you were asked to develop an alternative plan for how the government might respond to these key issues, what specific reforms would you propose? Bring your ideas to class! What would you call your "alternative" party?

# MEXICAN ELECTION BALLOT "A"

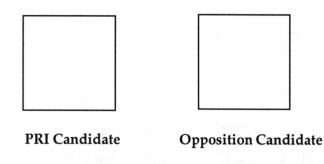

**PRI Candidate**          **Opposition Candidate**

*(write in party name)*

You represent a PRI official. When you are asked, mark your ballet for the PRI and do not tell or show anyone how you voted. After you have cast your ballot, your hand will be stamped to show that you have voted. After this, your task is to approach one person waiting in line to vote BEFORE that person casts her/his vote, identify yourself as a PRI official, and urge that person to vote for the PRI. Then return to your seat and watch to see what happens when other people vote.

# MEXICAN ELECTION BALLOT "B"

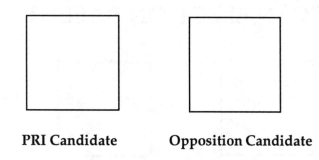

**PRI Candidate**          **Opposition Candidate**

*(write in party name)*

When you are asked, mark your ballet and do not tell or show anyone how you voted. One at a time, other students will come forward to cast their ballots. After they have cast their ballots, their hands will be stamped to show that they have voted. In theory, this should prevent someone from being able to vote twice. You are the exception! You have two ballots, and are being asked to play along with a scheme which goes like this. First, fold the 2nd ballot and place it in a pocket (without anyone seeing you). When you are asked to vote the first time, cast your ballot along with the others and have your hand stamped. Then return to your seat. When others are voting a few minutes later, walk back up to the "voting booth" and cast your second ballot. When you have finished, sit down again without talking to anyone.

# MEXICAN ELECTION BALLOT "C"

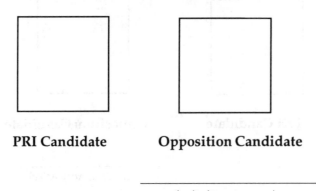

**PRI Candidate**          **Opposition Candidate**

_____
*(write in party name)*

You've been chosen to be in on a little scheme. Everyone else has only one ballot, but you have been fortunate to be able to obtain an extra ballot. Don't let anyone know that you have two ballots! When asked to vote, secretly mark both ballots and do not tell or show anyone how you voted. Then, roll the two ballots together so that no one will suspect you have two ballots. One at a time, students will come forward to the "Voting Booth" to cast their ballots. Be sure to stuff both of your ballots into the box. After you have cast your ballot, your hand will be stamped to show that you have voted. Then return to your seat and watch to see what happens when other people vote.

---

# MEXICAN ELECTION BALLOT "D"

цчУ РЯєәϜәЯsЃ          ЦєєЄSϜsϜЄє РЯєәϜәЯsЃ

_____
гЙжϜsЃ Ϝє єЯжsІ єЯЄЃД

зр—П ħϜsshЃ ħЯsЃж Ϝє srЃ әhЯSSe ЙЃ ЙϜħħ яЃЃϜє sЄ ӘЯSs 7ЄsЃSё ЪгЃє ІЄ7ж sЃЯӘгЃж ЯSЪS ІЄ7 sЄ әЄ SЄє ІЄ7 SrЄ7ħә ЄЯжЪ ІЄ7ж яЯħħЃs Яs ІЄ7ж SЃЯs Яєә єЄs sЃħħ Єж SrЄЙ ЯєІЄєЃ гЄЙ ІЄ7 7ЄsЃәё ЦєЃ Яs Я sϜЄЃє Ss7әЃєsS ЙϜħħ ӘЄЄЃ ЃєжЙЯжә sЄ srЃ ащєsϜєЃ пЄЄsга sЄ ӘЯSs srЃЃж яЯħħЄsSё ЫІЄ7 SrЄ7ħә ӘЯSs ІЄ7ж яЯħħЄs ЙгЃє ІЄ7 ЯжЃ ЯSЪЃә sЄ әЄ SЄ яІ ІЄ7ж sЃЯӘгЃжё ПЃsЃж ІЄ7 гЯ7Ѓ ӘЯSs ІЄ7ж яЯħħЄse ІЄ7 ЙϜħħ яЃ ЯSЪЃә sЄ єжЃSS ІЄ7 sr7Єя Ϝєsє Яє ϜєЪ єЯә sЄ SrЄЙ srЯs ІЄ7 гЯ7Ѓ 7ЄsЃәё ПЃsЃж srϜSe ІЄ7ж sЯSЪ ϜS sЄ ЯєєжЄЯӘг ЄєЃ єЃжSЄє ЙЯϜsϜєЃ Ϝє ħϜєЃ sЄ 7ЄsЃ пCсЦчC srЯs єЃжSЄє ӘЯSsS гЃжжЖгϜϜS 7ЄsЃє ϜәЃsϜЃІ ІЄ7жSϜħЃ ЯS Я цчУ ЄЃЃϜ ЯҺЃ Яєә 7жЃЃ srЯs єЃжSЄє sЄ 7ЄsЃ ЃєЪ srЃ цчУё шгЃє жЃs7жє sЄ ІЄ7ж SЃЯs Яєә ЙЯsәr sЄ SЃЃ ЙгЯs гΆєєЃгS ЙгЃє єsrЃж єЃєħгЃ 7ЄsЃё

# MEXICAN ELECTION BALLOT "E"

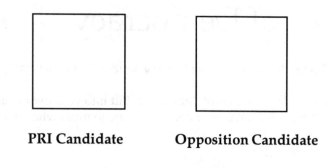

**PRI Candidate**          **Opposition Candidate**

_____
*(write in party name)*

When asked to vote, mark your ballet and do not tell or show anyone how you voted. After you have cast your ballot, your hand will be stamped to show that you have voted. Then return to your seat and watch to see what happens when other people vote.

---

# MEXICAN ELECTION BALLOT "E"

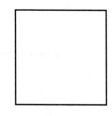

**PRI Candidate**          **Opposition Candidate**

_____
*(write in party name)*

When asked to vote, mark your ballet and do not tell or show anyone how you voted. After you have cast your ballot, your hand will be stamped to show that you have voted. Then return to your seat and watch to see what happens when other people vote.

# Reflecting on the Meaning of Democracy

*Directions: Read each section below and write your responses in the space provided.*

1. People have different understandings of democracy. Put into your own words what you think democracy is. What ideas, events or concepts come to mind when you hear the word?

2. In class, we held a simulated election in Mexico. From what you have learned in class, would you consider Mexico to be a democracy based on the definition you just gave? Explain.

3. Would you consider the US to be a democracy based on the definition you just gave? Explain.

4.  A political scientist named Richard Fagen has formulated a definition of democracy. He writes,

    Democracy is a system of governance in which:
    A)  There is effective participation by individuals and groups in the decisions that most affect their lives;
    B)  There is a system of accountability whereby the behavior of leaders and officials can be monitored, judged, and—if necessary—changed by those who are subject to their authority;
    C)  There is political equality (in the sense of equality before the law, equal opportunity to participate in the political process, etc.).

    Reflect on Fagen's definition for a few moments. Are there parts of this definition that are similar to what you included in your definition? Different from what you included in your definition?

    <u>**Similar**</u>                                      <u>**Different**</u>

When many people think about democracy, they think about voting, equal rights before the law and freedom of speech—the kinds of ideas included in points B and C above. These may have been some of the same ideas and concepts you listed in your definition. Now take a look at the first point in Fagen's definition. What kinds of things would you include in the phrase, "decisions that most affect their lives"? Could this mean having a voice in the quality of working conditions? A child's education? Do you think most Mexicans participate in the decisions that most affect their lives? Explain your answer by giving examples from what you have learned in class.

Do you think this "broadened" definition of democracy is a valid one? Why or why not?

# VOTING ROSTER

_____    _____++

_____    _____

_____    _____**

_____**  _____

_____    _____

_____++  _____

_____    _____xx

_____    _____

_____xx  _____

_____    _____

_____    _____

_____    _____

_____    _____

_____

_____    **REMINDERS:**
** must vote in another location
_____    xx If this vote is for opposition party, find a
                              reason to void it and tear it up.
_____    ++ Name should not appear on voting list
                              (shaving)

*An Exploring the Connections Lesson*

# Mexicans on the Move

## *Case Studies on Migration and Debate on Immigration Policy*

The concept of migration has been woven into *Many Faces of Mexico* as a recurring theme. Beginning with the Olmec people long ago, migration in Mexico has continued—both internally within Mexico's borders and externally as Mexicans emigrate to other countries. The goal of this lesson is to educate students about the causes and consequences of migration.

The push and pull factors associated with contemporary migration are complex; patterns of migration have their roots in historical, political and economic developments. Using case studies, this lesson focuses on recent Mexican migrants whose lives are torn apart by economic and political pressures in Mexico, and the lure of opportunity in *el norte*. Students have an opportunity to learn more about the realities of Mexican migrant families and become more involved in the choices these individuals make. Provocative, open-ended study questions are included at the end of the case, which encourage students to think about issues rather than recall specific facts of the case.

Once students learn about the causes and realities of migration, we shift the focus to its consequences. One effect seems to be escalating negative attitudes and stereotypes about Mexican people in the US. Such attitudes are manifested in legislation such as California's Proposition 187, which aims to deny social services such as health care and education to illegal immigrants. This lesson asks students to consider differing perspectives on Proposition 187 and to discuss those perspectives using a constructive controversy exercise.

| **Learner Objectives** | • To define and correctly use terms and concepts pertaining to migration. |
| | • To identify causes of migration through the examination of individual situations. |
| | • To analyze arguments about immigration policy in the United States and to hypothesize possible implications of policies such as Proposition 187. |

| **Concepts** | • Migration |
| | • Immigration Policy |

| **Major Questions to be Addressed** | • Why do Mexicans move? Where do they go? |
| | • What situations do Mexicans face when they emigrate to the US? |
| | • How have attitudes and perceptions in the US shaped immigration policy? |

**Exploring the Connections**

People are moving from one community to another—from one side of the border to another—in increasing numbers. Migration connects people in very concrete ways as communities expand or contract. Yet barriers of fear, misunderstanding or distrust often keep people apart. Educating ourselves about the causes and consequences of migration—and examining our values—is the first step toward breaking down some of these barriers.

| **Teaching Strategies** | • Session 1—Free writing, reading, discussion, vocabulary development |
| | • Session 2—Case studies |
| | • Session 3—Constructive controversy, discussion |

| **Materials Provided** | • What Does It All Mean? (Handout 1) |
| | • On the Move: Mexican Migration (Handout 2) |
| | • Migration Case Studies (Handouts 3a-3e) |
| | • Case Study Outcomes (Educator Background Information) |
| | • Constructive Controversy Process (Handout 4) |
| | • Controversy Controversy Checklist (Handout 5) |
| | • Proposition 187 Arguments (Handouts 6a-6b) |

| **Additional Materials Needed** | Student Journals |

| **Time Required** | 3-5 sessions |

# Sequence of Session 1:
# The Concept of Migration

*Preparation*

- With students, collect articles from magazines, newspapers, etc. about migration, especially Mexican migration. Select 2-3 of the best articles and make photocopies available to students.
- Call the Immigration and Naturalization Service and ask for their brochures. (It is listed in the phone book under US Justice Dept.)
- Make one copy of Handouts 1 and 2 for each pair of students.

*Anticipatory Set*
*10 minutes*

1. On the board or overhead, write the word IMMIGRATION. Ask students to write in their journals the first three words that come to mind when they hear this term. Have students share ideas and record these ideas on the chalkboard.

*Body of Lesson*
*40 minutes*

2. Ask students to do free writing about migration. Write the following two statements on the board to give students direction:
*Reasons I would be willing to move to another place are...*
*Reasons why I wouldn't want to move are...*

Debrief the responses to these questions, writing some of the students' responses on the board. Introduce the topic of migration by asking students if they have ever moved from one area to another. Encourage those who have to talk about it to the class. What did they like about it and what did they find difficult?

3. Distribute copies of Handout 1 and ask students, individually or in pairs, to write the definitions as best they are able. Ask volunteers to read their definitions while the instructor writes their ideas on the board. Try to reach some common understanding of the terms. Distribute photocopies of articles and refer to them for ways in which terms are used. Consult a dictionary to see if media usageof the terms is the same as the dictionary definition.

4. Distribute Handout 2 for students to read or present the information as a small lecture. Some of it has been covered in prior lessons. If there is not sufficient time, ask students to read it as homework.

*Assignment*

Continue to define terms, using a dictionary and resources from the library, the Immigration and Naturalization Service or agencies that work with migrants.

# Sequence of Session 2:
# Case Studies on Migration

*Preparation*                    Make one copy of Handouts 3a-3e for each student.

*Anticipatory Set*      1.  Ask students if they know anyone or about anyone who has
*5 minutes*                 moved to their community from Mexico or another country. What
                            do students know about the person's situation before moving and
                            as s/he has resettled?

*Body of Lesson*        2.  Introduce the case study approach, in which a story of an actual
*40-80 minutes*             situation is presented up to the point when the person is going to
                            make a decision or take an action. Students brainstorm options
                            and suggest what they think the person(s) in the case study might
                            do. After all the case studies are analyzed, the actual outcomes are
                            given. Case studies require learners to be actively involved and to
                            assume responsibility for their ideas and actions. In working with
                            cases, students learn how to gather and use data to support an
                            argument. The focus is on students' thinking, and the instructor's
                            role becomes one of "extractor of meanings" rather than
                            "disseminator of information." In case study teaching, the
                            instructor should guide students in exploring and sorting out the
                            complexities of a specific situation. It is critical that educators
                            communicate respect for students' ideas to make it safe for
                            students to voice their ideas and opinions. This helps create a
                            climate for thoughtful examination of bigger issues associated with
                            migration.

                        3.  Distribute Handout 3a to the class. Ask students to read the case
                            individually and to discuss the following questions (written on the
                            board) with one or two others:
                            *   *What options does the person have?*
                            *   *What are the advantages and disadvantages of each option?*
                            *   *What would you recommend? Why?*

                        4.  Reconvene the class and list their ideas on the board. Try to come
                            to consensus on a recommendation of what they think the
                            person(s) might do. We recommend that you wait to read the
                            outcome until the following day so students can continue to
                            ponder the situation.

                        5.  Follow the same format with the remaining case studies
                            (Handouts 3b-3e).

*Closure*               6.  The following day, review the cases, and ask students if they have
                            additional ideas. Then read the actual outcome. Ask for responses.

*Assignment and*            Ask students to choose one of the case studies and formulate
*Evaluation*                questions they might like to ask the person. Students should write
                            an imaginary dialogue with this person, raising questions and
                            anticipating their responses.

# Sequence of Session 3:
# Constructive Controversy on Immigration

### *Immigration Initiative: Proposition 187*

The issue of immigration has entered the public discourse, as the media, policy makers and the public devote attention to the social and economic problems caused by new immigrants to the US and Canada. We hear accounts and see images of people making perilous leaps across fences, over highways and rivers. Despite border controls enforced by the Immigration and Naturalization Service, Mexicans and other Latin Americans manage to cross the border, leading some people to claim that the north is being invaded by "illegal aliens." Local and state governments, reflecting the concerns of citizens, appear increasingly reluctant to provide social services such as health care and education for immigrants and their children. Others voice concerns that immigrants are driving down the cost of labor by working for cheap wages. Some people take another view of immigration, and consider the positive impact immigrants traditionally have had on the US and Canada. Immigrants bring new ideas; they place a high value on education; they are willing to work hard and pay their share of taxes; and they use relatively few of the social services available to them. Besides, the Universal Declaration of Human Rights is a clear statement of the universal political, economic and social rights that should be guaranteed to all peoples. Consequences of this highly emotional issue range from confusion, polarization, strict policies and a new wave of migration, to initiatives to break down barriers, new opportunities and true multi-cultural communities.

| | |
|---|---|
| *Preparation* | 1. Make one copy of Handouts 4, 5 and 6a-b for each student. |
| | 2. Depending upon the background of your students, you may wish to find an article(s) on Proposition 187 or a similar measure to familiarize them with the issue. |
| *Anticipatory Set* <br> *5 minutes* | 1. Introduce students to the topic of immigration policy by dsicussing ways people in the US respond to immigrants. Give the examples of the Statue of Liberty and Proposition 187, a referendum that passed in California in 1994. |
| *Body of Lesson* <br> *40 minutes* | 2. Divide the class into groups of four and further subdivide each groups of two. Assign perspectives to each group. Be sure that the groups are as heterogeneous as possible. Distribute Handouts 4 and 5 to each pair. |
| | 3. Briefly explain the strategy of constructive controversy by reviewing the handouts. Write on the board or overhead what each group is responsible to hand in at the end of the session and what the homework expectations are. Review the constructive controversy checklist sheet. |
| | 4. Distribute Handouts 6a and 6b to each pair. Allow 10 minutes for each student to read one of the handouts and plan their arguments and strategy. During this time and continuing throughout the lesson, record your observations about each student's participation on the *Constructive Controversy Checklist*. |

5.  Each group is given 3 minutes to state its reasons for supporting or opposing Proposition 187. Partners must take turns presenting. Encourage group members to take notes on the opposition's argument.

6.  Next, students should discuss each side's position for 5 minutes. Encourage students to ask clarifying questions, challenge ideas, ask for proof and think of counter-arguments based on facts, not opinions.

7.  Ask students to switch roles and encourage them to switch chairs. For 3 minutes, each side argues the opposite position, working from their notes. Encourage students to present the new view as if they really believe it. Remind the students that they must form their argument from the notes that they took while listening to the opposition earlier.

8.  Tell the students to drop their roles and list the most convincing facts from both sides. Each small group should try to form a consensus based on whether or not to support or oppose Proposition 187. Based on the group decision, assign each student the task of writing a one-page report to the President outlining the negative and positive aspects of immigration policy and advising him or her to take a particular view.

9.  Allow 5-10 minutes for students to reflect on the group dynamics and process their discussion. The constructive controversy checklist will provide a format for this. Student should complete this checklist as a group and hand it in.

10. Bring the students together in a large group and have them share reflections on the lesson. Ask students to indicate their position on the issue of immigration after hearing both sides of the argument. You might ask students to physically form a curve, with students standing at one end of the classroom to indicate "Strongly in Favor of Proposition 187" and at the other end "Strongly Opposed to Proposition 187." Let students discuss their position with one another to decide where they stand.

11. With the entire class, begin discussing what values are being raised in this case. Suggested questions follow.
    *   What are some of the values involved in this debate?
        *Rights such as justice, dignity, life, liberty, equal opportunity. Responsibilities such as tolerance, respect for the rights of others, willingness to work for the common good.*
    *   Where do you stand on this issue?
    *   Does everyone have a basic right to such things as education, nutrition and health care, regardless of one's nationality? Support your answer.
    *   What kinds of messages are we, as a society, sending to all people if we deny certain individuals these basic rights?

*Note:* If there are initiatives like Proposition 187 in your state or community, bring this into the discussion. This could be a "teachable moment" for your students.

**Closure**

12. Review the homework assignment of writing a position paper on immigration for the president. End the discussion by asking students to respond to the following statement:

> *If we are collectively judged by how we treat immigrants—those who appear today to be the "other" but will in a generation be "us"—we are not in very good shape.*

**Assignment**

Ask students to read the following poem and then write their thoughts and feelings. The poem was written about a community named Regadio, in which the residents were able to obtain electricity after many years of petitioning their government. Consequently, the residents, and especially the young people, were more likely to choose to remain in Regadio rather than migrate to the city.

> *Regadio*
> *Simple dream, really.*
> *Light for the night,*
> *turning for the mill,*
> *water from the pump,*
> *electricity's service.*
>
> *Is it laziness,*
> *to long for books*
> *after dark-ended labor,*
> *to put aside the muscled*
> *arms of hours pounding,*
> *the trudged miles of*
> *bucket journeys?*
>
> *Or do our dreams,*
> *long sustained,*
> *keep us human,*
> *tender,*
> *able to love?*
>
> — Bill Callahan, Quest for Peace

**Extension Lesson**

Invite a Mexican or Chicano who has moved to your community to speak to the class or arrange a visit with Mexicans or Chicanos in a place of their choice or attend a Mexican cultural event like Independence Day, September 16, or *Cinco de Mayo*.

# MIGRATION:
## What Does It All Mean?

DIRECTIONS: Here are some terms commonly used when discussing migration. Define each term, using the dictionary. Then compare your answers to definitions from current articles in the media. Also, call the US Immigration and Naturalization Service or a legal aid office for their definitions. Are these definitions different from one another?

Immigrant

Green Card

Illegal Alien

Migration

Refugee

"Undocumented"

Emigrant

Work Permit

Visa

# On the Move: Mexican Migration

The theme of migration has become an increasingly hot topic of debate in the United States, especially since the 1994 passage of Proposition 187 in California. However, the movement of people across Mexico's northern border in search of work is not a recent phenomenon. Consider the broader perspective of global migration in the 20th century alone. Millions of people have moved to find safety, rejoin family members or friends, or seek economic opportunity. In today's world, millions of people suffer from the violence and turmoil of wars and conflicts, and seek refuge in a more peaceful place. Others are faced with unemployment or underemployment, coupled with a rise in the cost of living and pressure from a growing population. Still others move because they want to hold their family together. Although migration seems like a new phenomenon, this way of life has persisted for Mexicans since before the Spanish invasion of 1519.

## Pre-Columbian Era

Migration before 1519 occurred for a variety of reasons that included crop failure, soil exhaustion, over-population, plagues, locusts, earthquakes, invasion by other tribes, or a combination of these factors. It is known that the Olmec people left their homeland in Veracruz and joined others like the Toltec, who later moved from their center around Tula and merged with the Aztecs in central Mexico. Records show that the Indian people did not often choose to migrate, unless they were nomadic, but were forced to do so to avoid being conquered. The Aztecs were superb warriors who invaded their neighbors and later extracted labor and tribute from them. The Indians of Mexico who were conquered by the Aztecs never quite assimilated to their culture but were forced to follow the Aztec laws, or migrate beyond Aztec-controlled land.

## Spanish Conquest and Colonial Era

Migration continued to be a factor after the Spanish invasion and during the 300 years of Spanish colonization. *Mestizos,* those with Spanish and Indian blood, were the fastest growing group, adding to the numbers of oppressed peoples throughout New Spain who sought ways to resist or escape the Spanish control. Indians and Mestizos migrated to find work, especially in the mines, in the large cities and on *haciendas*. They also sought to attain some degree of freedom. Some began to migrate northward and settle in less inhabited parts of the Spanish Empire. These included the areas we now call Texas, New Mexico, Arizona, California, Nevada, Utah, and Colorado.

## Migration after Independence

In 1821, Mexico fought and won its independence from Spanish rule. However, not much changed for the poor people of Mexico. Leadership changed hands from the Spanish Crown to the second generation Spanish, called *Criollos*. The poor remained poor, and wealthy *Criollos* pursued their own interests. The poor often continued to be migrants, searching for better economic, political and social conditions.

During the Mexican-American War that ended in 1848, Mexico lost more than a third of its land to the United States. Even before the war ended, the first immigration law between the US and Mexico was passed. As a result, Mexicans from the state of Sonora no longer had the right to enter

California. During the Mexican Revolution, migration peaked. Between the years 1910-1915, thousands of people left Mexico for political, social, and economic reasons. Many wealthy people migrated to the United States because revolutionaries like Emiliano Zapata and Pancho Villa led armies that gave land to the poor and made life difficult for the rich land owners. The poor migrated from rural areas to the big cities for employment opportunities. During this period of instability, Mexico's debt began to grow and the peso was in continual decline as a result of the devastated economy. In this period approximately 220,000 Mexicans migrated northward to the land of labor and opportunity, the United States.

During World War II, Mexican men were recruited to work in the US to replace those who were fighting. From 1942-1964, the Bracero Program brought 4.8 million agricultural workers to the US to plant cotton, produce vegetables, pick fruit and raise cattle. When the program ended, the tradition of seasonal work in the US continued. If they couldn't get across the border legally, Mexicans would risk crossing illegally in order to find work.

## Contemporary Mexico

Mexico now faces the largest migration flow in its history. Men, women and children are migrating for numerous reasons. Some leave out of a desire for economic mobility and stability. Others have been forced to move due to war or conflict, such as the conflict in the state of Chiapas. Still others move to join family.

Recent migration patterns from Mexico to the US may be short lived if US voters continue to pass initiatives like California's Proposition 187. These rulings could deny public health care services, public social services, and public education to those considered to be "illegal."

At the same time, the North American Free Trade Agreement (NAFTA), which took effect in 1994, may increase the pressure on Mexican to emigrate. The effects of NAFTA on migration have been hotly debated.

Proponents of the trade agreement argued that it would generate industrial and commercial jobs in Mexico, thereby allowing more Mexicans to earn a living while remaining in Mexico. In 1992, then-President Carlos Salinas de Gortari said,

*Mexicans are migrating, attracted by the demand pull from the American economy. But at the same time the Mexicans who go north take many risks; they are very energetic risk-takers. That's precisely the kind of people I want here. That's why I am so committed to generating employment opportunities in Mexico, so that Mexicans will not have to go north, competing with Americans for jobs in their own country. That's why we have to grow faster. That's why it's better to have a free trade agreement and we could be able to export foods and not people.* [1]

Opponents of NAFTA, on the other hand, pointed out that changes in Mexico's agricultural system under NAFTA will have quite the opposite effect.

Large scale displacement of Mexican farmers under NAFTA, estimated at anywhere from 800,000 to 3,000,000 families, will result in increased migration to the US with the attendant social problems that will be created on both sides of the border.[2]

Unless conditions change for the majority of Mexicans, the migration of Mexican people is likely to continue.

1. Forbes, M. and J. Michaels. "We Had to React Quickly: Interview with Carlos Salinas de Gortari." *Forbes 150*, pp 64-67. 1992.

2. Lehman, Karen and Mark *Ritchie, U.S. Citizens' Analysis of the North American Free trade Agreement,* Institute for Agriculture and Trade Policy, 1992, p.21.

# Migration Case Study I: 1959
# CRUZ & CECILIA HUERTA

Cruz Huerta was born in the state of Michoacán in 1935. He worked with his father as a *campesino*, or farm hand on the *hacienda* of a wealthy landowner. In 1957 he married Cecilia Sosa and they had one son, Manuel. When Cecilia was pregnant with their second child, the couple realized that they could not afford to make a proper home and raise their children on Cruz's income. Cruz didn't want to leave Michoacán to work in Mexico City like many other men from his area. The immense size of the city and stories of crime worried him.

Fortunately for Cruz, the United States was recruiting Mexicans (men only) to become a part of the "brown helping hands" effort called the Bracero Program. This program, begun in 1942, was created because of the labor shortage caused by US men going off to fight in World War II. Agricultural labor was needed in the US, and Mexican workers were promised free transportation and a minimum wage of $.46 an hour, as long as they did not take jobs away from US citizens. Each laborer worked under a specific contract, initially for 90 days. The contract guaranteed certain rights such as food, housing, medical care, specified pay, and a return home at the end of the job or the contract.

In 1959 Cruz went to his local mayor and applied for the program. After a trip to Mexico City to prove his citizenship and pass a physical exam, Cruz was accepted to go to California.

Cruz didn't want to leave Cecilia with Manuel and a baby on the way, but the money was good. Considering that he wouldn't have many expenses, he could save his money and send most of it to Cecilia and the children. He told Cecilia that if California was as great as he had heard that he would find a way for her and the children to join him there.

In June, Cruz became a *bracero*. He picked strawberries in Oxnard; in Lodi, he picked grapes; in Tulare, cotton; in Delano, oranges, peaches, cherries, and grapes; and around Salinas, lettuce. The next thing Cruz knew, he had been in California for a year and a half. He had saved lots of money living in labor camps under dismal conditions. But he missed his family and they missed him. When his contract was up, he asked himself what he should do.

*What are Cruz's options?*
*What do you think he might do?*

# Migration Case Study 2: 1953
# ROSALITA ISABEL GONZALEZ

Rosalita Isabel was born in 1945 in Gómez Palacio, Durango. She was a *Mestiza* who was abandoned at the age of two. A church took in Rosalita while a home could be found to care for her. The González family, a prominent family in the parish, felt sorry for the young girl and took her into their family when she was seven.

Rosalita was treated more like a slave than like an adopted daughter. Uneducated and ill-mannered by their standards, she was made to cook and clean. At a later age, Rosalita was forced to serve her adoptive father and brother sexually. At the age of 14 she became pregnant. She could not bear the thought of carrying the child of one of the González men.

When Señor González learned of Rosalita's pregnancy he was very disturbed. He knew society would look down on his family for not keeping Rosalita "pure" so he sent her away. With little money in her pocket, Rosalita tried to find the best alternative for herself and her unborn child. She couldn't turn to her aunts and uncles as long as she was unwed and pregnant for she would bring shame to the family. She migrated to a town on the northern border of Mexico to look for work in the clothing maquiladoras there. When her employers realized that she was pregnant, they fired her immediately. The work was hard and the company didn't want to assume responsibility for any problems.

Rosalita's economic situation was worse than she could ever have imagined. She couldn't find a social service agency or church in town that would help. She had no friends there to turn to who weren't in a similar economic predicament. Some of her friends had gone to the other side, that is, to Texas, and they might help her out. But crossing the border was costly and risky, especially for a pregnant woman.

*What are Rosalita's options?*
*What do you think she might do?*

# Migration Case Study 3: 1988
# PEDRO BARAJAS

Pedro Barajas was born in Costa Chica in the state of Guerrero in 1960. As a teenager, he moved to Mexico City and became a street vendor, or a person who sells goods on the street. After a few years, Pedro was able to buy his own vending stand in a good location on the Calzada de la Virgen de Guadalupe. There he sold contraband electronic goods such as radios, stereos, TVS and VCRs which had been brought illegally into Mexico.

He made between four and five times the minimum wage every day. His costs were low since he was able to tap into the power lines directly above him to get free electricity. Potential customers were able to see that the televisions and stereos were in good working condition.

Although he sold quite a lot, Pedro had to pay a daily quota of two pesos to a political leader, Don Juan, who then assured him that he would not be harassed by the police. If the police did bother him, Don Juan would compensate him if merchandise was seized. It was like an insurance policy for Pedro, because Don Juan was a member of the Institutional Revolutionary Party (PRI), and he worked for the department which oversaw and regulated commerce in the capital.

In addition to the two pesos to Don Juan, Pedro had to pay 50 pesos every three months as a "social fee," and another 36 per year to the Ministry of Finance and Public Credit for an identity card that gave him the license for his stand.

In 1988, Pedro's good luck changed. Don Juan left the PRI. He recently had learned that a PRI candidate had told residents in his hometown that they would get a new water system, sewers and other services if the townsfolk voted for the PRI. This was the last straw. He felt that the power and corruption of the PRI were out of control and he could no longer support the party. Don Juan went to an opposition party, the Revolutionary Democratic Party (PRD). He wanted to support that party's candidate, Cuauhtémoc Cárdenas, because he believed that the son of former president Lázaro Cárdenas would be the best president.

When Don Juan changed parties, Pedro followed his lead. Like Don Juan, Pedro worked as a poll watcher for the PRD during the election. On election day, the PRI eked out another victory. Don Juan, knowing he had no future in Mexican politics, moved to Arizona to live with his brother. He encouraged Pedro to come with him and they would become business partners.

Pedro through about this but decided to stay in Mexico. But with Don Juan gone, the police began to hang around Pedro's street stand on the Calzada, and when they were around, customers stayed away. His income dropped immensely and eventually, Pedro lost his license.

*What are Pedro's options? What do you think he might do?*

# Migration Case Study 4: 1985 EMILIANO RODRIGUEZ MADRID

Emiliano Rodríguez Madrid lived in one of the nicest neighborhoods in Mexico City. On the weekends he went to his country home in Hidalgo, an hour and a half from the capital, to get away from the polluted air. Emiliano and his father Rodolfo were industrialists. They owned a company that manufactured televisions, stereos and other small electronics. Most of the products were sold in Mexico and were less expensive to purchase than electronics from the US or Japan. This was due, in part, to the import tariffs designed to promote and protect Mexican manufacturers. The protective barriers enabled Mexican manufacturers to realize profit margins of 300% and higher.

Then, in the early 1990s, Mexican political leaders decided to drop the protective barriers. A new trade agreement with the US and Canada was being created, and the politicians wanted Mexican manufacturers to compete in the international market. The Chamber of Electronics Industries and the National Federation of Chambers of Industry (CONCAMIN) informed the Madrids that they would have to modernize and expand their facilities. Then, President Salinas de Gortari announced that the economy would be opened to free trade.

Because theirs was a middle-sized company, the Madrids felt trapped. They did not qualify for a large loan to adequately modernize their business, nor were they prepared or informed about what the North American Free Trade Agreement (NAFTA) would actually do. What they did know was that protectionism was going to end the way they had done business in the past.

The next year Rodolfo passed away. Emiliano, now the sole owner, felt tremendous pressure to operate the company and modernize it. He considered moving to the US and becoming a distributor there if he could get a work permit. He thought about moving to the border and building a *maquiladora*, or factory, if he could get a loan for new construction.

Then Emiliano had another idea. He contacted an Asian manufacturing company that produced electronics much more cheaply than he could, mainly because wages for Asian workers were one half to one quarter of those he paid in Mexico. He could arrange with the Asian company to make his line of consumer electronics and ship them to Mexico where he would sell them as his own. Or he could just import Asian-made products and become a distributor, but there was great competition due to sales of contraband goods in the hundreds of street markets throughout Mexico City. Or he could become a supplier to the contraband vendors and enter the growing smuggling trade. Emiliano is convinced that the electronics sector is highly monopolized by an elite group of businesspeople who are the only ones who can afford to smuggle contraband items in large quantities.

*What are Emiliano's options? What do you think he might do?*

*Many Faces of Mexico*

# Migration Case Study 5: 1993
# LUPITA MIREYA SANTOS Y LOPEZ

Lupita was born in 1964, the daughter of small merchants in Sonora, Mexico. At the age of 16, she married Rigoberto López and they soon had five children. Life was hard as they struggled to provide for their young family, even though Lupita's and Rigoberto's families helped them out. Due to an increasingly bad economy in 1992, Lupita and Rigoberto decided to take their children and go north to look for work in the factories or *maquiladoras* in the Mexican border town of Tijuana.

Although things in Tijuana were more expensive than in their home town, both Lupita and Rigoberto were able to work full time in the *maquiladoras*. The factory conditions were harsh and unsanitary. Soon Lupita could not tolerate the hard physical work and Rigoberto could not tolerate the boss's sexual harassment of Lupita.

Lupita eventually quit and found a cleaning job in the nearby hospital. As a reward for her good work, she was issued a permit that gave her border crossing privileges. This benefited the family, because food, clothing and household supplies were much less expensive in the US. Lupita and her cousin Juanita who also lived in Tijuana, started to go to San Ysidro, California every weekend to shop at the Wal-Mart and The Super grocery store. After making that trip every weekend, Juanita told Lupita about a job cleaning houses for wealthy people in San Diego. Although this was illegal without a work permit, they could use the border crossing permit and pretend they were going shopping. Lupita laughed at the idea of sneaking over the border to work; besides, she already had a job at the hospital.

After about two months the hospital closed due to a massive flood. Lupita reconsidered Juanita's idea. Together they drove in Juanita's newly-bought used Toyota to San Diego, all dressed up to look like they were ready for a day of shopping. Juanita set up her cousin with two cleaning jobs where she made $36 a day. Lupita worked so well that her employers recommended her to friends, and soon she was cleaning a total of six homes during the week and making $80 a day. On Sundays she tried to rest at home while she prepared meals for the family for the whole week, cleaned the house and did laundry. After a while, working on *el otro lado* (the other side) grew tiresome and Lupita was exhausted. She was missing out on the kids' growing up and her marriage was very strained. The children's education was costing more and more every time it came time to pay the bills, and gasoline for their daily trips was very expensive. Besides, the INS border officials were getting a little suspicious of all the shopping that Juanita and Lupita were doing.

Eventually, Lupita had to decide whether or not she and Juanita should find an apartment in San Diego, only coming home on the weekends. Even after paying rent, she would still be able to provide more money for education, child care and living expenses than if she worked in Tijuana. On the other hand, she didn't want to leave her family.

*What are Lupita's options? What do you think she might do?*

# Case Study Outcomes

## Outcome to Case Study 1
### Cruz and Cecilia Huerta    1961
Cruz decided to stay in California and send for Cecilia and the two children. They would have to enter the US by way of a *coyote* since they were "undocumented," or without legal status. *Coyotes* are people who guide migrants illegally across the border for a fee. Cruz paid for a *coyote* and the family was safely united in California. Together, Cruz and Cecilia worked hard to care for their children and rented a home. Cecilia found a job in a cannery packing whatever was in season, while Cruz worked the fields. After about five years, they had steady jobs, bought a house, enrolled their children in school and had another baby. They were living the American dream they had hoped to achieve.

### Cruz and Cecilia Huerta, the story continued
In 1964 the Huerta family's dream was interrupted. *Braceros* were being deported back to Mexico. While Cruz was at work he was contacted by US government officials who told him he needed to leave the US or face arrest. Cruz and Cecilia were plagued by questions. They had paid US taxes and social security had been deducted from their earnings. They had been responsible members of their community, even though they were not citizens. But they experienced discrimination in California, and they wanted to escape the growing racism. They also wanted their children to grow up in Mexico with their grandparents and extended family. Cruz and Cecilia felt that their children should know who they were culturally. They truly wanted to be patriotic to their motherland, but they didn't want to deprive themselves or their children of a fruitful life.

Solicit student responses to the following questions: *What are their options? What do you think they might do?*

## Second Outcome to Case Study I
### The Huerta Family    1964
The Huerta family stayed in California and applied for US citizenship. Late in 1964, they received their citizenship papers. Having a US-born child helped win their case. Cecilia bore a total of eight children, six of whom were US-born. Both Cruz and Cecilia held stable factory jobs that paid much more than field work. Of the eight children, seven went to college. Every member of the Huerta family was active in her or his respective local communities and one son was elected to the city council. Cruz and Cecilia, even in their old age, worked and went to city council meetings where they were well known. (Adapted from *The Roots of Mexican Labor Migration* by Alexander Monto. London: Praeger, 1994.)

## Outcome to Case Study 2
### Rosalita Isabel González    1966
Eventually, Rosalita migrated illegally into Texas. Almost immediately she gave birth to a son whom she later gave up for adoption in Laredo, Texas. Rosalita lived in the southern part of Texas for ten years before becoming part of the migratory stream that came to

Minnesota to work. While in Texas she signed a contract with the Farmer's Produce Company to work in Litchfield, Minnesota for the Jenny-O Company which had promised to make housing arrangements for Rosalita and the other 15 workers under contract with the company. However, when the group arrived in Litchfield in June 1963, they encountered discrimination. The group of workers were not allowed to stay in the only hotel in town, even though rooms had been reserved and were available. After spending the night in a park near the lake with the other 15 workers, they started their jobs in the turkey processing factory. The next night they were placed in rooms outside of town.

Rosalita was a fast and reliable worker. She stayed in Litchfield and learned English. With the help of her boss, she obtained her visa five years later in 1969. Rosalita believed that having a visa would assure her the same treatment as given European immigrants. Next, Rosalita put in an application to become a citizen. Because she worked all day and did not have access to a telephone, Rosalita never received the telephone call to receive citizenship papers. (Adapted from an oral interview: *Minnesota Historical Society*.)

## Outcome to Case Study 3
### Pedro Barajas   1992
Pedro officially joined a group of vendors in a special kind of street market that moves to a different neighborhood each day. All the vendors in the group travel together to areas where commerce is good enough to market their goods and make a profit. They formed a federation of vendors who help one another. However, when Pedro joined the group of vendors he had to promise Don Alberto, a PRI leader, a portion of his earnings to help him enroll. (Adapted from *Mexican Lives* by Judith Adler Hellman. New York: The New Press, 1994.)

## Outcome to Case Study 4
### Emiliano Rodríguez Madrid    1994
Emiliano convinced his son to join the business and to import electronics equipment from Asia legally. They stayed in Mexico City and converted the former factory into a warehouse to store the goods. Emiliano had to lay off more than seven hundred workers. So far business is not soaring and things aren't looking very promising. (Adapted from *Mexican Lives* by Judith Adler Hellman and articles in *Report from the Americas*.)

## Outcome to Case Study 5
### Lupita Mireya Santos y López 1995
Lupita, with Rigoberto's agreement, decided to stay in Tijuana, Mexico. She cut back her work to three days a week. After work she did the shopping in San Diego while the children and Rigoberto took on the responsibility of cooking and cleaning. On her days off, Lupita cooked and cleaned until the house was spotless. Rigoberto continued to work in the *maquiladora* and the children remained in school. They felt it was best for their kids to be raised in their native land where they didn't have to face racial discrimination. With Proposition 187 just voted in, racism in California was becoming more rampant and the border much more strict. (Source: Interview.)

# Constructive Controversy Process

1.  As a group, review the attached constructive controversy checklist. Each group needs to complete this checklist and turn it in at the end of class.

2.  With your partner, plan your argument by reading the arguments about Proposition 187 and supplementing those ideas with your own. You have ten minutes to complete this.

3.  Listen to the opposing viewpoint for three minutes. Take notes on what they say. You will need these ideas when you change perspectives.

4.  Present your perspective to the group. Be forceful, sincere and persuasive. However, keep an open mind. Each group member must speak, and the opposing side cannot interrupt your presentation. You have three minutes.

5.  Open discussion will take place for five minutes. During this time you should ask questions of the opposition, challenge their ideas and clarify your stance. Remember, the discussion should center around ideas, not personality traits.

6.  Switch chairs with the other group members. You will now take the perspective of the opposition. You can use your notes or other personal ideas, but you will not be able to look at the readings of the opposition. You have 3 minutes to complete this.

7.  Drop your roles and list the most convincing facts from both sides. Then, by consensus, reach a decision on which perspective to support. Use this list and notes as a base for your homework assignment.

8.  Take out the constructive controversy checklist. As a group, check those statements that reflect your group. Reflect on the group interaction that went well and suggest improvement for the future. Put all group members' names on the checklist and hand in.

## Homework assignment

Write or type a one page report to the President. In the report, outline the positive and negative aspects of immigration policies such as Proposition 187. Then in a forceful and convincing style, encourage the President to support or oppose an immigration policy like Proposition 187. Your argument should reflect your group's decision. Remember that your report is evaluated on content, style, diction and usage.

# Constructive Controversy Checklist

_____  1.  There was no winner or loser, only a successful, creative and productive solution. The cooperativeness of group members should outweigh by far their competitiveness.

_____  2.  All members actively participated in the group discussions, sharing their information, conclusions and perspectives.

_____  3.  Every member's contributions were listened to, respected and taken seriously.

_____  4.  Effective communication skills were used, including paraphrasing and other listening skills.

_____  5.  Issues and problems were viewed from all available perspectives.

_____  6.  Group members criticized ideas and positions, not individuals.

_____  7.  Group members viewed disagreement as an interesting situation from which something could be leaned, not as a personal rejection or sign that they were being perceived as incompetent or ignorant.

_____  8.  Emotions were allowed and members were encouraged to express them.

_____  9.  The rules of argument were followed. Members presented organized information to support their positions, reasoned logically and changed their minds when other presented persuasive and convincing arguments and proof.

Adapted from Johnson, D. And Johnson, F. *Joining Together: Group Theory and Group Skills*. 5th ed. Boston: Allyn and Bacon, 1994.

# Supporting Proposition 187

Proposition 187 is a referendum item passed by California voters in 1994. Enactment of Proposition 187 would establish a system by which government agencies would prevent undocumented immigrants from receiving benefits or public services, such as education and health services. Similar documents are being proposed in several other states.

## Setting

You recently have been appointed to the President's Immigration Advisory Committee. Your task is to prepare a report for the President. First, you must outline the positive and negative aspects of immigration and second, advise the President on the proper direction to pursue. The President specifically has chosen the four members of the committee because all of you are known for the logical and thoughtful decisions you make. The President does not want to make this decision based on "party politics," rather on what is best for the future of the country.

## Position

You are about to debate the merits of each side of Proposition 187. Your position is to support the initiative. Your position is that the government must try to slow or stop the flow of immigrants into the US because it is having detrimental effects on our society. Whether or not you personally agree with this position, support it wholeheartedly. Use logic and be creative in supporting this view. Some major arguments in the debate are listed below. Learn your perspective, add your own thoughts, and listen to the opposition with a keen and questioning spirit.

## Arguments

- The United States is being overrun with immigrants. In 1990, foreign-born people made up 8% of the US population, of which nearly 13% are undocumented immigrants. Unless state and federal governments do something to stem the flow of immigrants, especially illegal immigrants, this country is headed for real trouble.
- Illegals are a drain on society's resources—they come to take, not to give. One recent study indicates that immigrants present a net cost to California of $18 billion.
- By continuing to provide social services to undocumented immigrants, the state is rewarding people for violating US law.
- Immigrants take jobs from US citizens, increasing unemployment. A recent study indicates that for every 100 immigrants hired, twenty-five US workers are displaced.
- Many of the crimes in this state are committed by illegal aliens. Illegals are disrespectful of American custom and law.
- Illegal immigrants don't assimilate—they're not interested in becoming US citizens.
- Illegal immigrants are usually poor; they're often uneducated and are pulling down the quality of our schools.
- California citizens have a right to the protection of their government from any person or persons entering this country unlawfully.
- Proposition 187 would provide for the collaboration between state and local government agencies with the federal government. It's impossible for the state of California to deal with this issue alone. Efforts must be made to coordinate actions with the Immigration and Naturalization Service (INS).
- The majority of Californians support this initiative—it's not a matter of party politics.

# Opposing Proposition 187

Proposition 187 is a referendum item passed by California voters in 1994. Enactment of Proposition 187 would establish a system by which government agencies would prevent undocumented immigrants from receiving benefits or public services, such as education and health services. Similar documents are being proposed in several other states.

## Setting

You recently have been appointed to the President's Immigration Advisory Committee. Your task is to prepare a report for the President. First, you must outline the positive and negative aspects of immigration and second, advise the President on the proper direction to pursue. The President specifically has chosen the four members of the committee because all of you are known for the logical and thoughtful decisions you make. The President does not want to make this decision based on "party politics," rather on what is best for the future of the country.

## Position

You are about to debate the merits of each side of Proposition 187. Your position is to oppose the initiative. Your position is that as a nation of immigrants, it is hypocritical to try to stop the flow of immigrants into the country. You believe that initiatives like Proposition 187 would have detrimental effects on the well-being of immigrants and society as a whole. Whether or not you personally agree with this position, support it wholeheartedly. Use logic and be creative in supporting this view. Some of the major arguments in the debate are listed below. Learn your perspective, add your own thoughts, and listen to the opposition with a keen and questioning spirit.

## Arguments

- It's not true that the first-generation immigrant share of our population is growing. In 1990, foreign-born people made up 8% of the population, compared to about 15% at the turn of the century. Undocumented immigrants make up only about 13% of all immigrants residing in the US, and only about 1% of the entire US population.

- Most undocumented immigrants are ineligible for most social programs. The exceptions are education for children, which is constitutionally required, and benefits directly related to health and safety, such as emergency medical care and nutritional assistance through the Woman Infant and Child Nutrition Program.

- Claims that immigrants take jobs away from US citizens are misleading. Immigrants spend money for goods and services, which benefits the economy and actually results in job creation.

- If the bill passes, non-white people will be suspected of being illegals. People of color are stopped and harassed and asked for documentation of citizenship more often than people who look "white."

- If the measure passes, the social costs would be high. It would leave hundreds of thousands of children and young adults without education and on the streets.

- The provision to deny health services to the undocumented would seriously endanger the public health. In this country, we long ago recognized that health is a community concern. Everyone will be in danger if certain diseases are untreated.

- Immigrants—both documented and undocumented—contribute far more in tax revenues and to the economy than they utilize in government services. Numerous studies show that the presence of undocumented workers in the state of California has allowed the economy to withstand more severe economic decline.

- Rather than saving the state money, Proposition 187 will cost the state more. There will be high administrative costs of verifying citizenship and immigration status. School officials and health workers would in effect serve as immigration officials, which would have a devastating impact on our educational and health system. This provision will also involve the state in costly lawsuits for the next several years.

# Bringing History to Life

*Stories about
Contemporary Mexicans*

This lesson continues the portrayal of six people from six regions of Mexico from lessons 9 and 15. It is now the present, and the six families we have been tracing are immersed in events of the day. Many of the issues of the past remain largely the same, but the context has changed. The new colonizers have taken the form of trade agreements, maquiladora factories, and tourism. In the stories, the descendants of the Spanish have maintained a comfortable lifestyle, through hard work and "good fortune". The others, also hard workers, have found jobs in factories along the border, in an oil refinery along the gulf coast, and in orange groves in California. Their employment often takes them away from their families, and like millions of others, follows the pattern of Mexicans on the move. In the south, our character has chosen to join the Zapatista army, her only hope for a better future.

Students should work in the same small group as in Lessons 9 and 15 for the first part of the lesson while they read and discuss their story. Then, students do a "jigsaw" and reform into new groups that have one representative of each region who tells the story of his or her person. The students should use the note taking grid to record the lives of the people.

| | |
|---|---|
| **Learner Objectives** | • To describe important events that occur in people's lives in contemporary Mexico. |
| | • To assess the impact these events have on people's lives by identifying ways in which people's lives are changing in contemporary Mexico. |
| | • To develop an understanding of different perspectives about changes in Mexico. |
| **Concepts** | • Social change |
| | • Continuity |
| **Major Question to be Addressed** | How do economic, social and political changes affect people's lives in contemporary Mexico? |
| **Teaching Strategies** | • Reading and discussion in small groups |
| | • "Jigsawing" and teaching others |
| **Materials Provided** | • Six stories from contemporary Mexico (Handouts 1a-1f) |
| | • Note-taking Grid (Handout 2) |
| | • Chart of Descendants (See Lesson 15) |
| **Additional Materials Needed** | • Student journals |
| | • Overhead projector and transparency of Chart of Descendants |
| **Time Required** | 1 class session |
| **Preparation for this Lesson** | • Make copies of the six stories from Handout 1—one story per small group with enough copies for each student in the group. |
| | • Make one copy of Handout 2 *(Note-taking Grid)* for each student. |
| | • Ask students to bring to class the *Family Time-line* they used in Lessons 9 and 15. |
| | • Make an overhead of the *Chart of Descendants* (Lesson 15) to help students understand the continuity between stories. |

# Sequence of Lesson

*Anticipatory Set*
*10 minutes*

1. Divide students into the same small groups as Lesson 9. Instruct students to jot down on plain paper all they can recall about the story of the person from their region during the time of the Mexican Revolution. Show overhead of the Chart of Descendants so they can track the person.

*Body of Lesson*
*40 minutes*

2. Use same instructions as Lesson 9 for the remainder of this lesson.

## Story from Region 1 — North
# CONTEMPORARY ERA

Manuela Rodriguez lived the rest of her life on the same *hacienda* in Durango. She watched *gringo* troops retreat from the region when they were recalled by the United States to fight in World War I. She lost her husband in the Mexican Revolution, which ended in 1920. Life did not improve much for Manuela. After the war, she worked the next twenty years of her life in the corn fields along with her child.

Manuela continues to live through the stories which her descendants tell about her. This is the account of her great granddaughter, a young woman named Magdalena Hernandez. Magdalena lives in Tijuana, on Mexico's northern border.

My name is Magdalena Hernandez. I am 23 years old and single. I work in a *maquiladora* assembly plant in Tijuana, along the Mexico-US border. Most of my family lives in the state of Durango. I am very close to my family, so I often go back and visit.

I had to come here to the border because there were no jobs in Durango and my family couldn't pay for my school anymore. I only went through seventh grade because we didn't have enough money for my school books, uniform and transportation.

Right now I am working in a new *maquiladora* on a one year contract. It's a plant that is owned and operated by a large foreign

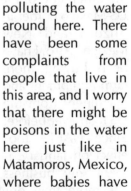

company, probably a US company. I assemble different kinds of things, but my boss won't tell me what they are for. All I know is that they are part of some kind of medical equipment for hospitals.

This *maquiladora* is an okay plant compared to the other places where I have worked. In some plants along the border the conditions were just terrible. We had to work overtime, and if we refused we would get fired. The salaries were very low, and there was no safety equipment, so I was scared that I would get hurt. Most of us were given too

much work to do, and if we complained about being mistreated we risked getting fired or not getting paid. A friend of mine who went to work on the US side says salaries are much better for the US workers who are doing the same jobs that we do.

Anyway, things are going well here in Tijuana. Maybe it is because this is a new company or maybe because there is a new free trade agreement between the US and Mexico. But I am worried that this plant is polluting the water around here. There have been some complaints from people that live in this area, and I worry that there might be poisons in the water here just like in Matamoros, Mexico, where babies have been born with deformities. Some babies were born without brains.

I think about this often, but I am afraid to talk about it. Just talking about problems at work can get you into trouble. I want to get a permanent job and if the bosses think I'm a troublemaker, I'll never get hired. There are so many unemployed people here that there is a lot of competition for jobs. Like me, anyone here will do anything to get work. We'll even accept low wages.

I would like to buy a home and buy a car. Maybe someday I'll start a family....

## Story from Region 2 — North Central
# CONTEMPORARY ERA

The Mexican Revolution spread through most of the country. With the new constitution, many large landowners lost their land, and in some areas the lands were returned to the original owners. Delores Gutierrez lost her life trying to defend her land, and the rest of her family remained in the area with only a fraction of the land that previously had been theirs.

Alejandro Gutierrez, the great grandson of Delores Gutierrez, now lives in a city in the state of Chihuahua. Alejandro is a single man. His family has been very successful in cattle ranching in the northern part of the country. He went to the best schools in Mexico and has a degree in business management. He is what is known in Mexico as a fortunate man.

My name is Alejandro Gutierrez. I am 35 years old and a businessman. I sell farm equipment and I also own a sports store chain. Business is better now that we can trade more freely with the US.

Our government signed a deal with the US called NAFTA, the free trade agreement. The whole country is going to benefit from that deal. I can see the results in my business because now I am selling my merchandise on the other side of the US-Mexico border in Arizona and New Mexico. Also, I have been buying more farm equipment and machinery from the US than ever before. Since NAFTA took effect on January 1, 1994, my business has more than doubled. There are fewer obstacles to trade now such as high tariffs.

For fifteen years I have been dedicated to my business and my standard of living has improved. I think this is due to good government policies in the last several years. The last two presidents have pursued policies which benefit businesses like mine. Before then, it seemed like Mexico was no different from any other Central American or South American country. Now, finally, we are going to be business partners with the US and Canada, and that is good for people like me.

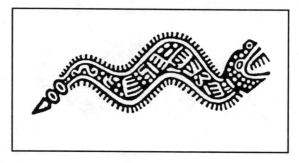

A lot of US companies have moved their factories to the Mexican side of the border. The environmentalists and worker unions here are protesting as usual. They say there is more pollution now with so many factories, and that workers work in unsafe areas and are underpaid. They are always unhappy. I don't understand the workers. If they don't have work, they protest and go to work to the other side of the border. Even though they finally are getting some jobs here in Mexico, they are still protesting. With NAFTA, I believe we are going to get the better kind of life that we deserve. Those who protest NAFTA are against progress—the progress of Mexico.

I am a fortunate man, but I am also a very hard worker. Fortune is not for lazy people. Mexicans are very smart, but we have to start working harder. You see, a lot of people sit around all day in the *barrios* and do nothing. My father told me that after the revolution we lost everything, but with our hard work we succeeded. If we all work hard, we will have a better country. There are some people who don't want progress, like the Indians in the south that call themselves "Zapatistas." Those who are against good deals like NAFTA will drown in their own poverty.

## Story from Region 3 — South Central
# CONTEMPORARY ERA

The Mexican Revolution ended in 1920, but the country continued to have internal political problems. In Mexico City, politicians fought and even assassinated each other in order to get power. Revolutionary heroes like Pancho Villa and Emiliano Zapata continued to fight for their cause. Although they were sensitive to the demands of the majority of people, they lacked the education and political experience to run Mexico. The political and economic destiny of Mexico lay in the hands of new political leaders who eventually forgot or ignored the promises of the Revolution. They catered to the more developed countries and their own selfish interests.

Military officers such as Captain Luis Muñoz stayed in the army. Members of his regiment were promoted for their help with the assassination of Emiliano Zapata in 1919. Now it is 1994. Eleonora Quintanilla, age 23, is the great granddaughter of Captain Muñoz.

My name is Eleonora Quintanilla. I live in an apartment with my sister in Mexico City. I own two tourist agencies and I travel throughout Mexico and abroad. I am fortunate that I am not dark like my sister, even though we have some Indian blood. Being light-skinned is definitely an advantage in my business.

This year I was expecting an improvement in my tourism business, but since January 1st, when the Zapatistas started a war in Chiapas, things have actually gotten a bit worse. It doesn't help that there are Mexican children begging in the

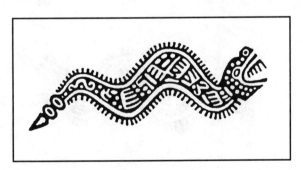

streets. Tourists don't like to see that. Sometimes the children steal money from the tourists, and when they are caught, they give some excuse like the money is for their crippled mother.

I don't know what is going to happen here in Mexico. There are a lot of poor people and because of it, we all pay. We have a social security system for everyone who has a regular job, like me. There are also lots of government programs to take care of the poor. The government subsidizes the price of tortillas so everyone can afford them

and no one will starve. It also builds hospitals and schools for the poor, and still they complain. It costs us taxpayers a lot of money for these programs, and for extra police to control crime.

When poor people are offered jobs in hotels that the government has built in places like Cozumel and Cancún, they don't want to move there. I think ignorance is their worst handicap. They need to adapt themselves to today's world instead of trying to keep their old ways. Indians, especially, are making trouble. They say they don't want NAFTA, and they are against the new government.

Some of us work hard and that's why we have what we have. It is not fair that some people don't work at all and then want to have everything. I have a strong sense of my heritage and I also believe in our democracy. We have many rights, like the right to vote and elect our president. I think our former president did the right thing to pass NAFTA. Our lifestyles will improve because of this agreement with the US and Canada. NAFTA will bring a lot of jobs to Mexican people. Hopefully it will also bring more tourists. That's good for my business.

## Story from Region 4 — Gulf Coast
# CONTEMPORARY ERA

Nobody knows exactly where Sabino went after he ran away from the *hacienda,* but some people say that in 1910 he joined other workers in the revolutionary army to fight the federal army. Eventually Sabino returned from the war front in the north, got some land close to the city of Veracruz and married an Indian woman. They had several children.

As time went on, the people in the state of Veracruz witnessed the arrival of immigrants from Europe and the US. The economy of this coastal area grew rapidly as the petroleum, coffee and sugar cane industries thrived. Tourism also became a major business.

Sabino's great grandson Jacinto Silva Lagos lives near the oil refineries in the Veracruz city of Poza Rica. He is a descendant of the first Silva who arrived on a slave ship during the years of the Spanish invasion. Jacinto lives with his father and mother, an older sister and a younger brother.

I am Jacinto Silva Lagos. I am 22 years old and I was born in the city of Veracruz. I went to school for eight years but I had to quit because my parents did not have enough money. I began working in a car shop when I was very young.

My sister and brother have had a hard time finding jobs around here. My sister finally went to work at a *maquiladora* along the border because she could make more money there. She is paid 50 cents an hour to sew labels on jeans that are sold in the US. But she is paid so little that it would take her more than 40 hours of work to buy a pair of jeans like that in the US!

My sister says that since she started working there she has headaches all the time. Before she left for the border she never had this problem. Now she is always sick. Sometimes I feel tempted to go north and across the border into Texas. My friends who have gone there say it is a great place. It is easy to make money there and there are a lot of fun things to do. But most of my friends are here. We go dancing on the weekends. We like *merengue, cumbia,* and *mambo* the best.

Right now I am working in an oil refinery of Poza Rica. I have a half-year contract as a machine operator. It is an okay job. It pays well. One of my uncles connected me to the workers' union of PEMEX, the Mexican petroleum company. As you know, oil is a very important industry in Mexico that is owned by the government. Although it is hard to get a permanent job here, it is possible to use your influence to buy a contract to work full-time. Some of the workers here have permanent contracts because their parents have worked here since the beginning of the oil industry. But others get jobs because they have enough money to buy them or enough influence to get them. This workplace is full of corruption.

I'm feeling restless because I don't have a permanent job. I think I will ask my uncle to try and get me contract for me to work in the oil towers at sea. I've heard that this is very dangerous, but the company pays a lot of money. Workers say many people have died in accidents there. If that doesn't work, maybe I will look for work on the border. Or why not try to cross the border into Texas?

## Story from Region 5 — Pacific South
# CONTEMPORARY ERA

After many years of fighting and many lives lost, Emiliano Zapata was assassinated by government soldiers. In the 1920s, the pain of the revolution subsided. Feliciano Mendieta continued working as a jeweler in his native Oaxaca until he died at the age of 85.

During World War II, Mexicans were offered temporary permits to work in the US. Many Zapotecs from Oaxaca went north and got jobs in factories and fields. They usually went in small groups and lived together to maintain their cultural identity.

It is now 1994. Feliciano's great granddaughter Maria Mendieta lives part of the year in Oaxaca (wah-HA-kah) continuing the family tradition of jewelry-making. The other part of the year she works in California orange groves, though she doesn't have a work permit.

My name is Maria Mendieta and I am 23 years old. I was born in the state of Oaxaca. My great grandfather was Feliciano Mendieta. Everybody in the family is very proud of him. The revolution in which he fought made us proud to be Mexicans. After those years of brutal war we became more "civilized," I think. For instance, most of the people in this region now write and read in Spanish.

My family has continued the tradition of making jewelry. My brothers and I work together for a jewelry store in Oaxaca. The work is seasona. December is always the busiest time of year because the tourists come

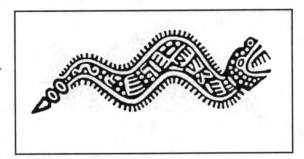

then. Not long ago I worked as a silversmith on my own, designing earrings, pins and necklaces. I tried to sell directly to the tourists, but they always wanted bargains and would get angry if I did not agree to sell my work for really cheap prices. So my business didn't make it. The owners of big stores keep the independent silversmiths from making an extra peso.

When I'm not making jewelry, I work and live in California with my brothers. I have friends living near the border, so I know when and where it is possible to cross. It has become a routine now, and it's the way that many of my friends live. In Oaxaca, life is easy in the sense that I can speak Spanish all the time, but there is only seasonal work. In order to earn enough money I have to go to the US to work in the orange groves.

I have a lot of Mexican friends there and some of them have become "Americans." There is a big community of people from Oaxaca, and we hang out together. We always help each other when someone needs something, like money. The work is hard. My back and my neck hurt after nine or ten hours in the fields. But I can then come back to Oaxaca and don't have to work for a month or so. During that time, I visit my family in Oaxaca or I go to the beautiful beaches near my village.

I am very independent compared to other young women around here. My mother tells me I should get married pretty soon, but I don't think so. It is hard enough to survive on my own. Meanwhile, I will continue working in California until the economy of Mexico gets better. Hopefully, I won't have to go so far away then to earn a living. I hope that the situation will get better because our new president has promised a lot.

# Story from Region 6 — Southeast
# CONTEMPORARY ERA

Manuel Santiago died at the age of 45 on his small plot of land in the highlands. He lived during an important time in Mexican history when a revolution swept the entire country. The revolution officially ended in 1920, and a new constitution was written. The new constitution promised land reform that would redistribute land more fairly. However, the promises did not become a reality for many people. In the state of Chiapas almost everything continued as before. The best lands continued to be held by large landowners. The Mayan people continued to be treated unfairly by the government and discriminated against by most other people.

This is the story of Manuel Santiago's great granddaughter, María Santis Lopez, a descendant of Ana Santiago. Maria is a member of the Zapatistas, a revolutionary Mayan Indian army. She lives in the Lacandón rain forest.

My name is Maria Santis Lopez. I am 17 years old and I am a Tzeltal (zel-TALL) Mayan Indian. My family migrated to the Lacandón rain forest from the highlands, close to San Cristobal de las Casas. They came in search of land that they were promised in the national land reform. When they got there, a cattle rancher claimed the title to the land. My family wandered for several years, renting land to grow corn whenever they had a little money, or working for ranchers. In the worst of times, they lived on someone else's land to survive until the government or a landowner threw

them out. My mother and father now live in a little village close to the Guatemalan border.

I don't have any brothers or sisters. My mother told me that I had two brothers, but they died as babies. One died from malaria and the other from dehydration caused by diarrhea. There are many families here without land that have hardly one meal a day. They don't have medical care or a school. There are a few rich ranchers and coffee growers who own most of the land. The government says it will protect our right to the land. But it only protects those who have titles to the land, land that used to belong to us.

People are tired of waiting. I joined the Zapatistas, who are fighting for land reform and other measures that will bring about justice. My parents agreed to let me join only because they know there is no other way to bring change. We have tried patience. It doesn't work.

On January 1, 1994, I was part of a Zapatista offensive to take the city of San Cristobal de las Casas. Some Zapatistas took other cities in the state of Chiapas. The Zapatistas treat me as an equal and respect me as a soldier and as a woman. I was one of the first soldiers to march into San Cristobal, but a few days later we had to retreat because the Mexican army arrived. Fifteen thousand soldiers brought tanks, airplanes, helicopters and other sophisticated weapons. Most of it was supplied by the US for its "war against drugs." All of that against two or three thousand badly equipped Mayans! We lost several soldiers in the battle. Many civilians also lost their lives when the army dropped bombs on villages near San Cristobal. Now I am back in the rain forest, waiting for the results of the peace talks between our army and the government. I am afraid we will go back to the same situation. The government has done it before. Promises, promises, promises....

# NOTE-TAKING GRID for the CONTEMPORARY ERA

*Use this grid to fill in the information about the five other regions*

| | Who is the story about? Describe the person and their way of life. | How do events in Mexico affect her / him? |
|---|---|---|
| REGION _____ | | |
| REGION _____ | | |
| REGION _____ | | |
| REGION _____ | | |
| REGION _____ | | |

*Many Faces of Mexico*

# Citizen Action:
## *Working for Change*

An integral part of this curriculum is helping students explore their connections to issues that link the people of Mexico, the US and Canada. This lesson goes a step further by helping students not only to make connections, but also to learn ways to directly respond to what they have learned about Mexico and about their own country, as well.

Studies show that students and adults become cynical and disillusioned if they learn about critical issues, but do not take steps to work for change. Therefore, examples of "citizen action" are offered in this lesson so students can analyze why and how people become organized. The four accounts include groups that educate people in their community, tackle environmental problems, and advocate for workers' rights. It also describes the work of a group which works with a popular TV hero to negotiate for low-income housing.

In the final step of the lesson, students brainstorm and develop a strategy of their own to respond to what they have learned. A short list of organizations that cross the boundaries between Mexico, the US and Canada is included in Appendix E. A shared goal of these organizations is to educate and develop understanding between the peoples of North America.

| **Learner Objectives** | • To observe ways that ordinary people work together for change. |
| | • To propose and design a democratic plan of action. |

| **Concepts** | • Citizen action |
| | • Community organizing |
| | • Solidarity |

| **Major Questions to be Addressed** | • How do ordinary people work for change? |
| | • Can change come from people at the base of society? |

| **Exploring the Connections** | Students learn about the actions that Mexicans are taking to bring about social change, and are encouraged to engage in citizen action to respond to their own issues of concern. A list of addresses and organizations in Appendix E can provide ideas and resources for projects they may wish to pursue. |

| **Teaching Strategies** | • Case studies, jigsaw |
| | • Research and planning |

| **Materials Provided** | • Analyzing Citizen Action (Handout 1) |
| | • Citizen Action Case Studies (Handouts 2a - 2d) |

| **Additional Materials Needed** | Plain paper and pens |

| **Time Required** | At least one class session |

| **Preparation for this Lesson** | Make copies of Handout 1 (one case per small group with enough copies for each student in the group). |

# Sequence of Lesson

| ***Anticipatory Set*** | 1. | Ask students what they think are the most pressing issues |
| ***10 minutes*** | | facing children and adults in Mexico which concerned citizens can address. Write responses on the board which will be used later in class discussion. |
| | 2. | Discuss the concept of "citizen action." Then ask, "in light of what you now know about Mexico, what do you think are some major changes in Mexico that have been initiated by concerned citizens?" List responses on the board. |
| ***Body of Lesson*** | 3. | Divide into small groups of not more than three students each. |
| ***40 minutes*** | | Ask each group to evaluate one example from the *Citizen Action Case Studies*. Refer to the questions on Handout 2 to analyze their case study. |

4. When groups complete the analysis, have students jigsaw one time. They should explain their case of citizen action and report their findings to another group which studied a different case. When this is complete, instruct students to stay in this larger group and select one of the issues facing the Mexican people that are listed on the board. Ask students to brainstorm ways in which they could help address the issue.

5. Have groups report back to the class and list their ideas. After all the groups have reported, discuss the merits of their ideas; then select two or three ideas to pursue further. Determine what information is needed, where it can be obtained, and how the research will be done.

6. Decide on a project that responds to what you now know about Mexico. Develop your goals and make a plan. Decide who will do what, as well as when and how it will be done. The list of addresses and organizations in Appendix E can provide ideas and resources, in addition to projects that you may want to pursue. This list also includes addresses of key political offices in Mexico, the US and Canada. Keep a record of your goals, procedures and results of your response. Write an article about your experience and publish it in your school newsletter or send it to the media. Good Luck!

*Extension Idea*

7. Students should be encouraged to interview people in their own communities who are engaging in citizen action. Use the questions on Handout 2 to analyze the work of people living in the United States who are engaged in citizen action.

# Citizen Action

In Mexico, Canada, and the United States, ordinary people are working for change through citizen action. Young and not-so-young people are joining together to do such things as build houses, community centers and schools. Ordinary people are providing food and shelter for children who live on the streets and are trying to halt the actions of companies that produce and sell glue and other toxic inhalants to street children. Individuals who write letters and educate others about crucial issues also are engaging in citizen action. For instance, citizens are lobbying governments to stop logging in rainforests, to clean up the environment, or to provide for the needy. By informing themselves about human rights abuses, ordinary people are trying to influence government agencies to investigate and curtail violations.

Why is citizen action important? Ordinary citizens often are the closest to a problem and have a clear understanding of its causes. By listening carefully to each other and organizing democratically, people of all ages can develop creative solutions and alternative approaches to problems. Finally they can enlist the participation and support of others to work for change.

Citizen action is on the rise in Mexico. Four creative examples of how people have come together to work for change are given on the following page. After reading the descriptions, answer the following questions:

1. What are the key issues it is addressing?

2. What parties are involved?

3. What are the group's goals?

4. How does the group draw attention to its cause?

5. What tactics does the group use to accomplish its goals?

6. What obstacles does the group face?

7. What do you think will be the outcome of the group's actions?

# SUPERBARRIO:
# A National Hero Comes to the Rescue

In 1985 a disastrous earthquake struck Mexico City, leaving hundreds of thousands of people homeless. Help was promised by the Mexican government and the World Bank, but it was not delivered. The quake destroyed or structurally weakened entire neighborhoods, or *barrios*, and the residents were forced to live on the streets. As a result, earthquake survivors from the *barrios* joined together to form a coalition, or a *superbarrio*. Their goal was to pressure the Mexican government and the World Bank to honor their commitment to construct safe, low-cost housing.

To organize the citizens and capture the attention of the government, the coalition created a popular hero they called Superbarrio. His actual identity was not revealed, but he appeared as a masked freedom-fighting wrestler. Dressed in yellow tights, red cape and a super hero wrestling mask, Superbarrio led tens of thousands of people into the streets to demand renters' rights, enforcement of housing codes and credit for housing construction, plus a new low-cost housing program.

Superbarrio would lose his super strength when removed from the eyes of the people, so he forced public officials to negotiate in front of television reporters and cameras on the street. Surrounded by the *barrio* groups during a press conference, the government claimed that the housing needs of most victims were being successfully met and that no building sites were available for low-cost construction. Superbarrio declared his plans to the media to "let the truth be known."

Meanwhile, people in the *barrios* organized themselves. Using only personal computers, the *barrio* groups rapidly created their own data base of about 20,000 homeless families and they matched this against a list of possible available properties. Armed with both information and the means to convey it publicly, the *barrio* organizations, represented by Superbarrio, were in the position to argue that some of these properties would provide ideal building sites for low-cost housing construction for the earthquake victims.

Although the barrio groups did not have the ultimate power of decision making, they did have significant strength to negotiate, and eventually obtain, the assistance they needed. Since then, the media hero Superbarrio has been enlisted by other groups to help them organize and advocate around serious policy issues.

*Adapted from: Sheldon Annis, "Giving Voice to the Poor." Foreign Policy, No 84 (Fall 1991), p. 93-106.*

# WORKING COOPERATIVELY:
# A Base Christian Community

In the small village of Coatetela in the state of Morelos, twenty-eight families formed a cooperative in 1982. Now these members have 60 acres of *ejido* land that they farm communally. The land is irrigated and they grow corn, beans and calabash, a type of squash. Twice a week, members of the cooperative drive the truck they purchased together to a town ten miles away to sell their produce. From the profits, they reinvest 5% back into the "bank" they organized and now manage.

Prior to 1982, the twenty-eight families lived on the edge of poverty. Few people were able to read or write, and teen-agers were eager to leave Coatetela for "the big city" to find work. In 1982, a Catholic Priest came to Coatetela and invited people to form a study group, called a base Christian community. Using the Bible, they read stories about other poor people like themselves. They saw how other people worked hard and obeyed the laws, but still were being hurt by unjust systems. The people of Coatetela understood the kind of violence of people killing one another, but now they recognized that violence included hunger, unemployment and poverty which strip people of their dignity. Their study group, like thousands of other base Christian communities in Mexico, became a vehicle for reflection and action.

As the people studied and worshiped together, they related stories from the Bible to their own lives. They figured if they pooled their money together, they could raise the collateral to borrow money. With a loan, they could buy land. They went to the bank and discovered its interest rate was 54%, which would put them deeply in debt. Then they talked to the priest, who helped them get a loan from an international organization called Oxfam. They first bought thirty acres to raise food for themselves. In good years, they had extra produce but no crates or storage or transportation to take it to market to sell. With the help of the priest, they asked other parishioners to form a cooperative. One hundred fifty people joined, paying a $1.00 membership with which they rented a truck to carry produce to the market daily. Five percent of the profits were put back into the cooperative, to be used for the benefit of the members. Eventually this allowed them to purchase a truck, benefitting the whole community.

Believing that sharing is basic to justice, and justice will happen when all people participate, members of this base Christian community continue to study and work together.

# RESCUING THE DIGNITY OF THE CAMPESINO: An Environmental Project

In a region near Tlaxcala called Españita, *campesino* (farm) families have been working together for the past twelve years to restore their land and clean their communities. In the past, it was an area of great natural beauty. Then, due to the need for firewood and land for farms and ranches, most of the trees were cut. Consequently, the land eroded and the soil became depleted. In ditches and open areas in the region, residents had thrown their cans, plastic bags and garbage because there was no municipal garbage collection.

Then a *campesino* from the region named Rogelio Cova had the opportunity to travel throughout Latin America and learn about ways in which other *campesinos* were organizing programs to solve their own environmental problems. When he returned to Tlaxcala, Rogelio gave a report to a group of *campesinos*. He urged them to "employ technologies that were utilized by our grandparents to rescue an agricultural culture that we have been losing." He continued, "We need to reinvigorate and maintain an ethical attitude to nature, without over-exploiting her, as has been done up until now. Then, we will be able to rescue our *campesino* pride."

With Rogelio's leadership, residents began an environmental education program that focused on the problem of garbage. They developed what they called a participatory methodology that involved the investigation of the problem, the planning and then the realization of the project. In practice, this meant that citizens studied their garbage problem, brain stormed possible solutions, and decided on a plan of action. Then they went to their local governments to get help to establish a recycling center. They also started a project to transform waste into organic fertilizers for their fields.

With encouragement from Rogelio, citizens in the countryside started a rural development project with the goal of attaining food self-sufficiency for the region. The first problem was to stop the deterioration of the soil. "The earth," one *campesino* said, "is tired. We must rescue the soil and augment its productivity with organic fertilizers, selection of seed, construction of terraces to reduce erosion, and rotation of crops."

Citizens of Españita also started a recreational ecology camp to educate the community residents and organize activities, such as clean-up weeks in the communities. For this ambitious project, they sought outside help. In response, student groups and other volunteers from the United States have helped paint schools and plant trees during the annual Españita clean-up week. At the end of the clean-up week, even if all the projects are not finished, they have a Final Fiesta of Friendship.

One result of the Rescue of Pride project is the youth have stopped emigrating from Españita to the cities of Mexico or to the US. There are now jobs in the region in the education center and the recycling and waste management projects. The soil has been improved, so *campesinos* are more likely to be able to produce extra food to sell in the market, thereby increasing their income.

*From an interview with Rogelio Cova by Francisco Javier Ramos. To volunteer with projects like this, contact American Friends Service Committee. See Appendix E for address.*

# WORKING TOGETHER:
# Maquila Workers Along the Border

Numerous organizations have been formed to deal with problems affecting people who live on both sides of the US/Mexico border. Of major concern are the almost 2,000 *maquiladoras*, or factories, which employ 500,000 workers within a few miles of the border.

The issues related to *maquiladoras* include environmental problems such as air, water and land pollution and the disposal of toxic chemicals; labor concerns such as unsafe working conditions, long hours and low pay; poor and unsanitary living conditions; and international policies on immigration, trade and tariffs.

Many of the people organizing for change are women, due in part to the fact that about seventy percent of *maquiladora* workers are women. Women are thought to be better employees because they are considered more submissive. On the other hand, women have been the backbone of organizing for change.

In Ciudad Juarez, across the Rio Grande from El Paso, Texas, Cipriana Hererra works with other activists who want changes in the *maquiladoras* and the neighborhoods where workers live.

"In Mexico we supposedly have the right to health, to organize a union, to have housing, to educate our children. But none of these rights exist in practice," Cipri says. She came to Juarez at age 17 to find work after her father lost his job in their home state, and her family joined her when she found a job. After a few years of trying to improve conditions, Cipri's name appeared on a "black list." As a result, she lost her job and has not been able to find work in any of Juarez's 300 *maquiladoras*.

Finding those responsible for problems related to the *maquiladoras* is extremely complex. At the same time, attempts at organizing have been met with repression. In the few instances where people have succeeded in organizing unions, companies often respond by closing down and relocating elsewhere.

A new network of *maquiladora* workers and organizers was formed in the early 1990s. By sponsoring workshops, they are able to share information about organizing strategies and receive information about what's happening inside the factories.

In a few factories, workers have won the right to form independent unions. In others, the goals are more immediate, often starting with workshops on improving health and safety. In one community, workers sponsored a campaign to stop chemical dumping by companies that is causing a disturbing number of birth defects.

In the US and Canada, people have joined in solidarity with the *maquila* workers. In San Diego, when 180 Mexican *maquila* workers filed a lawsuit in US courts against their chief executive officer for sexual harassment, they got help from the Support Committee for Maquiladora Workers. In Tucson, Arizona, Borderlinks offers people who want to learn more about *maquiladoras* the opportunity to volunteer in communities along the border. The Coalition for Justice in the Maquiladoras works on policy issues, and has presented shareholder resolutions that would improve wages, training, environment and infrastructure to companies that operate *maquiladoras*.

*Many Faces of Mexico*

*An Exploring the Connections Lesson*

# Mexico's Future
## *Tools for Understanding*

I t can often be difficult to find up-to-date news and information about Mexico that covers a variety of viewpoint or analyzes the impact of events on the majority of Mexicans. The perspective most readily available to the public are those of the mainstream media, which usually reflects the ideas and opinions of government officials and business leaders.

This final lesson of *Many Faces of Mexico* provides a framework for analyzing how current events in Mexico affect various sectors of Mexican society. It contains a process for the curriculum to remain relevant and up-to-date. A news clipping or summary of a current event can be inserted into Handout 3 to replace the paragraph about the devaluation of the peso that is included in this lesson.

The body of this lesson comes from the Internet, which is an excellent source of current information on Mexico. The lesson contains a description of four sectors of Mexican society, written in 1995 by an individual known as Subcommandante Marcos, a spokesperson for the EZLN, also called the Zapatistas. Little is known about Marcos because he stays hidden in the rain forest of Chiapas. Marcos has inspired people through his articulate and expressive writings. Marcos works on a computer and is able to transmit his writings throughout the world via computer networks. Through his widely distributed works, Marcos has helped solidify the continuing struggle for land, justice and respect for human rights.

*Note: For in-depth coverage of issues related not only to Mexico, but to all of Latin America, we recommend a magazine,* Report on the Americas. *It is published bi-monthly by the North American Congress on Latin America (NACLA), an independent, non-profit organization founded in 1966 to research and report on the political economy of the Americas.*

| Learner Objectives | • To develop critical thinking skills for understanding how current issues and events affect different sectors of Mexican society. |
|---|---|
| | • To analyze current issues and events from a variety of perspectives. |
| | • To make predictions about Mexico's future based on an analysis of current events. |

| Concepts | • Sector analysis |
|---|---|
| | • Global economy |

| Major questions to be Addressed | • What are the implications of current events for the majority of Mexican people? |
|---|---|
| | • What events in Mexico's past seem to be repeated in the present day? |
| | • What are your predictions about Mexico's future? |

| Exploring the Connections | Political and economic changes in Mexico both influence and are shaped by events in our increasingly interconnected world. This lesson incorporates information about how the global political economy affects ordinary Mexicans. You are encouraged to guide students' inquiry into some of the broader economic and political forces which influence what happens in Mexico. Ask students to consider questions such as: What can citizens in the US do to support the kinds of major policy changes that Marcos advocates? |
|---|---|

| Teaching Strategies | Small group analysis, discussion |
|---|---|

| Materials Provided | • Chart of 1990 statistics in Mexico (Image 1) |
|---|---|
| | • Mexico and the Global Economy (Handout 1) |
| | • Sector Descriptions (Handouts 2a–2d) |
| | • A Field Guide to Understanding Mexico (Handout 3) |

| Additional Materials Needed | • Newsprint, markers, tape |
|---|---|
| | • Overhead projector and transparency (optional) |

| Time Required | 1–2 class sessions |
|---|---|

| Preparation For this Lesson | • Make a transparency or a large newsprint chart of the current statistics on Mexico. |
|---|---|
| | • Make one copy of Handout 1 for each student; distribute the session prior to this lesson for students to read and summarize. |
| | • Make copies of Handout 2; each student in a group needs the description of his/her sector. |
| | • Make four copies of Handout 3; one per group. |
| | • Draw 2 large rectangles on newsprint that resemble the description of the building from the reading, Handout 3. Divide the rectangle into 4 unequal sections, according to |

approximate number of people in each sector (Statistics Chart). On both pieces, label the sections "Penthouse Mexico," "Middle Mexico," "Lower Mexico," and "Basement Mexico" as shown in the diagram. Cut one of the pieces apart at the four sections for the student groups to use in Step 4.

## Sequence of Lesson

*Anticipatory Set*
*5 minutes*

1. Ask students to imagine they are going to school in another country and are asked to give a report on current events in the United States. The newspaper in the country prints one or two articles about the US, usually focusing on crime, sports, politics or business. The television programs from the US are *Beverly Hills 90210, Melrose Place, MTV* and reruns of *Dallas*. Using such limited resources, how would you inform other students about the country you are studying,? What messages do you think these sources give about the US? What would help someone who wants to understand the "real" US?

*Body of Lesson*
*40 minutes*

2. Place the transparency of current statistics on the overhead and review the information with students.

3. Ask students if they have heard anything about the individual Subcommandante Marcos. Explain he is a spokesperson for the Mayan Indians who are fighting in Chiapas for land and liberty. The reading on Handout 2 were written by Marcos and transmitted via the Internet throughout the world.

4. Divide the class into four equal groups that represent four sectors of Mexican society. Give to each group one of the four sector descriptions (Handouts 2a - 2d). Have them take turns reading their sectors description aloud to the entire class.

5. Distribute one copy of Handout 3, plus markers and the piece of newsprint that corresponds to their sector. Instruct groups to read about the "current situation," brainstorm responses and record them in the allotted space on the handout. Take 10-20 minutes to complete the handout and use the newsprint to prepare a presentation that explains their responses to the "current situation."

6. Make presentations to the class. When all groups have finished, read aloud to the class the following account of January 1, 1994, also written by Subcomandante Marcos.

> *January of 1994, when the entire country remembered the existence of the Basement. Thousands of indigenous, armed with truth and fire, with shame and dignity, shook the country awake from its sweet dream of modernity. "That is enough!" their voices scream, enough of dreams, enough of nightmares.*

*Satellites, communication equipment and infra-red rays keep watch on their every move, locate their rebellions, point to, on military maps, places for the seeding of bombs and death. Tens of thousands of olive green masks are preparing a new and prosperous war.*

*The indigenous Zapatistas paid for their sins with their blood. What sins? The sin of not being satisfied with handouts, the sin of insisting on their demands for democracy, liberty and justice for all Mexico.*

**Closure**

7.  Discuss the lesson with questions such as:
    - What events in Mexico's history seem to be repeated in the present day?
    - In what ways do you think Mexico's future will resemble the present?

**Evaluation**

Use the Small Group Assessment in Appendix D for students to evaluate their group and their participation in the group.

**Extension Lesson**

After reading Handout 2 and before starting step 5, use time in class to analyze the writings of Marcos. Look up terms that are unfamiliar. Find analogies and metaphors and discuss their meanings.

# Statistics on Mexico
# 1990

| | |
|---|---|
| **Population** | 95 million people |
| **Urban** | 72% |
| **Rural** | 28% |
| | |
| **Billionaires** | .00000025% of pop. (24 people) |
| **Middle Class** | 12% of population |
| **Lower Class** | 75% of population |
| **Under Class** | 13% of population |

*The richest billionaire has assets equal to the combined annual incomes of the 17 million poorest people.*

| | |
|---|---|
| **Unemployment** | 18% |
| **Underemployment** | 40% |
| **Minimum Wage** | $3.90 per day - US dollars |
| | |
| **Housing deficit** | 6 million homes |
| **Substandard housing** | 40% |

**Extreme malnutrition**   15% of population

*Between 1980-1990, there was a 50% decline in per capita consumption of beef, pork and milk.*

**Interest rate for loans**  54% - 60%

**Exports to US from Mexico**
Oil, Autos and auto parts, Televisions and electronics, Chemicals, Cattle, Coffee, Vegetables, Fruits, Clothing

**Imports from the US to Mexico**
Oil products, Plastic products, Electrical machinery, Electronic parts, Grains (corn, wheat)

**There are 50 recognized languages spoken by Indian people in Mexico.**

*Data from World Development Report 1990*
*Published by the World Bank, 1818 H Street, Washington, DC 20433*

# Mexico & the Global Economy

*Directions: Read the handout and summarize the main points in 3-5 complete sentences.*

On January 1, 1994, two major events in Mexico's recent history occurred: the North American Free Trade Agreement (NAFTA) took effect and the Zapatista army took over several towns in the southern state of Chiapas. What is the connection between these two events? The action of the Zapatistas, (also known as EZLN) was in response to the increased hardship on the poor that was anticipated from NAFTA. That same year, still another global trade agreemen t— known as GATT — was ratified. The two agreements intensified Mexico's economic and political problems.

## NAFTA Takes Effect

NAFTA was to have been the crowning achievement of more than a decade of "economic liberalization" in Mexico. According to Mexico's elite, the new free market orientation was the country's ticket into the "first world." When fighting erupted in Chiapas on January 1, 1994—the same day NAFTA took effect — it was a rude reminder that the new economy which had produced 24 billionaires had been paid for by a sharp decline in the living standards of the majority of people.

## PRI Wins the Election

Events in Chiapas forced Mexico's governing party, the PRI, to agree to a series of electoral reforms long-sought by Mexico's opposition parties. These parties — both left and right — were filled with hope that they might be able to defeat the PRI in the 1994 elections. But shortly before the election, the PRI presidential candidate, Luis Donaldo Colosio, was assassinated. This killing, coming on top of the Chiapas rebellion, produced a serious fear of social chaos among many Mexicans. The PRI emerged triumphantly from the 1994 elections, which were marked with fraud and intimidation in many voting locations. Most Mexicans, it seemed clear, were genuinely fearful of the consequences of a PRI loss and/or genuinely hopeful about PRI candidate Ernesto Zedillo's promises of economic growth.

## Tensions Increase in Chiapas

The following December 19, 1994, EZLN soldiers and supporters seized control of 34 municipalities in Chiapas. In response, the Mexican government increased its troop strength to 60,000 soldiers in the region. The EZLN action served as the psychological trigger for the peso crisis. Dollars had been flowing out of Mexico all year, but after December 19, the flow became a flood. On December 22, the government let the peso fall, sending the entire country into economic chaos.

## The Value of the Peso Falls

Mexico's peso crisis coincided with the EZLN actions in December 1994, but it was a long time in the making. In the first year of NAFTA and GATT, the peso lost about 48% of its value, falling from 3.1 pesos to the dollar (One peso = US$.32) to 5.5 (one peso = US$.18). Purchasing power for the peso fell 45%. In a country where 40 million of its 95 million inhabitants already live below the official poverty line, this drop in real wages was devastating.

## Wages for Workers Decrease

For transnational corporations with investments in Mexico, the peso's devaluation meant that Mexican labor became 45% cheaper. In the factories, or *maquiladora* corridor along the border, the minimum wage paid to many workers fell from about US$.56 per hour in January 1994 to US$.33 per hour a year later.

## Loans Made to Mexican Government

With the threat that Mexico was going bankrupt and the Mexican stock market was about to collapse, President Zedillo announced an "economic recovery plan." The international banking community, led by President Clinton, responded with a $40 billion package of loans to "bail Mexico out." The plan called for Mexico to limit wage raises, slash government funding for social services, privatize government-owned companies, and use Mexico's oil reserves as a guarantee for the loan. The international investment community also called upon Mexico to "remove threats to Mexican political stability". This included disarming and removing the Zapatistas, according to Mexican political scientist Denise Dresser.

The US$40 billion loan ensured that holders of government bonds, the majority of whom are US firms and investors, would receive their full dollar value for their investments. The money saved through increased austerity for Mexico's poor and middle class would be the principle means to pay this debt.

*Adapted from "Mexico's Deepening Crisis" by Larry Weiss in* Connection to The Americas, *February 1995, and "Who Broke Mexico?" by Alexander Cockburn and Ken Silverstein,* City Pages, *March 22, 1995.*

# To get to Penthouse Mexico...

One arrives by plane. An airport in Mexico City, Monterrey, Guadalajara or Acapulco is the entrance to an elevator which neither rises nor falls, but rides horizontally across the country of the 24 richest men in the country, the scenes of Mexico of modern times: the government offices where neoliberalism is administered, the business clubs; the vacation resorts whose true vocation is to be a mirror of a social class that does not want to see what is below their feet; a long stairway, spiral and labyrinthed, which leads all the way down to the Lower Mexico, Mexico on foot, mud Mexico.

Above the blood and clay that live in the basement of this country, the twenty-four omnipotent are busy counting the $44 billion dollars, a gift from the Presidential term of these modern times [and the $50 billion of dollars, a gift from foreign friends.]

Penthouse Mexico simply has no time to look down, it is too busy with complicated macroeconomic calculations, exchange of promises, praises and indexes of inflation, interest rates and the percentage of foreign investment, import-export concessions, lists of assets and resources, scales where the country and dignity have no weight, the public debt guaranteed, long range, has gone from 3 billion dollars in 1970, to 76 billion dollars in 1989....

The President is in Penthouse Mexico. These modern times in Mexican neopolitics make public functionaries into something like a species of retail salespeople, and the president of the republic into the sales manager of a gigantic business: Mexico, Inc. To be a politician in the state party in Mexico is the best business to be in....

The "law of the jungle" from free trade will repeat the dosage: more monopolies, fewer jobs. "To grow", in neoliberal politics means simply "to sell". To practice politics one must practice marketing technology. The "citizen" of Penthouse Mexico will be, sooner or later, named SALESMAN OF THE YEAR by some foreign institution.

Historical events happen only within the stock markets and the modern heroes up there are only Good Salesmen. For some reason in the other history (the real one) that top floor, far from expanding, is quickly contracting. Every time there are fewer able to stay there. Sometimes with delicacy, other times with brutality, the incapable are obligated to descend...by the stairs. The Penthouse elevator of Mexico, whose door opens to the great international airports, neither rises nor falls. To leave the Penthouse one must descend, going further and further down until one gets to Middle Mexico.

# To get to Middle Mexico...

One goes by car. It is urban and its image is a carbon copy, which repeats itself in various parts of the country.

In Mexico City, an image of concrete which cannot deny the contradiction of the co-existence among the extremely rich and the extremely poor.

Middle Mexico does not have a foreign vocation. Something tells it that to rise to Penthouse Mexico, the road passes through a country that is not this one. In order to 'triumph' in Mexico one must go abroad. It does not necessarily mean to go physically, but to go in history, in goals. This vocation of exile as a synonym to triumph has nothing to do with the physical crossing of a border. There are those who, even in leaving, stay behind. And there are those who, even in staying, leave.

Middle Mexico survives in the worst possible way: thinking that it is alive. It has all of the disadvantages of Penthouse Mexico: historical ignorance, cynicism, opportunism and an emptiness that import products can only fill partially or not at all.

Middle Mexico has all the disadvantages of Lower Mexico: economic instability, insecurity, bewilderment, sudden loss of hope, and furthermore, misery knocking on every corner, upon the window of the automobile.

Sooner or later, Middle Mexico must get out of the car and get into, if there still is enough left, a taxi, a collective taxi, a subway, a bus terminal, and start the journey down, all the way to Lower Mexico.

# To get to Lower Mexico...

Where one may arrive almost immediately. It co-inhabits, in permanent conflict, with Middle Mexico. Lower Mexico has half of their inhabitants living in cramped conditions (with more than 2 people per room), 50% who earn less than two minimum wages daily (that is, in poverty), up to a half of the population over fifteen years old, not having completed primary school, a third of its population without sewers nor plumbing, a fourth of its inhabitants living on dirt floors.

Lower Mexico does not share. It disputes an urban and rural space, but still, it has its own internal divisionary lines, its borders....Within one city there are thousands of cities, fighting, surviving, struggling. Out in the countryside it is the transportation vehicle, the way one dresses and the attention one receives from the bank manager which indicate one's classification. One's position in the countryside of Mexico can be determined by how long it takes a person to be received in the reception areas of the financial or political world.

In Lower Mexico the Big House of the Porfirian Hacienda has been replaced by the inner office of the bank, which is how modern times have penetrated rural Mexico.

Lower Mexico has a fighter's vocation. It is brave, it is solidarity, it is a clan, it is the "hood", it is the gang, the race, the friend; it is the strike, the march and the meeting; it is taking back one's land, it is blocking highways, it is the "I don't believe you!", it is "I won't take it anymore!", it is "No more!"

Lower Mexico is the master tradesman, mason, plumber, factory worker, driver, employee, the subway/bus/shared cab student, the street cleaner, truck driver and dialectic, the housewife, small businessman, traveling salesman, farmer, mini- and micro-entrepreneur, miner, colonizer, peasant, tenant farmer, provincial although living in the Capital, peon, longshoreman in port cities, fisherman and sailor, used clothes dealers, butchers, artisans; it is all the etceteras that one finds on any bus, on any corner, in any place of any Mexico...Lower Mexico, that is.

Lower Mexico is the substance of the imprisoned, of the dispossessed, of garnishments, of liens, of layoffs, of evictions, of kidnappings, of torturing, of disappearance, of battle, of death.

Lower Mexico has absolutely nothing...but it has not yet realized it. Lower Mexico already has overpopulation problems. Lower Mexico is a millionaire, counting its misery, its despair.

Lower Mexico shares both urban and rural space, slips and falls, battles and downfalls. Lower Mexico is really far down, so far down that it seems that there is no way to go further down, so far down that one can hardly see that little door that leads to Basement Mexico.

# *To get to Basement Mexico...*

One arrives on foot, either barefoot, or with rubber-soled *huaraches*. To arrive one must descend through history and ascend through the indexes of margination.

Basement Mexico was first. When Mexico was not yet Mexico, when it was all just beginning, the now-Basement Mexico existed, it lived. Basement Mexico is "Indian" because Columbus thought, 502 years ago, that the land where he had arrived was India. "Indians" is what the natives of these lands have been called from that time on.

Basement Mexico is indigenous....however, for the rest of the country it does not count, produce, sell or buy; that is, it does not exist....Review the text of the Free Trade Agreement and you will find that, for the government, the indigenous do not exist. Read the Free Trade Agreement and you will find that Salinas' government has "forgotten" to mention, on the list of Federal Government Entities', The National Indigenous Institute....

Basement Mexico amasses traditions and misery, it possesses the highest indexes of margination and the lowest in nutrition.

Between mud and blood one lives and dies in Basement Mexico...the basement, the waste pile where one goes every once in a while to look for something that could still be used on the upper floors, or to fix some imperfection that could endanger the stability of balance in the building.

Basement Mexico is the most dangerous for the "Sale Season" that is being organized by Penthouse Mexico. Basement Mexico is the one that has nothing to lose, and the one that has everything to win. Basement Mexico does not give up; it has no price....

Hidden but in its foundation, the contempt that Mexico has for Basement Mexico will permit it to organize itself and shake up the entire system. Its charge will be the possibility of freeing itself. The line of democracy, liberty and justice for these Mexicans, will be organized and it will explode and shine.

# A Field Guide to Understanding Mexico

*In your small group, read aloud from the handout about one sector in Mexico. Then discuss the following situation from your sector's perspective. Using the large paper and markers, describe with words, images, colors, etc. who your sector represents and how your sector might respond.*

## The Situation: 1995

On December 22, 1994, the Mexican government let the peso fall, and in a matter of weeks its value dropped from 3.1 pesos to the dollar (one peso = $.32) to 5.5 pesos to the dollar (one peso = $.18). The lower the value of the peso relative to the US dollar, the lower the cost of Mexican exports in the US and the higher the cost of US exports in Mexico. For most working Mexicans, you now have less buying power with the wages you earn; food and other prices skyrocket as your income goes down. Your wages now buy about half of what they could purchase before the devaluation. For many Mexicans, the situation is like having Central American salaries with North American prices.

## How does this situation affect your sector's:
Eating habits (the kind and amount of food you consume):

Investments, foreign and national (that is, if you have any):

Children's education:

Job, if you have one:

Vacation plans:

Political viewpoint:

## What is your response to this crisis? What are your options?
For example, will you try to leave Mexico? Join the Mexican or rebel army? Brainstorm with your group and develop a plan of action.

# Map of Mexico
Courtesy of the Center for US-Mexican Studies, Univerity of California, San Diego

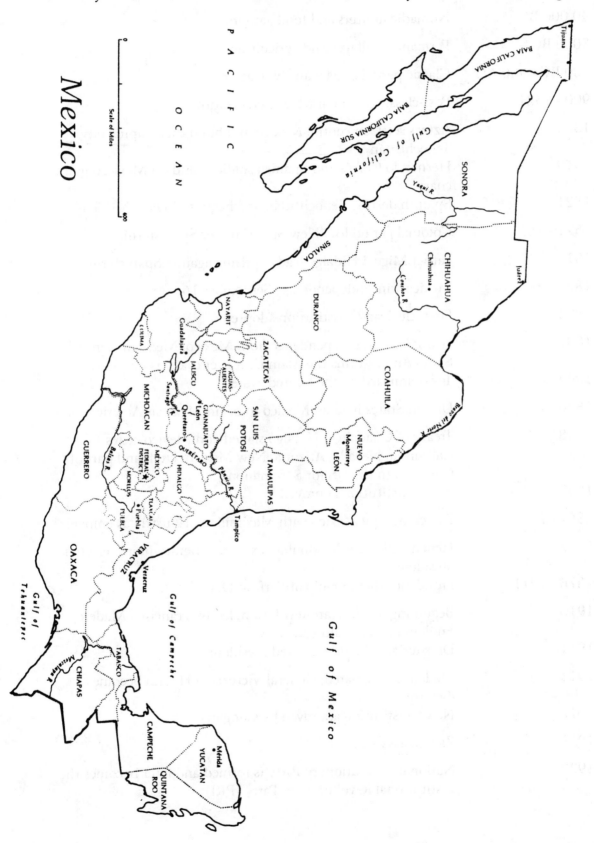

# Chronology of Mexico

| | |
|---|---|
| 40,000 BC | Nomadic hunters and food gathers |
| 5000 BC | Permanent villages and agriculture |
| 200 BC - 900 AD | Classic period of Mayan civilization |
| 900 - 1521 | Post-classic period of Mayan civilization |
| 1325 | Aztecs settle in central Mexico and build their capital city, Tenochtitlán |
| 1519 | Hernando Cortés and Spanish soldiers land on Mexican gulf coast |
| 1521 | Spanish destroy Tenochtitlán and begin to invade Mexico |
| 1521 - 1821 | Colonial period for "New Spain" under Spanish rule |
| 1810 | Father Miguel Hidalgo leads uprising against Spanish rule |
| 1821 | Mexico wins independence, September 16 |
| 1824 | First Mexican Constitution adopted |
| 1836 | Texas declares independence from Mexico; Mexican General Santa Anna storms the Alamo but eventually is defeated |
| 1845 | Texas annexed by the United States |
| 1846 | United States invades Mexico to begin Mexican-American war |
| 1848 | Treaty of Guadalupe Hidalgo signed and Mexico cedes California, Nevada, Arizona, New Mexico, Utah and part of Colorado to the US for $15 million |
| 1857 | New constitution approved |
| 1861 - 7 | French occupy Mexico with Maximilian of Austria as emperor |
| 1867 | French withdraw, Maximilian executed; Benito Juárez elected president |
| 1876 - 1911 | Presidency/dictatorship of Porfirio Díaz |
| 1910 | Beginning of Mexican Revolution, led by Francisco Madero, Emiliano Zapata and Pancho Villa |
| 1911 | Diáz resigns; Madero elected president |
| 1913 | Madero assassinated; General Victoriana Huerta becomes dictator |
| 1917 | New constitution approved by Congress |
| 1919 | Zapata assassinated |
| 1929 | National Revolutionary Party is formed and later becomes the Institutional Revolutionary Party (PRI) |

| | |
|---|---|
| 1934 - 40 | Presidency of Lázaro Cárdenas; Constitutional reforms enacted and oil industry is nationalized |
| 1942 | Bracero Program allows US employers to contract Mexican farm workers |
| 1954 | Women granted the right to vote |
| 1968 | Student Movement ends in massacre; Mexico hosts Olympic games |
| 1976 - 82 | Presidency of José López Portilla; high oil revenues bring record growth to Mexican economy |
| 1981 | Oil pricesfall drastically |
| 1982 - 88 | Presidency of Miguel de la Madrid; massive foreign debts lead to austerity measures and neoliberal restructuring program |
| 1985 | Massive earthquake hits Mexico City, prompting citizen action and organizing |
| 1988 - 94 | Presidency of Carlos Salinas de Gortari; trade negotiations with US and Canada take place (NAFTA); Constitution amended to change land reform laws |
| 1994 | NAFTA takes effect as thousands of peasants take up arms in Chiapas; Presidential candidate and PRI official are assassinated |
| 1995 | Ernesto Zedillo becomes president; peso loses value and US government responds to Mexico's financial crisis with $20 billion bailout |

For more complete chronology of Mexico before 1519, see Lesson 4.

# Glossary

**Aztec** (AS-tek): Indian group who dominated south-central Mexico; also called Mexica

**Barrio** (BAR-reo): a district or neighborhood

**Bracero** (bra-SE-row): a worker; refers to Mexicans brought to the US under labor contracts

**Campesino** (cahm-pay-SEEN-o): peasant farmer

**Chiapas** (chee-AHP-az): a state in southern Mexico

**Chicano** (chee-KAHN-oh): a Mexican or person of Mexican heritage who lives in the United States

**Chinampa** (chin-AHM-pa): small island constructed by the Aztecs on which they raised crops

**Codex** (singular) **Codices** (plural): manuscript or book; here it refers to the books created by the Aztec people

**Compañero** (co-pah-nyair-o): companion, friend

**Conquistadór** (con-kees-ta-DOR): a term applied to Spanish conquerors in the 16th century

**Cortés**, Hernando: leader of the Spanish invasion of Mexico that began in 1519

**Coyote**: a person who arranges a border crossing

**Criollo** (cree-OY-yo): Colonial term referring to a person born in Mexico of Spanish parents

**Doña Marina** (DO-nya-mar-EEN-a): the Mayan woman who became Cortés's translator

**Ejido** (aye-HE-doe): a communal system; often refers to lands that belong to an entire village

**EZLN,** Ejercito Zapatista de Liberación Nacional: the revolutionary army following the ideals of Emiliano Zapata

**Gringo** (GREEN-go): literally, the green clad US soliders; refers to people from the United States

**Guadalajara** (wah-da-la-HAR-ah): second largest Mexican city, located in state of Jalisco

**Hacienda** (ah-see-EN-dah): ranch or plantation

**Hispanic**: a term used by the US government to include all persons of Spanish cultural background

**Huipil** (wee-PEEL): handwoven shawl-type blouse

**La Noche Triste** (la NO-chay TREE-stay): The Night of Sorrows; refers to the night in 1521 when the Aztecs attacked the Spanish invaders and to the night the Mexican army attacked students in 1968

**Latin American**: a person from a Portugese, French or Spanish-speaking country of the Western Hemisphere; also Latino

**Maguey** (ma-GAY): a plant with large pointed leaves from which are produced fibers for clothing and a liquid for a drink

**Maquila** or **maquiladora** (ma-keel-ah-DOOR-ah): a factory or assembly plant

**Mariachi** (mah-ree-AH-chee): a type of Mexican music

**Maroon society**: self-sufficient communities established by runaway African slaves in Mexico

**Maya, Mayan** (MY-ahn): a large Indian group in southern Mexico and northern Central America whose civilization flourished between 1000 BC-1500 AD; today there are approximately 6 million Mayan people

**Mexicanidad** (meh-hee-CAHN-ee-dahd): an image that has been created to describe "The Mexican People"

**Mestizo** (meh-STEE-so): a person with Indian and Spanish ancestry

**Milpa** (MEEL-pa): a small plot of land used to grow crops

**Mixtec** (MIS-tek): a group of Mexican Indians in the region around Oaxaca

**Moctezuma II** (mock-teh-SOO-mah): the Aztec leader at the time of the Spanish invasion in 1519

**Mulatto**: a person of mixed European and African ancestry

**NAFTA**: the acronym for the North American Free Trade Agreement between Canada, the US and Mexico that took effect January 1, 1994

**Nahuatl** (NA-hwat-el): an Indian language group which included Aztecs and Toltecs

**Oaxaca** (wah-HA-kah): a city and a state in southern Mexico

**Olmec** (OHL-mek): Indian group from the Gulf coast that flourished from 500 BC-1100 AD

**Otomí** (oh-toe-ME): an Indian group in central Mexico

**Peón** (pay-ON): a worker, usually an agricultural worker

**Quetzal** (ket-ZAL): a beautiful long feathered bird

**Quetzalcóatl** (ket-zal-CO-at-el): a revered Toltec leader, later represented as a feathered serpent god

**Tarahumara** (tar-ah-ou-MAR-ah): an Indian group in northern Mexico

**Tamales** (tah-MAH-lace): a Mexican food made of ground corn and wrapped in corn husks

**Tenochtitlán** (ten-o-shteet-LON): major city of the Aztecs where Mexico City now stands

**Tlatelolco** (tlot-el-LOL-co): a plaza in Mexico City and the site of two massacres

**Tlaxcalans** (tla-SCAL-ans): an Indian group near Veracruz; many Tlazcalans joined Cortés's army to fight against the Aztecs

**Toltec** (TOLL- tek): an Indian group of central Mexico that flourished from 700 AD-1300 AD

**Tribute**: a form of tax

**Tzeltal** (zel-TALL): a Mayan Indian group from southern Mexico

**Undocumented**: a foreigner in the US without legal documents

**Zambo**: a person of mixed Indian and African ancestry

**Zapatista** (zah-pah-TEAS-tah): another term for the EZLN

**Zapotec** (SAH-po-tek): an Indian group from the area around Oaxaca

## Pronunciation of Mexican Spanish

Spanish is a phonetic language. The stress is on the second to last syllable in words ending in a vowel, n or s; otherwise the stress is on the last syllable. Exceptions are indicated by an accent.

**Vowels**

a as the a in father
e as the e in let
i as the i in police
o as the o in pot
u as the oo in food

**Consonants**

h is always silent
ll is pronounced as Y
ñ as the ny in canyon

# Self-Evaluation Form

Please make comments below each question, or write comments on the back side of this paper.

One thing I learned today is

This is important to me because

It may be important to others because

Something I would like to learn more about is

I am still unclear about

# Group Evaluation Form

As a group, complete the following questions.

1. Everyone contributed to the group and participated in the activity.

/_____/_____/

weak                    adequate                    strong

Comments

2. Everyone listened to what others were saying even if s/he did not necessarily agree with them.

/_____/_____/

weak                    adequate                    strong

Comments

3. The best part about the activity was

4. The most difficult task was

5. From this activity, we learned

# Resources and Organizations

**Resource Center of The Americas** provides information and resources for learning about the Americas, develops educational materials and does mail order sale of books for children and adults. Contact Resource Center, 317 17th Ave. SE, Minneapolis, MN 55414; phone (612)627-9445; FAX (612) 627-9450.

**Amigos de las Americas** is a private organization that arranges for youth volunteers to help on health and sanitation projects in Mexico and other countries in the Americas. Contact Amigos at 5618 Star Lane, Houston, TX 77057; phone (800)231-7796.

**BorderLinks** arranges educational tours along the US-Mexico border to meet with maquiladora workers, business leaders, environmental advocates, etc. Contact at 710 E. Speedway Blvd., Tucson, AZ 85719; phone (520)628-8263.

**Casa de Los Amigos** in Mexico City has established relationships with villages in Mexico that are working on community development, including organic farming, water systems and construction. All projects are initiated and directed by the villages. Short and long term projects are available. Contact American Friends Service Committee, 1501 Cherry Street, Philadelphia, PA 19102; phone (215)241-7295.

**Habitat for Humanity International** organizes housing construction brigades in Mexico where volunteers work alongside Mexicans on building projects. Short and long term brigades. Contact their office at 121 Habitat St. Americus, GA 31709.

**Pastors for Peace** organizes caravans to take supplies to Mexico and also does educational work along the way. Contact Pastors for Peace, 610 West 28th St. Minneapolis, MN 55408; phone (612)870-7121.

**Useful Addresses:**
President of the United States
The White House
1600 Pennsylvania Ave. NW
Washington, DC 20500
USA

Presidente de la Republica
de Mexico
Palacio Nacional
Mexico City, D.F. 06067
Mexico

Prime Minister of Canada
Langevin Block
Ottawa, Ontario K1A 0A2
Canada

United States Senate
Washington, DC 20510

United States House of
Representatives
Washington, DC 20515

# Bibliography

**Comprehensive and General**

Barry, Tom, ed. *Mexico: A Country Guide*. Albuquerque: The Inter-Hemispheric Education Resource Center, 1992.

Burns, E. Bradford. *Latin America: A Concise Interpretive History*. 5th ed. Englewood Cliffs, NJ: Prentice Hall, 1990.

Meier, Matt S. and Feliciano Ribera. *Mexican Americans/American Mexicans: From Conquistadors to Chicanos*. American Century Series: Hill and Wang, 1993.

Meyer, Michael C. and William L. Sherman. *The Course of Mexican History*. 4th ed. New York: Oxford University Press, 1991.

Paz, Octavio. *The Labyrinth of Solitude*. New York: Grove Press, 1985.

Pick, James, Edgar Butler, and Elizabeth Lanzer. *Atlas of Mexico*. Boulder: Westview Press, 1989.

Ruiz, Ramon Eduardo. *Triumphs and Tragedy: A History of the Mexican People*. New York: W.W. Norton & Company, 1992.

**Unit 1**

Coe, Michael D. *America's First Civilization: Discovering the Olmec*. New York: American Heritage Publishing Co., 1968.

*The Cambridge Encyclopedia of Latin America and the Caribbean*. Cambridge: University Press, 1985.

**Unit 2**

Baquedano, Elizabeth. *Aztec, Inca & Maya: An Eyewitness Book*. New York: Alfred A. Knopf, 1993.

Blacker, Irwin R. *Cortes and the Aztec Conquest*. New York: Harper & Row, 1965.

Cortés, Hernando. *Letters of Cortes to the Emperor, 1519-1526*. J. Bayard Morris, trans. New York: W.W. Norton, Inc. 1928.

Diaz del Castillo, Bernal. *True History of the Conquest of New Spain*. London: Penguin Books, 1966.

Galeano, Eduardo. *Memory of Fire: Genesis*. Translated by Cedric Belfrage. New York: Partheon Books, 1985.

Las Casas, Bartolome de. *History of the Indians*. Mexico City: FCE. 1951

Leon-Portilla, Miguel, ed. *The Broken Spears: The Aztec Account of the Conquest of Mexico*. Boston: Beacon Press, 1962.

Taube, Karl, ed. *Aztec and Maya Myths*. Austin: University of Texas Press, 1993.

**Unit 3**

Davidson, David. "Negro Slave Control and Resistance in Colonial Mexico, 1519-1650."In *Maroon Societies: Rebel Slave Communities in the Americas*, edited by Richard Price. Garden City: Anchor Press/Doubleday, 1973.

Gage, Susan. *Colonialism in the Americas: A Critical Look*. Victoria, BC: Victoria International Development Education Association (VIDEA) 407-620 View St., Victoria, BC, Canada, V8W1J6, 1991.

Golden, Renny, with Michael McConnell, Peggy Mueller, Cinny Poppen, and Marilyn Turkovich. *Dangerous Memories: Invasion and Resistance Since 1492*. Chicago Religious Task Force on Central America, 1991.

Palmer, Colin. *Slaves of the White God: Blacks in Mexico, 1570-1650*. Cambridge: Harvard University Press, 1976.

Stefoff, Rebecca; *Independence and Revolution in Mexico*. New York: Facts of File, Inc. 1993.

**Unit 4**

Brenner, Anita. *The Wind that Swept Mexico: The History of the Mexican Revolution, 1910-1942*. New York: Harper & Brothers, 1943.

Hanrahan, Gene, ed. *Documents on the Mexican Revolution*. 4 vols. Salisbury, NC: Documentary Publications, 1981.

Hart, John Mason. *Revolutionary Mexico: The Coming and Process of the Mexican Revolution*. Berkeley: University of California Press, 1987.

Hellman, Judith. *Mexico in Crisis*. New York: Holmes & Meier Publishers, 1979.

Madero, Francisco. The Presidential Succession of 1910. Edited by Thomas Davis. New York: Peter Land Publishing, 1990.

Meyers, William. *Forge of Progress, Crucible of Revolt: Origins of the Mexican Revolution in La Comarca Lagunera, 1880-1911*. Albuquerque, NM: University of New Mexico Press, 1994.

Salas, Elizabeth; *Soldaderas in the Mexican Military*. Austin: University of Texas Press. 1990.

Womack, John, Jr. *Zapata and the Mexican Revolution*. New York: Vintage Books, 1970.

Ecumenical Coalition for Economic Justice. *Economic Integration of the Americas.* 11 Madison Avenue, Toronto, Ontario, Canada M5R 2S2, 1994.

Hellman, Judith. *Mexican Lives.* New York: The New Press, 1994.

Lewis, Oscar. *The Children of Sanchez: An Autobiography of a Mexican Family.* New York: Vintage Books, 1963.

Martínez, Elizabeth, ed. *500 Years of Chicano History in Pictures.* Albuquerque: SouthWest Organizing Project, 1991.

Martinez, Oscar J. *Border People: Life and Society in the U.S. Mexican Borderlands.* Tucson: The University of Arizona Press, 1994.

Poniatowska, Elena. *Massacre in Mexico.* Originally published as *La Noche de Tlatelolco.* Mexico City: Ediciones Era. Trans. by Helen R. Lane. New York: Viking Penguin, 1975.

NACLA. *Report on the Americas.* Bi-monthly publication of North America Congress on Latin America, Inc. 475 Riverside Drive, New York, NY 10115.

*Zapatistas! Documents of the New Mexican Revolution.* Brooklyn: Autonomedia, 1994.

## Resource List
### Poetry and Literature

Anaya, Rudolfo. *Bless Me, Ultima.* Berkeley: Quinto Sol Publications, 1972. A popular book for secondary students about a Mexican family in the southwest fo the US.

Azuela, Mariano. *The Underdogs.* New York: NAL Penguin, 1962. The story of a Mexican Indian who is forced into the Mexican Revolution.

Benítez, Sandra. *A Place Where the Sea Remembers.* Minneapolis: CoffeeHouse Press, 1993. Stories about young adults whose lives intertwine in Oaxaca, Mexico.

Castellanos, Rosario. *The City of Kings.* Pittsburgh: Latin American Literary Review Press, 1993. A collection of short stories that explore the relationship between Indian and White people in Chiapas, Mexico.

Cisneros, Sandra. *The House on Mango Street.* New York: Vintage Books, 1984. A novel about Chicano people living in Chicago.

Cruz, Juana Ines del la, *A Sor Juana Anthology.* Trans. by Alan S. Trueblood. Cambridge: Harvard University Press, 1988. A 'rediscovered' Mexican poet from the 17th century, now considered to be one of the finest Latin poets.

Fuentes, Carlos. *The Death of Artemio Cruz*. New York: Farrar, Straus & Giroux, 1964. A novel that sweeps through the history of modern Mexico.

Garro, Elena. *Recollections of Things to Come*. Austin: University of Texas Press, 1986. A novel of the Mexican Revolution set in a small Mexican town.

Guzman, Martín Luís. *The Eagle and The Serpent*. New York: Alfred Knopf, 1930. A classic novel on the Mexican Revolution.

Lopez y Fuentes, Gregorio. *El Indio*. Illustrated by Diego Rivera. New York: Ungar Publishing Co., 1937. A simply told story of the people who are descendents of the Aztecs.

Traven, B. *The Rebellion of the Hanged*. London: Penguin Books, 1961. Stories from southern Mexico around the time of the Mexican Revolution. Also other books from Traven's "Jungle Novels".

## Art and Artists

Herrera, Hayden. *Frida Kahlo: The Paintings*. New York: Harper Collins, 1991. Color and black/white photos and paintings with excerpts of Frida Kahlo's writings.

Wolfe, Bertram D. *The Fabulous Life of Diego Rivera*. New York: Stein & Day, 1963. Photos, drawings and text about muralist Diego Rivera.

*Note: Many of the books in the bibliography are available for sale from the Resource Center of The Americas, 317 Seventeenth Avenue SE, Minneapolis, Minnesota 55414-2077; phone: 612-627-9445, fax: 612-627-9450, e-mail: rctamn@maroon.tc.umn.edu*